WHEN THERE WAS NO AID

When There Was No Aid

War and Peace in Somaliland

Sarah G. Phillips

Cornell University Press

Ithaca and London

First published 2020 by Cornell University Press

Printed in the United States of America

Library of Congress Cataloging-in-Publication Data

Names: Phillips, Sarah, 1977– author.
Title: When there was no aid : war and peace in Somaliland / Sarah G.
    Phillips.
Description: Ithaca : Cornell University Press, 2020. | Includes
    bibliographical references and index.
Identifiers: LCCN 2019032183 (print) | LCCN 2019032184 (ebook) |
    ISBN 9781501747151 (cloth) | ISBN 9781501747168 (pdf) |
    ISBN 9781501747175 (epub)
Subjects: LCSH: Humanitarian intervention—Somalia. | Peace-building—
    Somaliland (Secessionist government, 1991–) | Violence—Somaliland
    (Secessionist government, 1991–) | Postwar reconstruction—
    Somaliland (Secessionist government, 1991–) | Somaliland (Secessionist
    government, 1991–)—Politics and government. | Somalia—Politics
    and government—1991–
Classification: LCC DT407.4 .P45 2020 (print) | LCC DT407.4
    (ebook) | DDC 967.7305/3—dc23
LC record available at https://lccn.loc.gov/2019032183
LC ebook record available at https://lccn.loc.gov/2019032184

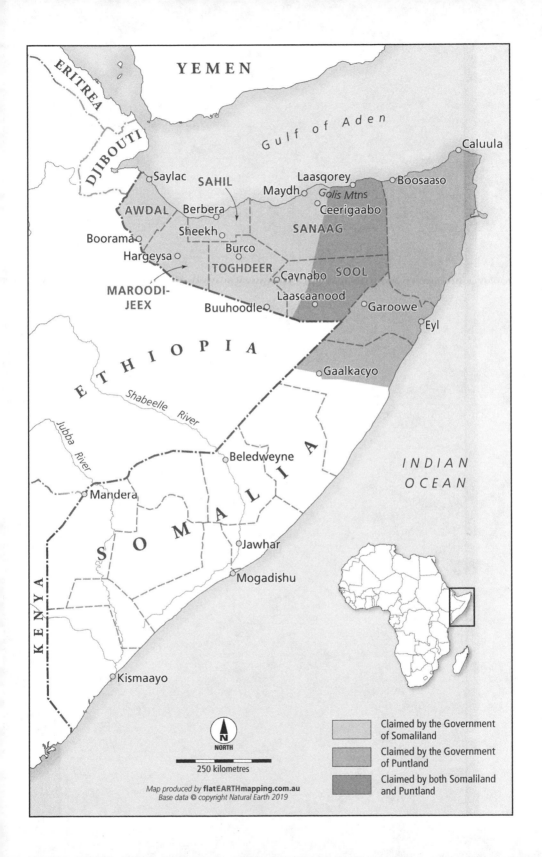

CONTENTS

Acknowledgments

I am enormously grateful to the many Somalilanders who so kindly offered me their time and wisdom in coming to grips with the political contours of their fascinating country. Somaliland is a small place, and the level of interest that it generates from foreign researchers is relatively high, meaning that Somalilanders (particularly those fluent in English and based in Hargeisa) spend a lot of time and energy helping to familiarize each of us. This level of generosity is widely remarked upon and extremely appreciated. Special thanks are due (in alphabetical order) to Adan Abokor, Mustafa Awad, Hassan Bulbul, Ahmed Dualeh, Mohamed Dualeh, Weli Egal, Mohamed Fadal, Khadra Omer Hassan, Abdirahman Hussein, Jama Musse Jama, Abdulkadir Omar, Khadar Omar, and Abdifattah Ahmed Yusuf. I hope that I have faithfully applied the many lessons I learned from each of you and, if I haven't, the responsibility is entirely my own.

Mark Bradbury at the Rift Valley Institute was very helpful in putting me in touch with people in Hargeisa as I began my research there. Jama Musse Jama organized a public talk for me at the Hargeisa Cultural Centre in 2015 where the insightful comments from the audience gave me much to reflect upon. Particular thanks are due to Mohamed Ahmed Ali (Amin), who made the fieldwork as fun as it was informative. I will never look at passport application procedures, personal security protocols, or mobile phone use in the same way. As always, I must single out two giants in my intellectual life, Abdul-Ghani al-Iryani and Adrian Leftwich, who helped me not only to think better but also (hopefully) to be kinder.

I have had some wonderful research assistants throughout the life of this project, and I would like to thank Mohamed Ahmed Ali, Aishwarrya Balaji, Ahmed Dualeh, Chrisanthi Giotis, Eda Gunaydin, Barkhad Kaariye, and Melinda Rankin for their great work and friendship. Thanks also to my colleagues in the Department of Government and International Relations at the University of Sydney for making the office a happy and supportive place to be. Roger Haydon at Cornell University Press is an incredible editor and I am very grateful to him, the rest of the editorial team at Cornell, and to the anonymous peer reviewers for their incisive comments on previous drafts of this book.

The Developmental Leadership Program generously funded the first phase of this research, and the Australian Research Council (DE130101468; DP130103966) funded its subsequent phases. Without their support, this work could not have been conducted.

Parts of chapters 2, 3, and 4 have been adapted from a working paper that I published with the Developmental Leadership Program in late 2013. Some of the material throughout this book (particularly in the introduction and chapter 5) has been adapted from Sarah G. Phillips, 2019, "Proximities of Violence: Civil Order beyond Governance Institutions," *International Studies Quarterly* 63, no. 3: 680–91. (Republished by permission of Oxford University Press on behalf of the International Studies Association.) Parts of chapter 1 and the conclusion have been adapted from Sarah G. Phillips, 2020 (forthcoming), "The Localisation of Harm: Why Local-Context Based Approaches to Poverty and Insecurity Still Tinker in the Margins," *Australian Journal of International Affairs*. Some passages about the influence of Sheekh School have been adapted from Sarah G. Phillips, 2016, "When Less Was More: External Assistance and the Political Settlement in Somaliland," *International Affairs* 92, no. 3: 629–45. Some of the primary interviews and analysis about piracy in Somaliland are adapted from Justin V. Hastings and Sarah G. Phillips, 2018, "Order beyond the State: Explaining Somaliland's Avoidance of Maritime Piracy,"

Journal of Modern African Studies 56, no. 1: 5–30, and are reproduced with permission.

Finally, I am so lucky to have had Hamish with me throughout this project. His happy acceptance of honeymoon travel to Somaliland and Yemen confirmed what I already knew. Torben and Maxwell came along a bit later and also helped in their own wonderful (if not always immediately obvious) ways.

Brief Timeline of Events

Somaliland's postcolonial, pre-independence period (1960–1991)

- **June 1960**—British Somaliland becomes independent and is recognized by thirty-four United Nations member states as an independent state (the State of Somaliland) for a period of five days before voluntarily unifying with the Republic of Somalia.
- **June 1961**—Referendum on the unitary constitution of Somalia is widely boycotted in the north of the country.
- **October 1969**—General Siyad Barre overthrows the civilian government of Mohamed Haji Ibrahim Egal (who later becomes Somaliland's second president).
- **1974**—Devastating drought and famine, centered in the north of Somalia.
- **1977–1978**—Somali–Ethiopian (Ogaden) war, culminating in Somalia's defeat.

- **April 1981**—The Somali National Movement (SNM) is officially established in London.
- **June 1981**—The SNM publishes its first edition of the opposition paper, *Somalia Uncensored*.
- **February 1982**—Student demonstrations over the trial of members of the Hargeysa-based self-help group, Uffo. Several were killed and hundreds arrested. The regime crackdown is popularly remembered within Somaliland as being the origin of the Somali civil war. President Siyad Barre announces state of emergency in the northwest.
- **1988**—Peace treaty signed between Somalia and Ethiopia. President Barre's oppression of the northwest peaks when he launches a devastating bombing campaign on urban centers in Somaliland, particularly the cities of Hargeysa and Borco. An estimated 50,000 people are killed in these attacks and the SNM insurgency is galvanized against the regime.
- **January 1991**—Siyad Barre's regime overthrown; Barre goes into exile.

Somaliland's key formative period (1991–2001)

- **February 1991**—The SNM leadership engages the clan elders in the northwest of Somalia to negotiate a ceasefire with the other northern militias and establish consent for the political leadership of the SNM in the region.
- **April–May 1991**—Grand Conference of Northern Clans held in Borco (Somaliland).
- **May 1991**—Somaliland proclaims its independence from Somalia at the Borco conference. SNM chairman, Abdirahman Ali Tuur is nominated as the first president of the Republic of Somaliland.
- **June 1991**—Creation of the (small) United Nations Operation in Somalia I (UNOSOM I), which consisted primarily of a food airlift and a tiny UN peacekeeping mission.
- **1992**—Berbera (Somaliland) Port and Borco conflict. Fighting breaks out in Berbera and Borco between Habar Yunis (Garhajis) and Habar Awal/Issa Musa militias after President Tuur attempts to organize a national military force to disarm militias. A violent

power struggle ensues over control of public infrastructure and revenue at Berbera Port.

- **October 1992**—The Sheekh Clan Conference (Somaliland) ends the conflict in Berbera and sets general principles for a forthcoming peace conference to be held in Boorama. The conference also established a framework—expanded at Boorama—through which the clan leaders would participate in key governance issues in a more formalized manner.

- **December 1992**—United Nations (Resolution 794) authorizes the creation of the Unified Task Force (UNITAF) to use all necessary means to provide a secure environment for the provision of humanitarian assistance in Somalia.

- **December 1992**—US-led Operation Restore Hope sends 30,000 American troops to Somalia and 10,000 allied troops for peacekeeping missions.

- **January–May 1993**—The Boorama (Somaliland) Clan Conference consolidates a peace charter and national charter for Somaliland. The charter establishes a bicameral legislature with an elected House of Representatives, a nonelected House of Elders (the Guurti), an elected presidential executive, and an independent judiciary. Under the peace charter it is agreed that all militias must be stood down and that all militia weapons be surrendered to become government property.

  The conference at Boorama also sees the transition from the SNM to a civilian administration, and nearly two-thirds of the 150 official delegates at Boorama voted President Abdirahman Ali Tuur out of office. Mohamed Haji Ibrahim Egal becomes Somaliland's second president with Abdirahman Aw Ali (Gadabursi) selected to serve as vice president in a transitional government with Egal.

- **March 1993**—Operation Restore Hope hands over to United Nations Operation in Somalia II (UNOSOM II).

- **June 1993**—(Somali) General Mohamed Farah Aideed's forces kill twenty-four Pakistani UNOSOM II peacekeeping troops.

- **October 1993**—(Somali) General Aideed's forces shoot down two Black Hawk helicopters, killing eighteen US soldiers, one Pakistani soldier, and one Malaysian soldier, prompting US President Clinton to announce the withdrawal of US troops by March 1994.

- **November 1994–October 1996**—Hargeysa airport conflict. In a mirrored reflection of the Berbera conflict in 1992 (in which the Habar Awal defied the government by claiming Berbera as its territory), members of the Idagalle (Garhajis) clan begin agitating for control of Hargeysa airport and the revenue that passed through it. By March 1995 the conflict had spread to Borco, continuing until 1996 and causing extensive destruction in both Hargeysa and Borco.
- **September 1994**—The Somaliland shilling is introduced as a new national currency, providing a financial windfall to the small circle of business elites who funded its creation.
- **January 1995**—The Somali shilling ceases to be legal tender within Somaliland.
- **March 1995**—UNOSOM II ends.
- **1995**—A national army of around five thousand people is established in Somaliland, largely from disarmed militiamen.
- **October 1996–February 1997**—The Hargeysa National Conference (*shir qameed*). Unlike the conference at Boorama, where the incumbent president was unseated, the Hargeysa conference reinstates both President Egal and the Parliament. Also unlike the previous conferences, it is the Somaliland government which funds the Hargeysa conference—rather than local communities.
- **August 1998**—The neighboring territory of Puntland declares itself as an autonomous region of Somalia, under the Puntland State of Somalia. Unlike Somaliland, Puntland does not seek outright independence from Somalia.

The ratification of the Constitution to the present

- **May 2001**—Somaliland referendum to ratify the constitution held, with around 97 percent of voters officially voting in favor of it.
- **May 2002**—President Mohamed Ibrahim Egal dies; Vice President Dahir Rayale Kahin is sworn in.
- **December 2002**—First local council elections.
- **April 2003**—First presidential elections. The incumbent is returned to office by an almost infinitesimal margin.
- **September 2005**—First parliamentary elections.

- **December 2005**—President Dahir Rayale Kahin presents the case for Somaliland's independence to the African Union.
- **September 2009**—Saudi Arabia officially lifts the ban on live cattle exports from Somaliland.
- **June 2010**—Second presidential elections. Ahmed Mohamed Mahamoud Silanyo defeats Dahir Rayale Kahin.
- **May 2011**—The controversial NGO Act is signed into law. This act tried to bring the UN and other INGOs under greater government oversight.
- **April 2011**—The Silanyo administration tables the controversial Telecommunications Act in Parliament—an ambitious attempt to extract greater tax from the telecommunications sector but which was ultimately undone by internal inconsistencies.
- **November 2012**—Second local council elections held.
- **November 2013**—Memorandum of Understanding for the Somaliland Development Fund (SDF) signed between the governments of Somaliland, United Kingdom, and Denmark. The SDF provides money that is administered by an external (private, for-profit) fund manager. The fund offers the Somaliland government a channel through which it can apply for external funds without the money going through the central budget.
- **March 2015**—Presidential and House of Representatives elections scheduled for June 2015 postponed. Ultimately rescheduled for November 2017.
- **March 2015**—Talks stall between Somalia and Somaliland about Somaliland's political status.
- **July 2015**—Saudi Arabia and the United Arab Emirates (UAE) request permission to use Berbera Port and Airport in their war in Yemen. This marks a sharp increase in Somaliland's entanglement in Middle Eastern power struggles.
- **September 2016**—The governments of Somaliland and the UAE sign a deal for the Emirates to fund a $250 million highway from Berbera Port to Ethiopia (the Berbera Corridor). Dubai Ports World was also awarded a $442 million thirty-year concession to develop and manage Berbera Port. The port concession includes the condition that 35 percent of annual revenue will go the Somaliland government.

- **March 2017**—The UAE government signs a controversial deal with the government of Somaliland to establish a military base in Berbera.
- **Mid-2017**—Crippling drought and starvation spread across much of Somalia and Somaliland.
- **November 2017**—President Silanyo's term ends and Musa Bihi Abdi is elected president with an outright majority in elections that international observers hailed as having minor flaws but being generally orderly and peaceful. The UAE contributed substantial amounts of money to Abdi's electoral campaign.
- **January–October 2018**—Skirmishes break out between Somaliland and Puntland forces around the border town of Tukaraq, which was captured by Somaliland in May. The fighting reportedly kills more than 100 people and raises fears that more conflict may be likely in the future.

A Note on Spellings

It is common to find books and maps that mix Somali spellings of names and locations with (often inconsistent) English transliterations. Some Somalis also move between Somali spellings and English transliterations (particularly for the letter "x," which has a hard "H" or Arabic letter ح/Ha sound, and for the letter "c," which has a hard "A" or Arabic letter ع/'ayn sound). Wherever possible, for people's names I have used the spelling each person uses for his or her name (though this also sometimes changes according to context). I have used Somali spellings for place names and list them here, with their most common English transliterations in brackets.

Boorama [Borama]
Boosaaso [Bosaso]
Burco [Borao]
Ceerigaabo [Erigabo]
Gaalkacyo [Galkayo]
Garoowe [Garowe]

Hargeysa [Hargeisa]
Laascaanood [Las Anood]
Laasqorey [Las Qoray]
Maroodi-Jeex [Maroodi-Jeeh]
Saaxil [Sahil]
Saylac [Sayla]

When There Was No Aid

INTRODUCTION

What if We Don't Intervene?

Anyone who has visited Hargeysa, the capital of Somaliland, knows that the country's peace-building process elicits proud assertions of Somalilanders' ability to end a brutal war with almost no external assistance. Widely heard refrains include the notion that peace "works because Somalilanders want it to work," and that, because of the lack of policing capacity, the country "runs on trust."[1] Researchers readily accumulate stories about how peace was painstakingly negotiated under the trees at dozens of clan-based conferences (1991–1997) while the world focused on the bloodletting in Mogadishu. Meanwhile, delegates from the rest of Somalia negotiated in five-star hotels funded by the United Nations to no avail against a complex emergency that killed hundreds of thousands of civilians and displaced many more.[2]

Within these stories, Somaliland's gold merchants—women who sit on bustling streets selling large quantities of gold without any visible protection from theft—hold a prominent position. After being repeatedly directed to visit Hargeysa's gold market and witness the level of security and social cohesion that their enterprise revealed, the merchants responded to my presence in similar terms: "See, there is peace and stability here. Take a photo and go show people!" Not only did they want me to understand what I saw in the same terms as those directing me to them, but they also understood the mileage to be gained from a foreigner photographing them going about their trade without any obvious form of security. However, by inviting the comparison with Somaliland's recent past (and, indeed, with the Somali Republic from which it claimed independence in 1991), these widespread stories about peace and cohesion are infused with the specter of violence. The implicit coda to the gold merchants' story is: and yet, things were very different not so long ago. War and peace are intermingled, with each understood through its proximity to the other.

The Lingering Place of War in Peace

The shadow of war pervades Somaliland's built environment. War is physically present across its cityscapes, even though its public monuments mark it as a relic of another time. The memorial to the antiregime struggle on Hargeysa's Independence Avenue, which displays a Somalia-flagged fighter plane (shot down as it attacked Somaliland's main cities in 1988) and large frescos of civilians draped in the national flag being massacred; the tank monument to Somaliland's own process of demobilization that brought its internal wars to an end in 1996; the Museum of War and Peace; the preservation of mass grave sites; the statues of a dove and of a fist raised to the sky holding a map of an independent Somaliland; the rusted Soviet tanks that still line the country's largest highway as it enters the port city of Berbera; and the prominent place that photographs of these monuments receive in official government publications and in hotels and restaurants, all underline the way that traumatic memories of war are kept present in daily life.

These artifacts are a physical reminder that peace (or at least the absence of war) is the basis upon which Somaliland was built and has since been sustained. References to peace are everywhere. The title of the national anthem is "Long Life with Peace" (*samo ku waar*). Peace is mentioned six times in the Constitution, which designates it as the basis of the national political system, while defining the protection of the peace as one of the president's constitutional responsibilities. But a preoccupation with peace tells of an intimacy with war. Everywhere its presence is so barely concealed that one is reminded that a careless outburst could unearth it.

Somalilanders' historically grounded fear about the velocity of war—and the irrelevance of international actors to containing its spread—is foregrounded such that in times of crisis, mobilizing for political violence is largely bracketed out as a viable, or perhaps even logical, course of action. This book argues that the intimacy of the relationship between war and peace has been harnessed, albeit uneasily and by no means inevitably, as a source of civil order.

All societies must manage the problem of violence if they are to endure (North, Wallis, and Weingast 2009, 13). In modern times, this responsibility is typically understood as belonging to the state, defined as the set of institutions that successfully and legitimately monopolize violence and enforce its rules (Weber 1919/1946). Let us put aside until the next chapter the fact that many states do not exercise that monopoly without descending into violence and consider only the idealized version of the Weberian state with its unambiguous monopoly on legitimate force. Even in that state, violence is almost always imputed without being realized. No state rules through coercion alone, no matter how brutal it is. It is the means by which this imputation is sustained—the coercive threat implicit to lawful governance (Barkawi 2016, 205)—that should concern us then, rather than the actual capacity of the state's institutions to forcefully uphold its rules. I show how the imputed violence that underpins civil order in Somaliland resides less in the threat of state- or clan-based coercion than in the discursive reproduction of past violence and the violence that continued in other Somalia. The idea that the discursive reproduction of violence limits actual violence has implications beyond Somaliland. It suggests that to understand how violence is managed we must ask how it is remembered and anticipated, rather than focusing only on the institutions that enforce sanctions against its use.

There is a vast literature about the role of war in the formation of states that manage violence (reasonably) effectively, within which two broad threads are most relevant to my purpose in this book. One draws largely from the experiences of European and other northern states to explore the ostensibly productive qualities of war. This body of work investigates the ways in which military violence underpins the construction of cohesive national identities, the consolidation of legitimate institutions and through these institutions, the maintenance of political order.[3] Crudely, this is the war-makes-states thesis that Charles Tilly (1990, 75) so famously advanced. A crude rendering of the other thread is that "war breaks states" (Hampel 2015, 1629). Scholars writing in this vein argue that globalization (or sometimes postcolonialism) negates war's supposedly generative properties, with political violence creating conflict traps that structurally impede security and economic growth without providing the opportunities for renewal that northern states may have experienced.[4] This second thread is typified by Paul Collier's argument that "civil war is development in reverse" (2007, 27). Collier's work is influential among those who see the fragility of state institutions in the Global South as a problem that calls for international intervention, a point that is taken up in chapter 1.

While both positions provide rich insights into the sociology of war, I deviate by seeking to establish neither the productive nor destructive qualities of war. Instead I explore the constitutive relationship between war and peace by illustrating the way that each seeps into and structures the other. In brief my argument is this: war and peace are not cleanly alternating phases where one begins as the other ends (Barkawi 2016, 201) but that they exist in constant tension, with neither one fully subsuming the other. Somaliland's experience reveals with unusual clarity that war's absence is sustained by its ongoing presence in daily life, in the ways that its memory and anticipation configure how actions become either possible or unthinkable.

Crucially, international interventions in conflict-affected areas (whether through state-building programs, peacekeeping or stabilization operations, support for belligerent parties, arms transfers, international loans, or overseas development assistance) are inexorably bound up in the ways that war reverberates through society. Interveners pick which group/s should benefit from violence and support that vision with resources that reshape economies, politics, and local networks of trust. The fact that some form of international intervention in situations of large-scale violence is all but assured in a globalized world affects how people anticipate political violence and how they act as a result. This book examines how the absence of international intervention during its formational years helped to foster a prolonged period of peace in Somaliland. It does so while noting that the internationalized war in neighboring Yemen (ongoing from 2015), the escalating geostrategic competition along the Red Sea, and the increasing relevance of Somaliland to both, represents a challenge to the longevity of that peaceful period.

The unrecognized breakaway Republic of Somaliland declared independence from Somalia shortly after the collapse of Somalia's military regime in 1991. Residents of northwestern Somalia—Somaliland—endured extreme brutality under President Siyad Barre (in power 1969–1991) from the early 1980s. The violence against them peaked in 1988 when the regime responded to a military offensive by the Somali National Movement (SNM) with a ground and aerial assault that killed up to 50,000 civilians and destroyed most of the physical infrastructure in the cities of Hargeysa and Burco. Mark Bradbury recalled that in 1991, "Hargeisa from the air, resembled a city of dry swimming pools, which on closer inspection were shells of houses whose roofs had been systematically looted during the war" (Bradbury 2008, 3). Approximately half of the population either fled abroad or to refugee camps, and the ground was strewn with landmines and other deadly ordinance. Many Somalilanders remember the events of the late 1980s as an act of genocide against the majority Isaaq clan, and some refer to it as the Hargeysa holocaust (Ingiriis 2016). The violence was so overwhelming that it established a widespread belief that the security of Isaaq clan members could only be guaranteed by a permanent separation from Somalia—and a rejection of the unitary state model that had enabled such violence by one group against another.

The removal of Barre's forces from Somaliland in January 1991 transformed the conflict but did not end it and local clan-based militias continued to cause widespread, if intermittent, violence until late 1996. Alex de Waal (2015, 132) argues that the intensity of Somaliland's civil war in 1992 was so high that it "threatened to bring Somaliland to disintegration even faster than (southern) Somalia." By the time Somalilanders had negotiated an end to the destructive interclan violence, the population had experienced a decade and a half of conflict and displacement.

The devastating violence across Somaliland ended in late 1996 for reasons that are taken up throughout the rest of this book. What is important to note at the outset is the extraordinary divergence in the levels of violence experienced by Somaliland and the Republic of Somalia since that time. Somaliland is not perfectly harmonious or conflict-free, and over three hundred people (mostly government forces) were killed between 1997 and 2018 in an intermittent border dispute with neighboring Puntland.[5] However, the Uppsala Conflict Data Program (UCDP) estimates that there were 25,793 conflict deaths in the rest of Somalia over roughly the same period (1997–2017).[6]

That is, from the time Somaliland's internal wars ended in late 1996, it has experienced around 1 percent of the fatalities from conflict than were suffered in the rest of Somalia.[7]

The Puzzle of Somaliland's Institutions

I selected Somaliland as a case study for three reasons: its successful transition out of civil war; the dearth of external intervention it experienced during the key phase of that transition; and the perceived inability of its state and clan-based governance institutions to provide a reliable ongoing deterrent to violence. Leveraging the conditions for a natural experiment that secessionist entities can offer, the book poses a simple overarching question: Why did the large-scale violence end in Somaliland while continuing elsewhere in Somalia? As the title suggests, it is particularly concerned with the conditions fostered by the most obvious difference between the two cases: the virtual absence of external intervention in Somaliland during its period of internal war (1991–1996) compared to the overwhelming international attention that the war in the rest of Somalia received over the same period.

The most common conclusion about the political impact of the vastly different levels of external intervention across Somalia (indeed one that I also reached previously—Phillips 2013) centers on institutional quality (Bradbury 2008; Renders 2012; Phillips 2013, 2016; Walls 2014; Richards 2015). This position is elaborated in chapter 4 but is essentially that the dearth of external interest in Somaliland's wars gave its people the time and political space to establish locally responsive and contextually appropriate (though not necessarily inclusive) governance institutions. That space was not available to other Somalis, who instead had to contend with a multitude of often conflicting political patrons, sources of revenue, and normative expectations about what a peaceful Somali state should look like. The core contention is thus that Somaliland's governance institutions (whether formal, informal, or a hybrid version of the two) established legitimate rules and that the actual or imputed enforcement of these rules determined the prospects for peace and civil order. This contention is squarely in line with new institutionalism scholarship, wherein institutions are the regularized patterns of behavior or "rules of the game" that make an ordered political, social, or economic life possible (North 1990, 3). The stronger an institution is, the idea goes, the greater the level of predictability, and thus civil order, it creates. The weaker it is, the less it permits (Schedler 2013, 23). From this it follows, if implicitly, that institutions are ontologically prior to the order they engender.

While not diminishing the importance of Somaliland's governance institutions to its transition from war, this book challenges the assumption that they ontologically preceded it, arguing instead that institutions have a constitutive relationship with sociopolitical order. That is, institutions may help produce order but only in so far as they are simultaneously products of it. This is best explained by considering the puzzle that Somaliland's institutions pose, which is that their inability to provide a reliable security guarantee helped, counterintuitively, to stabilize a prolonged period of peace. This suggests that even ineffective governance institutions—those that do not reliably embed or enforce Douglass North's rules of the game—may still help to produce civil order rather than subvert it. If this is possible then the relationship between the quality of institutions and the level of order a society experiences is not a straightforward one of cause and effect but one of coproduction.

I argue that in Somaliland this coproduction can be seen in a discourse that emphasizes the fragility of the country's hard-won peace. I will refer to this as the "independence discourse" throughout the rest of this book. I understand the independence discourse to consist of the belief—evident through speeches, texts, practices, material artifacts, and proclamations by a wide variety of Somalilanders in the areas that support secession from Somalia—that Somaliland should be independent because it is peaceful, and that peace depends on the ongoing conscious effort of Somalilanders. This discourse limits the possibilities for violent action by reiterating the catastrophic consequences that violence risks unleashing—a risk that is credibly amplified by the very weakness of other institutional constraints.

Somaliland's independence discourse consists of three core strands. One emphasizes the purportedly exceptional nature of the Somalilander identity. It suggests that Somaliland's achievement of postconflict peace demonstrates that Somalilanders are exceptional to other Somalis (who remain beset by violence), and that this peaceful identity warrants Somaliland's formal independence from Somalia. Unity with Somalia is therefore bracketed out as illogical because unity would subvert the peacefulness upon which Somaliland's identity rests. Another strand emphasizes Somaliland's autonomy, particularly from the international structural and normative constraints that usually apply to states emerging from conflict. In this, it serves as a counter-point to the dominant discourse about fragile states that is the subject of chapter 1. The other, and subtlest strand, is that violence is a choice which, if taken, is unlikely to be contained by the country's governance institutions and so must not be chosen. Somaliland's apparent propensity to war—as expressed in this discourse—is therefore a constitutive element of its ability to maintain peace.[8] By excluding certain behaviors (particularly political violence) from obvious consideration, it organizes and stabilizes peace in ways that Somaliland's governance institutions have not.

This stands in contrast to the widely-made suggestion that when a state's institutional deterrents to violence are weak, powerful actors are likely to see violence as a viable political strategy by perceiving that they may "[do] well out of war" (Collier 2000; Fearon and Laitin 2003; Walter 2015). Rather than only providing a structural opportunity for political violence, poorly constraining governance institutions may also generate popular ideas about violence that act to limit its use. This has important implications beyond Somaliland. If institutional weakness can underwrite both the legitimization and the delegitimization of violence, then we must reconsider the conventional wisdom about how governance institutions constrain violence and examine instead the ways that institutions simultaneously generate and reflect shared ideas about violence. Doing so destabilizes a central assumption of state-building and other development interventions for which violence is almost exclusively the product of dysfunctional domestic institutions.

Somaliland's Independence from the International

Somaliland's proclaimed sovereignty is not recognized by any state (nor, indeed, all its inhabitants), and it is still legally part of the Federal Republic of Somalia. The United Nations deals with Somaliland under its Assistance Mission in Somalia (UNSOM) and often uses the names of the "18 pre-war regions of Somalia" in official publications, allowing it to avoid reference to Somaliland as a single political entity (see for example UNFPA 2014). Treating Somaliland as independent is contentious within the rest of Somalia, which stridently rejects Somaliland's claim of independence. As a result of Somaliland's unrecognized status, and of Somalia's loan defaults during President Siyad Barre's thirty-two-year rule, Somaliland's government has had negligible access to external capital, whether through official development assistance (ODA), loans from international lending bodies such as the IMF, foreign investment, or rents for either strategic or natural resources. This has meant that it has no large international debts to service; no requirement that it perform structural adjustments, implement macroeconomic austerity measures, impose budgetary constraints, or apply other neoliberal conditionalities that are usually associated with Poverty Reduction Strategies by the World Bank and IMF. Private investors are also constrained, being unable to access commercial insurance or seek recourse through international commercial law because of Somaliland's unrecognized status (Reno 2006, 168). This has served as a considerable—though not entirely prohibitive—disincentive for non-Somalilanders to invest in the country and has further limited the government's ability to generate wealth through normal external channels, particularly those that are typically espoused by international financial institutions like the IMF and World Bank. The country is also excluded from international banking and postal systems, which has made its residents reliant on private enterprises, like money transfer companies and courier services, to provide similar services and plug gaps caused by the lack of sovereign recognition. Thus, throughout its existence, though particularly during its first decade or so, the government of Somaliland has been more reliant on its ability to access internal revenue than governments in most developing countries.[9]

Somaliland is also subject to the United Nations arms embargo on Somalia (Security Council Resolution 733, January 1992). Although the resolution was amended in 2014 to permit the importation of weapons, ammunition, or military equipment, the permission was "intended solely for the development of the Somali National Security Forces" (UN Resolution 2142, 2014). That is, Somaliland's police force (SLPF) and armed forces still cannot legally acquire arms under the conditions of the Somali embargo, which means that all members of Somaliland's police force must supply their own private weapons as a condition of their employment.

In addition to being overlooked by international donors, lenders, development agencies, and arms exporters, Somaliland was also peripheral to the interests of the foreign militaries that were active in Somalia in the 1990s. Their focus was firmly on and around the capital of Mogadishu, where together the United States and United Nations spent nearly $4 billion on military operations and peace-building processes (Prunier 1998, 227; Ahmad

2012).[10] International aid agencies also provided billions of dollars' worth of food aid to help counter the famine that was devastating the southern parts of Somalia, with the diversion of this aid becoming the linchpin of an entrenched conflict economy (Ahmad 2012). On the other hand, no external power attempted to end (or prolong) Somaliland's civil wars, which dramatically limited access to external revenue for its belligerents. The total amount of international funding that Somaliland received for its peace process between 1991 and 1997 appears to be around $100,000, which was supplied by two organizations (one Swedish and one American) to the Boorama Conference in 1993. That Somaliland was not the target of international intervention is a historical fact. However, the independence discourse assigns meaning to that lack of intervention, particularly the notion that it made Somalilanders more self-reliant and that, as a result, the peace that they forged is more resilient than it might otherwise have been.

It is important to emphasize that Somaliland is at a critical juncture. Its geostrategic significance has changed dramatically since the Gulf Cooperation Council (GCC) began its military intervention in Yemen in 2015, and as intra-GCC disputes have since manifested across the Horn of Africa. In 2017, the United Arab Emirates (UAE) and Somaliland signed a deal for the Emirates to fund a $250 million dollar highway from Berbera Port to Ethiopia (the Berbera Corridor) that will grant landlocked Ethiopia easier access to the Red Sea. The Emirati company Dubai Ports World was also awarded a $442 million, thirty-year concession to develop and manage Berbera Port. The port concession includes the condition that 35 percent of annual revenue will go the Somaliland government (*Indian Ocean Newsletter* 2017). Although most of the money is yet to be released at the time of writing, the expectations of an impending fiscal windfall are widespread. The UAE is also negotiating a deal to build a military base in Berbera, which will further embed Somaliland within international military, political, and economic structures— something that it was so detached from during its formational years.

The Somaliland Counterfactual

For all the doubts raised about the effectiveness of international assistance in advancing peace and development,[11] there are precious few examples of developing countries that are even relatively untouched by it. As a result, we generally lack the ability to conduct counterfactual or what-if analyses to determine whether outcomes would have been better for certain communities without aid (Stuckler and Basu 2010, 5). David Stuckler and Sanjay Basu point out that in the apparent absence of genuine counterfactual cases—countries that receive no aid and thus offer direct points of comparison to those that do—scholars are left with the awkward problem of trying to determine reverse causality, which leaves them subject to a number of methodological biases (5). They note that Dambisa Moyo's bestselling critique of international aid, *Dead Aid* (2009), tried to get around this problem by inventing the fictitious Republic of Dongo as hypothetical (and thus misleading) evidence for her argument about the problems caused by Western aid to Africa (5).

I contend that Somaliland's level of isolation from the international system during its foundational years (roughly 1991–2001)[12] is so unusual that it offers as close as we may come to a counterfactual case for the internationalized model of peace/state-building that is the norm. True, Somaliland does not have sovereign recognition and so is not technically a state in a legal sense, and since around 2001 it has also received an increasing amount of (largely indirect) international assistance. However, its first postindependence decade as a state-like entity offers scholars an unusually clear case of postconflict reconstruction in the absence of significant external involvement that offers purchase on the "what if there was no aid" question. That the normal internationalized model of peace/state-building was so powerfully enacted throughout the rest of Somalia from 1991 further enhances the relevance of Somaliland's early years as a comparative case. This period thus presents a rare case in which the drivers of peace, relative order, and institutional formation may be examined in the absence of aid and other forms of intervention as significant factors.

The chief significance of Somaliland as a counterfactual case is that it challenges one of the most engrained presumptions about violence and poverty in the Global South: that external intervention is self-evidently useful in ending them (see Koddenbrock 2014, 673). My aim is not only to explore a case when such intervention did not occur, important though the examination throughout chapters 2–4 is. Neither is it necessarily a call to either slash or double down on overseas development assistance. Rather, it is an attempt to situate the impulse to intervene against war and poverty within the larger universe of power exchanges between north and south (Engel 2014, 1382) and the effects of the ideational baggage that this exchange inevitably carries with it. In the case of Somaliland, I argue that this baggage was mobilized within the counterhegemonic independence discourse, which frames autonomy from the international system as a source of strength.

Methodology

Single case studies are often dismissed as sui generis, or too "highly idiosyncratic and context specific" to offer lessons "in a cross-national setting" (Gleditsch, Skrede, and Ruggeri 2010, 300) in the international relations literature. However, case studies from the Global South also offer analytical purchase on aspects of statehood that are rendered less visible by the often implicit prioritization of northern institutional frameworks. That is, they may afford "privileged insights into the workings of the world at large" (Comaroff and Comaroff 2012, 114) and alternative perspectives from which to theorize international politics.

To build a detailed empirical base, I have engaged a wide range of discursive sources—linguistic, practice-based, and material—that narrate Somaliland's transition from conflict, its proclaimed independence from Somalia, and its relative detachment from the international system. I made numerous visits to Somaliland between 2011 and 2015, and also spent seven months in Nairobi, Kenya in 2013 (where the head offices of most international agencies working on Somalia/Somaliland are located). During this period, I interviewed current and former ministers, deputy ministers, and bureaucrats across key ministries (finance, planning and international cooperation, interior, information, telecommunications, foreign affairs, justice, and education); members of the House of Representatives; the *Guurti* (essentially a parliamentary upper house of appointed clan elders); the Somali National Movement (SNM) that fought the regime of Siyad Barre; political parties (ruling and opposition); clan elites; women's rights activists, unionists, telecommunications companies; large- and small-scale businesspeople; academics; university students; school teachers; diplomats; journalists; civil society groups; international/nongovernmental organizations (I/NGOs); UN agencies; local and international security services; and a variety of national and international consultants working across numerous sectors in both Somaliland and Somalia.[13]

Some people (particularly senior government officials and those working for international organizations) requested anonymity for some or all of what they told me during interviews. Others requested that I use my judgement to determine which comments were sensitive (and thus nonattributable), and which were not (and thus attributable). In these cases, I have erred on the side of caution and treated the whole interview as anonymous, even where the comments may seem fairly innocuous when presented here. In the interests of participant confidentiality, therefore, most interviews are cited without specific reference to the person's name, although care was given to provide sufficient information about their position and level of access to information. Where participants have requested that their names be given, I have done so.

The sometimes-heavy use of quotes from interviews is intended to reflect, as closely as possible, how Somalilanders narrated their understanding of peace, independence, and external intervention to me. I must stress, however, that in reproducing comments made during interviews, I do not claim to speak for those I am quoting. Part of the research process is to select comments that are either representative of those made by others or are particularly incisive, both of which inevitably invoke the judgement of the researcher. Another researcher may have made different selections to mine, and my arguments remain an interpretation of what I saw and heard during the research process. Moreover, they may differ to the interpretations of Somalilanders, whose insightful scholarship deserves wide attention (see, for example, the research published by the Academy for Peace and Development, Adnan Abokor, Nasir M. Ali, Rashiid Sheekh Cabdullahi, Abdirahman Yusuf Duale (Bobe), Mohammed Hassan Ibrahim, Mohamed Haji Ingiiris, Jama Muse Jama, Cabdiraxmaan Jimcaale, Haroon Yusuf, Abdi Ismail Samatar, and Siham Rayale, to name a few). As Somali scholars attached to the #CadaanStudies movement, which critiques the authority that is attached to white (*cadaan*) scholars at the expense of Somali scholars, rightly argue: "Somali-produced scholarship will be central to academic knowledge" (Aidid 2015).[14] My position as a non-Somali researcher in this field is thus discussed further in this chapter.

In addition to information gained during interviews, I have used other language-based sources such as scholarship by local authors (including those mentioned previously), official government publications and speeches, interviews with Somalilanders published by other researchers, the speeches and political press releases issued in an attempt to mitigate domestic crises, translations of Somali language poetry about war and peace, opinion polling, secondary survey data, the country's constitution and other laws, and feedback that I received from an audience in Hargeysa when I presented an earlier version of my research about the nature of Somaliland's governance institutions.

I have also analyzed various practices, like the response to the 2003 electoral crisis, the peaceful way that power has been transferred, Somalilanders' lack of participation in maritime piracy, and also material artifacts, such as prominent memorials to war, demobilization, peace, and independence throughout the parts of the country that produce the independence discourse. These practices and artifacts are discussed in greater detail in chapter 5, but it is worth highlighting some of the everyday performances of security that helped to shape my understanding of how ideas about peace and security constitute the processes by which they are maintained. In addition to the story about the gold merchants that opened this introduction, another incident stands out. During a trip to the Borco district, I wanted to enter the grounds of a school to interview some teachers. Behind the school fence sat two guards who would not allow my Somalilander colleagues and I to enter until we could demonstrate that there was a personal connection that linked us, on one side of the fence, to them on the other. My colleagues began telephoning person after person, moving first through a chain of acquaintances, and then strangers, until they eventually found someone who happened to know one of the guards personally. When the guard confirmed that he knew the person we had finally stumbled upon, the gate was opened, and we were allowed to walk through the school grounds unaccompanied.

The people on the other end of the phone clearly did not know either my colleagues or me, and so could vouch for neither our purpose nor our integrity. Presumably, they could not be held directly accountable for our actions once we were inside the school either. My colleagues and the guards were acting out the discovery of a previously unknown personal connection between us, as outsiders, and the local community. However obviously strained this discovery was to all involved, it was nevertheless vital to perform it in exchange for entry. The security of the school that the guards were there to protect was thus upheld by a performance enacting our clearly fictitious connections to the local community and thus our implied trustworthiness. The performance was based on mutual deference to legitimate ideas, particularly that security is maintained through the implied obligations of being connected to those around you and that once that obligation is established, violating that contract of trust becomes almost illogical. Nowhere, of course, was there any sense of an external enforcement mechanism. Rather, the deference to those shared ideas about security and social cohesion *was* the enforcement mechanism.

This material was all supplemented by a small quantitative component that captured basic biographical details (such as the educational, geographical, and traditional backgrounds) of Somaliland's 150 or so most influential political and economic actors—although it is important to recognize the element of subjectivity inherent to the creation of any such list. This provided an empirical basis for understanding the pre-existing networks of trust that invariably influence the setting within which political contestation occurs.

Studying Discourse

To make sense of my interview data and field observations, I follow the well-established discourse literature in understanding discourse as a set of ideas, concepts, and categories that frame a particular object in ways that limit the actions that are considered possible in relation to that object (Epstein 2008, 2; see also Milliken 1999; Hansen 2006, chapter 2). Discourse is about more than just the things that people say or the communication of the ideas that people hold. It also incorporates practices and material artifacts as signs of how shared meanings are constructed and sustained. Here, the object of interest is Somaliland's legitimate independence from Somalia.

Discourses are fluid and rely on repetition to maintain their truth effect (Foucault 1980). If repetition is necessary to maintain how true a discourse appears to be, it is clear that discourse is not simply an articulation of a fixed and unmediated reality but that it is underpinned by power relations that promote the articulation (and re-articulation) of one particular representation of reality to the exclusion of others. When a discourse is powerful, it is widely accepted as presenting a self-evident or commonsensical understanding of the way that something naturally is. It does so, however, not because it presents the only logical understanding of that thing but because alternative ways of understanding it have been actively excluded (Epstein 2008, 9, cited in Hastings and Phillips 2018, 9), rendering them inappropriate, wrong, or even unthinkable. Discursive power does not imply an ability to persuade people to alter their view of something but rather to leave them "no choice but to talk (and act) in a certain way" because of how the meaning of that thing has been constructed (Epstein 2008, 9). Carolyn Nordstrom writes in her keenly observed anthropological study of political violence, *The Shadows of War* (2004, 233), that "power rests in part on the very illusion that power exists." I follow Nordstrom in understanding power as the capacity to maintain its own illusion, which it achieves not by the capacity to enforce sanctions but by generating and reproducing meanings that make sanctions appear self-evidently necessary.

This begs an obvious question: If discourse makes some things seem necessary and others not, does discourse cause behavior? The issue of causality is central to this book because I make claims about how and why discourse matters in the context of establishing and maintaining peace in Somaliland.

Poststructuralists are unwilling to directly assign causal properties to discourse, whereas critical realists argue that if discourses have consequences (as poststructuralists maintain) then they have implicit, if nonpositivist and nondeterministic, causal force (Kurki 2007, 375; Banta 2012, 385; Vucetic 2011, 1310). I am sympathetic to the poststructuralist claim because causing something to occur is not the same as structuring the conditions of possibility such that some actions seem necessary and others impossible. Discourse does not passively reflect an objectively knowable social world; it assigns meanings to that world and so simultaneously constructs it. This is what it means to say that the effects of discourse are constitutive rather than straightforwardly causal.

Returning to the case at hand, this means that Somaliland's discourse about independence does not cause peace in any mechanistic way. It is not a case of more discourse, more peace. But the meanings that are ascribed to independence within the discourse render certain actions normal or sensible, while others become dangerous or unthinkable. Therefore, Somaliland has not experienced large-scale violence since late 1996 in part because of how the independence discourse structures the conditions under which political violence can occur. Courting violence is rendered illogical not only because it could easily spiral into war but also because returning to war dissolves the separation that the discourse constructs between Somaliland and Somalia on the basis of who is inclined toward peaceful behavior and who is not. If

Somalilanders return to war, they become just as susceptible to violence as other Somalis.

For those producing Somaliland's independence discourse, the idea that Somaliland should not be recognized internationally as independent from Somalia contradicts both the obvious evidence of its de facto independence and the disparities in the level of conflict and insecurity within Somalia and Somaliland that are taken to render the two logically separate. Within the areas of Somaliland that participate in the independence discourse, the notion that peace and orderliness are inherent to the identity of Somaliland—and are what separates it from Somalia—exhibits a high degree of consistency across the sources that I surveyed.

I am sensitive to the fact that one of the core goals of Somaliland's independence discourse is to convince an international audience of the viability and legitimacy of its proclaimed independence, and that spoken aspects of the discourse (such as in interviews) may be particularly pronounced when articulated to a nonnative audience. I attempt to balance some of the distortions that this could bring through triangulation with the sources referred to previously, particularly those that are material or practice-based, and thus unable to be altered in response to my individual presence.

In researching the social world, my efforts to gather data invariably implicates my presence as a researcher. By the acts of observing, interviewing, and interacting with others, I am inevitably intervening in networks and relationships of power (Pachirat 2017, 19). While I, and other postpositivists, believe that this is an inescapable aspect of researching the social, it is glaringly apparent when researching an issue as politically charged as one group's desire to be formally recognized by the very group that I, as a white Western passport holder, may be taken to represent: the powerfully amorphous international community. It is entirely possible that some of those I interacted with presumed me to possess far greater access to people with decision-making authority than I do, which could have amplified aspects of the discourse that I observed. Moreover, it is likely that as a researcher from an affluent Western country (Australia), my access to powerful systems of knowledge production, including influential media outlets and academic publications, was presumed to be greater than that of those I interacted with, which again may have distorted what people were inclined to tell me. It is crucial, therefore, that I acknowledge that my position as a researcher may have lead, at least to an extent, to a cogeneration of data rather than to maintain the illusion that I simply collected existing packages of social data as if they were "rocks lying about in a field" (Pachirat 2017, 18). That is to say that this is inductive research and is offered as an interpretive piece of work.

Acknowledging the use of judgement in the selection of sources raises methodological issues regarding the basis upon which sources are deemed representative. Being interpretive and critically reflective, the validity of a piece of discourse analysis hinges upon the level of coherence and consistency it finds across its database of sources. Jennifer Milliken argues that an analysis may be considered valid when adding new texts to the database does not change the theoretical categories that have already been generated (Milliken 1999, 234; see also Jørgensen and Phillips 2002, 125; Epstein 2008, 173). Therefore, my argument about the power of Somaliland's independence discourse to influence behavior rests on there being a high level of internal consistency among the sources that I have surveyed and identified as constituting the discourse. My triangulation methods thus warrant further explanation.

First, I spoke to as wide a group of Somalilanders as I could. While a majority would be classed as elites, they were not universally so, although most still came into reasonably regular contact with foreigners and spoke at least some English. Second, where appropriate, I asked people directly about whether they felt that Somaliland's peacefulness and claim of independence is portrayed to foreigners in ways that differ from how it is understood by Somalilanders. This helped me to gain an appreciation of the strategic consciousness with which certain views may be expressed to me as a foreign researcher. One person was particularly direct on this point, lamenting his own role as a senior researcher in an externally funded research institute, saying that his job was to mythologize Somaliland's peacefulness and progressiveness for *both* an international and a local audience. He felt that he was a rare critic of this myth, and that this isolated him from the majority of Somalilanders who genuinely believe in it and from the foreigners who are eager for a good news story from Somalia: "The mythology is created and launched in the dialectic of Somalilanders who believe the myth and the [foreigners] who echo it."[15] He felt, however, that to openly challenge this mythology would jeopardize his job because there were strong, if implicit, normative expectations for the research he was hired to produce. Another, a former minister, cautioned me:

In Somaliland, two out of the five [now three out of the six] regions have claimed the country. Sool, Sanaag, and Awdal don't want [an independent] Somaliland. There is no media covering that. VOA [Voice of America] and BBC Somalia are both managed by [the] Isaaq [clan]. People elsewhere in the world don't hear the voice of the other three regions.[16]

That local sceptics of Somaliland's claim of peacefulness and progressiveness reported to feel isolated by the community at large suggests that the independence discourse is dominant among Somalilanders in the predominantly Isaaq clan areas, regardless of whether external observers are an intended audience. This point was underscored for me at a public talk I gave in Hargeysa in 2015, where I discussed some of the findings of my research. There, a local journalist read a quote back to me from a research paper that I published in late 2013 (and which forms the basis of some of this book) where I wrote:

> In spite of the general popularity of independence, anti-independence narratives are nevertheless evident even among the Hargeisa-based elite. A former minister argued, for example: "There are only two of five regions that want independence, the other three do not." (Phillips 2013, 28)

The journalist expressed what appeared to be genuine surprise that people in Hargeysa had spoken against independence to me and asked me to elaborate. From my (obviously subjective) reading of the room at the time, the journalist was not alone in his surprise.

Another way that I attempted to gain purchase on the way that the independence discourse affects political practices was through an analysis of the material artifacts and practices referred to above. Other visual sources included the near ubiquity of the national flag painted on privately owned shops, cars, fences, restaurants, construction sites, and in people's homes. Of course, it could be that outward portrayals of nationalism are a way of currying favor with a proindependence elite, though this is probably an overly reductive interpretation, and also one that attributes too much coercive capacity to the government. I consider the highly conspicuous public displays of the national flag an enactment of the discourse about independence.

Finally, I conducted an extensive survey of sources produced by other foreign researchers about Somaliland's postconflict reconstruction and desire for independence. As chapter 5 shows, there is a striking level of thematic consistency across much of the English language about Somaliland's post-conflict recovery, particularly in work produced by researchers who spent the bulk of their time within the capital city of Hargeysa.[17] This work tends to highlight the remarkable success of Somaliland, despite (but often because of) its inability to access many forms of international revenue, particularly development assistance (Kaplan 2008; Lewis 2009; Eubank 2012; Pham 2012; Mills 2015) In this, it generally articulates the key tenets of the independence discourse that is produced in the capital (and the more heavily populated middle section of the country that covers Hargeysa, Gabiley, Berbera, Oodweyne, and Burco) where foreign researchers are better able to access. Of course, such consistency across sources could mean that the discourse is internally consistent, or it could mean that it is consciously narrated to foreigners in a very deliberate manner. As suggested in chapter 5, these are not mutually exclusive possibilities: it appears to be widely believed (to the point of being quite internally consistent) *and* strategically reiterated to an external audience.

I must hasten to add that the majority of my own fieldwork within Somaliland was also undertaken in Hargeysa. Anthropologist Markus Hoehne rightly critiques the tendency of foreigners to spend time only in the capital and assuming that it represents the rest of the country (Hoehne 2015, 106–7). Having problematized the independence discourse, I do not suggest that it is representative beyond the areas in which it is produced, the epicenter of which is Hargeysa. As one might expect, Somaliland's independence discourse is only dominant in the parts of Somaliland that support the claim of independence. It is far less influential among the (predominantly non-Isaaq clan) residents of the east, and parts of the far west where the idea of independence from Somalia is commonly rejected. The eastern regions of Sool, Sanaag, and south-eastern Togdheer (the latter is known as Cayn to those who reject Somaliland's independence) are simultaneously claimed by Puntland, a region that declared semiautonomy (though not independence) from the Federal Republic of Somalia in 1998 and remains a member state of the Republic of Somalia. Markus Hoehne suggests that about 20 percent of Somaliland's population oppose independence (Hoehne 2011, 323).

Outline of the Book

The first chapter of this book sets the scene for Somaliland's place within debates about the utility of northern intervention against violence and poverty in various southern contexts. It explores the way that the dominant discourse about state fragility frames the quality of domestic governance institutions in the Global South as both cause of, and solution to, the prevalence of conflict and poverty. In so doing, it brackets out alternative—nondomestic and noninstitutional—ways of understanding peace and development in the Global South. These exclusions also frame international intervention as self-evidently useful in making the world more peaceful and prosperous. I argue that this dramatically overstates the impact that development or state-building interventions have because they constitute a small part of the means by which power and resources move between north and south.

The rest of the book focuses on the specific challenge that Somaliland's experience—reflected and produced by the independence discourse—poses to the powerful fragile states discourse. Each chapter examines a different explanation for what set Somaliland apart from the Somali Republic once it declared its independence in 1991.[18] These are: the country's relative isolation from global political and economic structures (chapter 2); the strong degree of mutual dependence between key elites and networks that this isolation fostered (chapter 3); and the local ownership that was attached to Somaliland's political and economic institutions, which was also substantially a function of its detachment from the international system (chapter 4).

The argument throughout these three chapters is that without the level of international isolation experienced by Somaliland during its early formational period, its key actors would have almost certainly been under pressure to adhere—or at least appear to adhere—to external expectations of, first good governance through strong and vertically inclusive institutions, and second, the progressively effective pursuit of state-monopolized violence. The fact that the peace process in the 1990s unfolded without an attempt to arrive at the institutional endpoints favored by international donor organizations allowed local incentives to drive elite interactions. Somalilanders had the freedom to cherry-pick from local and international institutional governance models and to experiment with what was seen as likely to work given the local context—an option that was closed to other Somalis (and those in many other conflict-affected states).

These chapters also reinforce one of the uncomfortable insights from some of the literature about elite pacts: that vertically exclusive distributions of power and resources—that exclude most nonelites—may be more likely to augur short–medium term political stability than those that are vertically inclusive (Phillips 2013, 363; see Hickey 2013, 10; Laws 2012, 2, 18–20; see also Lindeman 2011). They demonstrate that some of Somaliland's relative stability can be attributed to the collusive commercial arrangements that were established to end the fighting around the port city of Berbera between in 1993. Alex de Waal's observation that Somaliland emerged initially as "a profit sharing agreement among the dominant livestock traders with a constitution appended" (de Waal 1996) is appropriate. Somaliland's second president, Mohamed Ibrahim Egal, secured huge amounts of money for his supporters and simultaneously indebted them to him while also providing security dividends for the wider population. By combining exclusive business practices with somewhat greater control over the means of coercion, Egal and his coalition were also able to edge out their competitors to dominate the economy, putting Egal in a position to increasingly centralize patronage around his presidency. The political and economic elite consolidated an arrangement that excluded many but that laid the groundwork for relative peace. Exclusive though it was, Egal's ability to extract—and lavishly reimburse with public money—was, and remains, widely accepted within Somaliland as having been a legitimate course of action. While this relatively insular and collusive model of development chimes with historical analyses of state-building in Europe by Charles Tilly (1975, 1985, 1990) and others (Evans, Rueschemeyer and Skocpol 1985; Elias 1994, 351; Giddens 1985; Porter 1994), it is out of step with contemporary international expectations that peace and development should begin as inclusive, liberal processes, conducted through the channel of formal state institutions.

However, the confluence of permissive structures, elite pacts, and contextually appropriate governance institutions does not imply that a prolonged period of peace was inevitable. Chapter 5 spotlights the powerful discourse about independence that re/produced shared meanings about each of these elements, demonstrating their contingent nature. It argues that the maintenance of peace is less a function of institutional strength than of a discourse that structures the conditions of possibility such that political violence seems illogical or dangerous. The discourse articulates engrained popular ideas about the proximity—and dangerous unpredictability—of violence (see

Coburn 2011, 219). The visible consequences of failing to negotiate a peace settlement in Somalia undoubtedly reinforced Somalilanders' motivations to succeed in doing so. For Somalilanders, the war in and around Mogadishu provided a tangible worst-case scenario that graphically illustrated the potential for violence to spiral out of control in structural circumstances that closely resembled Somaliland's. It suggests that the maintenance of peace rests, to a significant degree, on the reproduction of a belief that violence is undesirable, rather than the enforcement capacity of the institutions that articulate that belief.

The independence discourse is imbued with a sense of barely-contained violence. This sense is inscribed in its references to Somaliland's physical proximity to the violence that continued in Somalia and in the temporal proximity to its own violent past. However, it is also inscribed in the fact that its clan-based institutions were central to establishing peace while also fueling its wars and those in the rest of Somalia. Thus, whereas the imputed violence in an ideal Weberian state principally resides in the state's institutions, in Somaliland it resides in the discursive reproduction of proximate violence.

Crucially, violence is also inscribed in the clear proximity of international intervention. On the one hand intervention is seen as having destroyed Somalia but on the other it represents the possibility of Somaliland being recognized as a sovereign state. Even Somaliland's quest for legal independence—so widely seen as the ultimate reward for its ability to maintain peace in such challenging circumstances—is tinged with plausible violence.

Chapter 1

The Imperative of Intervention

Somaliland received almost no official development assistance (ODA) during its early years.[1] Indeed, not only did Somaliland receive no ODA, it received (almost) no international charitable contributions, no support for state-building or peace-building, no peacekeeping missions, no political support for belligerents in its civil war, no military assistance, no access to the licit international weapons trade, no significant involvement in extractive industries, minimal foreign investment, and no access to international loans. And it was unencumbered with international debt repayments.[2] Other than the remittances Somalilanders were sending home from abroad, the country was remarkably free from external involvement of any kind during its formative years, in sharp distinction to the rest of Somalia. And yet, as the World Bank (2017, 5) recently wrote, "Somalia is a fragile state, while Somaliland seems to be doing well."

This chapter argues that intervention in so-called fragile states is so widely seen as beneficial (or at least inevitable) that only its form is open to debate. The idea of fragile statehood is produced by a powerful discourse about the ostensible harms certain states cause their citizens and the wider world—a discourse powerful not because it is empirically grounded but because it resonates with the ideologies and organizational mandates of northern policy makers as they try to manage the effects of globalization (Richards 2005, 6).

The experience of state formation in Somaliland challenges the assumptions that hold the fragile states discourse together. The first of these assumptions is that the causes of state fragility are primarily, if not wholly, domestic in origin. This is usually illustrated by emphasizing domestic corruption, patronage politics, social cleavages, and weak governance institutions in a country's experience of violence and/or poverty.[3] At the same time, the discourse disregards the ways that external intervention can exacerbate conflict and economic malaise in the states it designates as fragile. The second assumption is that the intervention of northern actors is self-evidently useful for overcoming these problems. More broadly, these assumptions deflect responsibility for global conflict and poverty to the south, and the levers for change within northern states are left largely ignored. By revealing how Somalilanders speak of their exclusion from the international system throughout the 1990s as generally beneficial, I provide some empirical footholds from which to challenge these assumptions.

Somalia is widely deigned the quintessential case of fragile or failed statehood. In 2008, *The Economist* referred to it as the "world's most comprehensively failed state" (see also Kaplan 2006), and it was ranked in first place by the *Fragile States Index* for all but two years of the index's first decade (2006–2016). A paradigmatic example of how Somalia's experience of conflict is framed can be found in Greg Mills, J. Peter Pham, and David Kilcullen's 2013 book, *Somalia—Fixing Africa's Most Failed State*:

> Many Somalis are quick to point to external reasons for failure . . . [and] often refer to the Cold War and its undoubted manipulations. . . . A few might go back even further and speak about the injustices of colonialism, though these memories pale against recent scars. On paper, Somalis would seem to have a point. . . . Currently, however, the threats to Somali security can be grouped into three different but related clusters, *all of which are internally generated*: first, that of Al-Shabaab . . . the second issue is the absence of government and governance. . . . This situation is related to, third, the most intractable problem in recent Somali history: the clan system, once a basis of social stability and consensus, today a basis of power and control outside of

government. Indeed, this history shows that the central problem of Somalia is the virtual impossibility of governing Somalis, from without and also within. (2013, Kindle Location 306–333, emphasis added).

This short passage provides a snapshot of the conventional wisdom about Somalia's troubles, particularly the insistence that they are detached from recent interventions by powerful states (other than on paper) and that as a result, its problems are all internally generated. In fact, as chapter 2 details, none of the three threats that the authors point to can be understood in isolation from the interventions that shaped Somalia from the colonial era to the present.

Making Intervention Inevitable

In 2019, the *Fragile States Index* listed 119 out of 178 countries at warning level or higher (Fund for Peace 2019, 6–7). Considering the diversity of those 119 countries it is not surprising that a large literature critiques the use of general terms like "fragile," "failing," or "failed," which suggests they all share certain fundamental defects along a spectrum of dysfunction.[4] Yet despite this, such terms remain integral to mainstream security and development policy doctrine in northern states. They provide the primary lens through which violence and poverty in the Global South are understood by major development agencies, think tanks, university research centers, the United Nations, and multilateral organizations like the OECD, World Bank, Asian Development Bank, and African Development Bank. Every year, international organizations monitor, measure, rank, and compare the political, economic, and social characteristics that supposedly define states as fragile and, as such, render them in need of remedial action.[5]

Despite an engrained trope about the importance of local ownership in solving state fragility, and the ineffectiveness of one-size-fits-all models for exiting the condition, practitioners adhere to a reasonably specific template. The World Bank's influential *World Development Report 2011* emphasizes that while local context matters, "a basic set of tools emerging from experience" can be adapted to suit different places (World Bank 2011, 16). These tools invariably focus on enhancing the capacity of state institutions to deliver security and political and economic goods to citizens through programs that reform the security sector, increase judicial capacity, manage elections, enhance citizen empowerment, improve livelihood opportunities, and develop macroeconomic policy (Westendorf 2015, 230). Development professionals continue to advocate for these tools despite the simultaneous acknowledgment that they have not achieved their stated objectives.

Those who produce the fragile states discourse readily admit that the precise meaning of fragile statehood is contested.[6] However, they agree that external assistance is an efficient, even necessary, way of breaking domestic cycles or traps of conflict and poverty.[7] Australia's Department of Foreign Affairs and Trade (DFAT, then AusAid) put the case plainly, stating that fragile states "have little chance of overcoming such serious problems alone. In fact, if left unassisted, they may experience fragility and development stagnation for generations" (DFAT 2005, 7). Britain's Department for International Development (DFID) made a similar claim five years later: "Eliminating global poverty and achieving the [Millennium Development Goals] will not be possible unless the international community tackles conflict and fragility more effectively" (DFID 2010, 10).

Paul Collier, the author of widely cited academic papers, popular books (2008; 2011), and some of the World Bank's most influential research papers, argues for a highly interventionist approach to development. He suggests that failed or failing states have "structural characteristics which gravely impede . . . the provision of public goods," particularly security and accountability (Collier 2009, 219). The key to turning the situation around lies "partly in a phase of international provision of the key public goods, partly in enhanced regional pooling of sovereignty, and partly in institutional innovation to make the domestic provision of public goods less demanding of the state" (220; see also Mallaby 2002; Krasner 2004; Fearon and Laitin 2004). A guiding assumption in this argument, and which is also central to the discourse, is that the international provision of key public goods will be contextually appropriate, benevolent, and disconnected from transnational systems that reproduce inequalities. It also assumes that human agency follows institutionalized incentives in a predictable manner. However, as we shall see in chapter 2, these assumptions obscure some important possibilities for autonomous recovery (see Weinstein 2005; Rutazibwa 2013).

Vast sums of money hinge upon the label of fragility. Chandy, Seidel, and Zhang (2016, 2) report that in 2012, a median fragile state relied on foreign aid for about half of its foreign capital. Large portions of northern states'

ODA budgets are also reserved specifically for states that have been designated as fragile. In 2016, Britain's DFID committed to spending 50 percent of its annual budget in fragile states and regions. The World Bank and other donors made similar commitments to increase the proportion of their budgets allocated to fragile states.

Not surprisingly, organizations and the professionals whose careers they sustain seek to spend the money they are allocated in order to secure further funding. There is strong pressure for staff to meet the burn rate—a measure of the rate at which an organization or its partners spends its budget. Within the United States Agency for International Development (USAID), for instance, it is commonly understood that faster spending means faster replenishment from Congress (Arnoldy 2010) and that project success is measured, in no small part, by the speed at which funds are disbursed (Munter 2016). This is not specific to USAID though. A World Bank Report from 1992 found that Bank employees widely saw the timely dispersal of funds as "the dominant institutional value" and that demonstrating an ability to secure loan approvals quickly was a means for staff to "achiev[e] personal recognition" (World Bank 1992, 16, 14). Both Ngaire Woods (2006, 39), and Alnoor Ebrahim and Steven Herz (2011, 66) found that these incentive structures had changed little since that report, suggesting that internal corporate objectives and reward structures constitute at least part of the reason that nonintervention is almost never seriously considered as a solution by development agencies.

A multitude of indexes categorize, rank, and thereby determine the amount of funding that fragile states receive. This helps to produce the realities that they describe. The coproduction of fragile states and donor entities can be seen clearly in the World Bank's *Country Policy and Institutional Assessment* (*CPIA*), which is the most influential index of state fragility. Its findings drive resource allocation for the World Bank's International Development Association (IDA), African Development Bank, Asian Development Bank, the International Monetary Fund (IMF), the Organisation for Economic Co-operation and Development's Development Assistance Committee (OECD-DAC), the Millennium Challenge Account, and the governments of Scandinavia, France, and the UK, among others (see Rocha De Siqueria 2014, 271; Nay 2014, 216). The *CPIA* defines a state as fragile and conflict-affected when its score across sixteen indicators is 3.2 or below or it has experienced a regional or UN peacekeeping or political/peacebuilding operation within the last three years. Sitting above a score of 3.2 renders a state ineligible for fragile states funding from many of the biggest international donors. The fact that significant pools of funding are linked to a determination of fragility hardens the incentives for states to accept the term and, presumably, perpetuates its use.[8]

But the role of the major development agencies in the production of state fragility goes beyond simply designating some states as fragile and dispensing money accordingly. The very definition of fragility expresses the identity and corporate mandate of the agencies that define the term such that they are indivisible from it. All that the World Bank's *CPIA* measures across its sixteen indicators is clear from the four clusters into which they are grouped: economic management, structural policies, policies for social inclusion and equity, and public-sector management and institutions. As Mick Moore (2016) notes, these are essentially the criteria upon which international lenders like the World Bank rate the creditworthiness of potential borrowers. They have nothing to do with political factors like the prevalence of violence or the perceived likelihood of a major political breakdown. They are also silent on human security and harm minimization, despite the central role that both play in the justification for intervening in fragile states. The most influential tool for determining whether a state is classed as fragile is therefore based on criteria that fit the World Bank's institutional mandate of providing loans—not the specific needs of countries that it ostensibly seeks to assist. The policy tools surrounding state fragility are principally about creating efficiencies within existing modes of distributing development assistance and, by extension, the power arrangements nested within those modes. They are not about unsettling these arrangements in the name of human security or equality. Fragile states and the development agencies that define states as fragile are coproduced. They do exist without each other.

Susan Woodward (2017, 135) quotes a representative from the OECD-DAC, who bluntly explains his own understanding of what constitutes fragile statehood: fragile states are "environments where international agencies cannot use their preferred aid effectiveness modalities." A senior official at Australia's DFAT told me something similar, that the idea of fragile statehood was developed by major international development agencies "to explain why their incentivized business models weren't working in these places."[9] Indeed, the consistency with which development agencies note their own failure to reverse state fragility is striking. The World Bank's *World*

Development Report 2011 concedes that: "No low-income fragile or conflict-affected state has yet achieved a single Millennium Development Goal (MDG)" (World Bank 2011, 50). The codirector of that report, Nigel Roberts, went further elsewhere:

> If you look at the experience of low-income, fragile states over the last 25 years, the lack of progress in health and education is pretty stunning. . . . No single low income fragile state has achieved or will achieve any of the Millennium Development Goals. And believe me, this is not for lack of trying, it is not for lack of investment in health and education, it is for a lack of success in transforming institutions. (Roberts 2011)

I will return to the institutional fix that this statement presumes. For now, however, note the circular reasoning implicit in the failure of development agencies to reduce state fragility: development projects are more effective in states that already have stronger governance institutions (see Hellman 2013). The World Bank's 2004 *Annual Review of Development Effectiveness* was clear on this point:

> The Bank's efforts have been more successful in countries that are politically stable; where there is strong ownership of reform; where the executive, legislature, and the bureaucracy are working for common purposes; and where the country has the administrative capacity to implement reforms. The Bank's efforts have been less successful where one or all of these elements have been lacking. (cited in Woodward 2017, 59)

Of course, stronger governance institutions would presumably negate the state's supposed fragility and thus the reason for Bank intervention in the first place. The paradox is striking: the interventions used to tackle state fragility work better when states are not fragile. An Independent Evaluation Group made a similar observation in 2016: "The Bank has been adept at responding and at adjusting its strategies and analytical support to situations of violence and conflict, but its operational response has been constrained by its limited menu of instrument choices" (IEG 2016). However, this failure has not generated a broader call to fundamentally alter either the menu of instruments or the assumptions about the domestic transformation required for a transition from fragility. This circularity illustrates how the fragile states discourse reproduces its own assumptions, particularly the notion that external intervention is necessary to enhance security and development in the Global South.

Where policy documents from key donor agencies refer to international actors, they generally portray them as straightforwardly benevolent or, if their self-interest is acknowledged, as working in good faith.[10] The World Bank's World Development Report (2017, 29) emphasizes, for example, the need to account for power asymmetries when designing institutional capacity building programs, though these asymmetries are discussed only in domestic policy arenas and not between donor and recipient. The report mentions "power asymmetries" forty-three times, but not once do they extend beyond the boundaries of the state that is to be intervened in. At one point the report explicitly brushes off the significance of asymmetries between countries:

> Although income inequality *between* countries has declined over the last 20 years as low-and middle-income countries have grown faster than those at the top of the world income distribution, the level of income inequality *within* countries has increased. (World Bank 2017, 170—emphasis in original)

As the following section shows, asymmetries between countries tend to be observed more acutely by those experiencing intervention.

De-Historicizing Intervention

Citizens of so-called fragile states regularly challenge the idea that external assistance is inherently useful. Most members of the African Union, the thirty-eight states that were initially listed as fragile by the OECD in 2006 (Nay 2014, 223), and Papua New Guinea, have rejected the terms "fragility" and "failure" as pejorative, seeing them as permutations of imperialism and an encroachment on sovereignty (Lambach 2006, 413). The president of Burundi articulated his concerns to the United Nations General Assembly in 2009:

> The terminology "fragile states" should only be used with caution. . . . I strongly feel that it is not a neutral terminology. Apart from the emotional implications, it has financial and political implications. Moreover, it gives us a bad image in the eyes of the investors we so badly need. (President Pierre Nkurunziza, quoted in Grimm, Lemay-Hébert, and Nay 2014, 197)

At times, international agencies have altered their language in response to such critiques. The Asian Development Bank's *Country Partnership Strategy* for Papua New Guinea (PNG) notes, for example, that it "does not refer to PNG as a fragile state as such," while adding that: "the main issues and problems . . . are clearly those which are common in situations of fragility" (ADB 2011, 1). This caveat did not alter the substance of the policy, which stated that the bank would treat PNG as it does other fragile states regardless of the label it applied.

Highlighting the historical amnesia embedded in the term *fragility*, we might note that the vast majority of fragile states experienced European colonialism, and many were also sites of Cold War proxy conflicts. On the "List of Fragile Situations" published by the OECD's Development Assistance Committee (DAC) in 2015 (OECD DAC 2015) (which is based on a combination of data provided by the World Bank, the Asian Development Bank, and the Fragile States Index), almost all of the fifty states included (except, in Europe, Kosovo, and Bosnia and Herzegovina), experienced European colonial rule. The three exceptions were partial: Ethiopia (occupied by Italy for five years but not formally colonized), Nepal (a British protectorate but not formally colonized), and North Korea (colonized by Japan). By the publication of the 2018 list there were only thirty-six states included, each of which had been colonized by a European state. By declining to reflect on this striking correlation, those who produce the discourse confine the significance of colonialism to the past even though its continuities are well established by postcolonial scholars.[11] By papering over a "violent and exploitative world order that has historically violated the integrity of African" and other postcolonial societies, the discourse creates the impression that all states were created with equal opportunities to advance, and that failure is theirs alone (Wai 2018, 52).[12]

Others emphasize that the notion of state fragility ignores how European states acquired their wealth and power. Christopher Cramer (2006, 36) argues, for example: "every country that is now industrialized got there through the four-wheel drive mechanism of protection against free trade and with the differential lock device of state intervention preventing the wheels of production from spinning endlessly in the mud." The international financial institutions that emerged after World War II conditioned access to international capital on the absence of such protections, thereby obstructing industrialization in postcolonial states. Moreover, wealthy European states attained global dominance through economic collusion, racketeering, and the application of ruthless violence to their citizens, neighboring populations, and the populations they kidnapped as slaves, colonized, and plundered. The "civilianisation of government and domestic politics" was, as Charles Tilly famously pointed out, essentially an unintended by-product (Tilly 1990, 206) of international military rivalry and power struggles between local elites. It was not the result of pressure from civil society for better services (Eriksen 2011, 231) or deliberations over constitutional design, elections, empowerment of the citizenry, or any of the other liberal democratic processes that are widely recommended as recovery mechanisms for fragile states. Neither was it internally bounded. Violence leapt over and redrew boundaries between peoples, just as the wealth stolen from the colonies reconstituted both the colonizers and the colonized.

The World Bank's influential *World Development Report* series provides a yearly indicator of where mainstream thinking broadly sits in the field of economic development. The 2017 report, *Governance and the Law,* implies that fragility is a stage that states inevitably pass through before progressing to the monopolization of legitimate violence:[13]

> Even the countries that enjoy the highest per capita incomes and most peaceful societies in the world, such as most of Europe, emerged from wars and violent contests for power (Tilly 1985, 1990). They were "fragile states" for most of their historical trajectory. (World Bank 2017, 112)

Continuing with the sense that fragility is a transitional point in the evolution of modern governance, the report notes: "Today, millions of people live under the rule of nonstate armed groups, contemporary equivalents of the medieval violence specialists who gave rise to the western European states" (112). Strikingly, it concludes this passage with reference to Somaliland, which, it argues, "provides a compelling illustration of the sustainability of the governance arrangements that arise organically—and without donor intervention—from the bargains struck among armed rebels, business communities, and civilians" (112). By ending its narrative of Europe's formation in this way, the report inscribes the European experience of taming violence as natural, suggesting that Somaliland transitioned from fragility (5) because it emulated that experience.

The Institutional Fix

The discourse about state fragility consistently frames helping states to build strong institutions as the most effective means of preventing war and civil disorder.[14] The relationship between institutional capacity and violence is presented as causal, and effective state institutions are rendered "preconditions for domestic peace" (Paris 2006, 438). The first key message that the World Bank offers in its 2011 *World Development Report* is that without effective and legitimate state institutions "the likelihood of violent conflict increases" (World Bank 2011 xi-xii). The report proposes that the "underlying reason for societies' inability to resist stresses is that their institutions are too weak to mediate them peacefully" (86).[15] Others argue that "peacebuilding is dependent upon a government's ability to exercise effective authority in economic, political, and military matters" (DeRouen et al. 2010, 333; see also Doyle and Sambanis 2006); that "successful peacebuilding can occur only in the context of capable state institutions" (Call and Cousens 2008); and that consolidating peace requires a "laser-like focus on the institutions of the state" (Sisk 2013, 168). Citing an "extensive study of all countries since 1946" by James Fearon, Barbara Walter concludes that "the shoddier the governance and the weaker the institutions, the more likely a country was to experience civil war" (Walter 2015, 5, citing Fearon 2010).

The idea that greater institutional capacity reduces violence is so common that the terms "state-building" (enhancing the capacity of state institutions) and "peace-building" (establishing foundations for a durable peace) tend to be used interchangeably by scholars and policy makers alike (Chandler 2017, 4; see for example Paris and Sisk 2009, 1; International Dialogue on Peacebuilding and Statebuilding 2011). The conflation of these terms highlights the degree to which state institutions are presented as the inevitable vehicles of peace and civil order.

Assuming that the relationship between state institutional capacity and reduced violence is causal, rather than correlative or reflexive, the literature supports interventions to increase the capacity of state institutions as a pathway out of conflict. In a paradigmatic example of the tendency to see governance institutions as the direct cause of civil order, Barbara F. Walter (2015, 1) argues that the best predictor of whether a country will return to civil war is the degree to which its leaders are "constrain[ed]" by:

political and legal institutions . . . [that] serve as a check on executive power, help incumbent elites credibly commit to political reform, and create a situation where rebels need not maintain militias as a supplementary mechanism to hold political elites in line.

But which comes first, the institutional arrangements that shape the behavior or the underlying willingness and/or ability of people to create and submit to those arrangements? If it is the latter (or a matter of coproduction) there are unbounded possibilities for the origins of that willingness. The former reading thus offers an appealing parsimony.

In Walter's account, institutional weaknesses "make it . . . attractive and . . . necessary for rebels to return to war" (Walter 2015, 23). However, the underlying suggestion that (institutional) constraints are necessary to constrain actors' behavior opens a chicken and egg problem (see Blyth 2002, 25): effective institutions are necessary to produce constraint, and constraint is the measure of institutional effectiveness. This problem is inherent in the literature that attributes political and economic outcomes directly to the quality of institutions. Writing about the possibilities for "preventing civil war through institutional design," Alan Kuperman (2015, 226) argues:

> The good news is that if institutionalized appropriately, either [of the two main models of constitutional design] can provide resilience against such shocks. However, if improperly institutionalized, either design may leave countries highly vulnerable to shocks, thereby magnifying the risks of political instability up to and including civil war and genocide.

As with Walter's argument, this formulation begs the question of how one knows whether a state's constitution has been institutionalized properly or improperly other than by the results—in this case, apparent level of political stability. The relationship between the variables (level of stability and institutional quality) is presented as causal even though the generator of in/stability has not been observed directly (see Blyth 2011, 90; Geddes 1990). The logic is circular: stronger institutions produce greater levels of stability, while greater levels of stability are evidence of stronger institutions.

Such arguments bring us no closer to understanding the reasons that effective institutions are established in some places and not in others and, therefore, no closer to understanding the underlying relationship between governance institutions and political order. The focus is on establishing the causal force of governance institutions rather than the means by which institutions are internally constructed and reflexively sustained such that they both produce and reflect their environment.

There is an additional chicken and egg problem posed by the impulse to strengthen state institutions against violence: that it is routinely offered as the solution to violent state institutions. For example, after detailing the pervasive collusion of state officials and rebels in the Democratic Republic of the Congo to steal billions of dollars' worth of natural resources, the UN Panel of Experts advised that "a step towards halting the exploitation of natural resources will be the early establishment of an all-inclusive transitional government . . . which would ensure that central government control is reinstated" (UNSC 2002, 30). How bringing officials and rebels "together in a state would reduce rather than magnify their exploitative behavior was not demonstrated" (Englebert 2006, 135). More recently, a report by the International Growth Center's Commission on State Fragility, Growth and Development, chaired by former UK prime minister David Cameron, declared that fragile states "are blighted by conflict and corruption. Their governments lack the legitimacy and capacity to deliver the jobs, public services, and opportunities their people need" (IGC 2018, 4). At the same time the report emphasizes that "only governments can lift societies out of fragility" (18), begging the question of how beneficial it might be to strengthen such blighted governments. Furthermore, there is no guarantee that enhancing the technical capacity of state institutions will strengthen only the liberal democratic impulses within them. Congolese scholar Patience Kabamba (2012, n.p.) writes:

> The state in the Congolese context is the problem and the internal dynamics are working to make it as weak as possible while the external dynamics supported by the UN and the international community is making it stronger. The war is prolonged by this obsession with the state . . . which emasculates the Congolese and gives the major role to the international community.

Similarly, in Somalia, the international community's fixation on institutional capacity building has repeatedly exacerbated political infighting by giving factions more to fight over (Balthasar 2014, 5) and increasing the risks posed by exclusion from the state apparatus. In fact, in some of the world's most fragile states, it is less their institutional weakness that citizens decry than the strength that the state gains by leveraging their supposed fragility (Phillips 2017). As Aasim Akhtar and Ali Ahmad write (2015, 95), Pakistanis

> do not view the state in terms of its strength or weakness . . . even when expressing their discontent . . . [rather] the state is implicitly represented as willingly and successfully renting out its sovereignty to imperial interests for the enrichment of a corrupt, collaborative elite that controls the levers of domestic power.

It is this constitutive relationship between local elites and international networks that the fragile states discourse entirely misses.

The Hybrid Institutional Fix

The idea that rational state institutions are central to development is critiqued by scholars who explore hybrid governance institutions. This literature challenges the presumed necessity of state institutions to the prospects for peace and sociopolitical order by exploring "informal and non-standard systems of governance that have arisen in conflict affected contexts" (Mac Ginty and Richmond 2016, 219).[16] It emphasizes that local informal (particularly customary or indigenous) institutions can provide governance without government (Lund 2006; Menkhaus 2006/2007; Raeymaekers, Vlassenroot, and Menkhaus 2008; Titeca and De Herdt 2011) and thus serve as "functional equivalents," or "replacement[s] of," state institutions (Börzel and Risse 2016, 150; Belloni 2012, 25, respectively).

However, by selecting cases of functional equivalency—informal agents and institutions that provide basic state-like services such as security, policing, justice, mediation, financial services, welfare, consultation, or tax extraction—the hybrid governance literature also tends to exclude rules of the game that engender civil order but do not have obvious counterparts within the rational-legal state apparatus. Specifically, it excludes the reflexive nature of ideas about civil order (and the discourses that give those ideas a measure of continuity), presumably because they do not provide governance mechanisms that are paralleled by states. In a widely cited piece, Tobias Hagmann and Markus Hoehne (2007, 21) note that:

> Scholars from traditionally state-centered disciplines such as political science or international relations have difficulty imagining that life can continue in the absence of the state. . . . In reality, however, alternative actors perform the core state functions that the state no longer fulfils when it abandons a certain space. (cited in Boege et al. 2009, 611)

This is a necessary counterpoint to Eurocentric notions of statehood that hold states as inevitable to the maintenance of sociopolitical order. However, by focusing on the ability of nonstate actors and institutions to reproduce the functions of a state in its absence, the hybrid governance literature affirms the state-centric ontology of the literature it critiques. It suggests that it is only states or the entities that directly mimic them that produce order. This leaves no room for ordering processes that do not simulate those provided by the state. It also constructs institutions as ontologically prior to (rather than constitutive of) the ideas that give them legitimacy.

Doing Development Differently: The Local Context Turn

The insights of the hybrid governance literature are reflected in the efforts of some development practitioners to better account for forms of legitimacy that do not derive from effective state institutions. The OECD was an early leader in this, noting that: "Absent a careful understanding of the way in which the political and social fabric of society is expressed institutionally, investment in recreating or building new institutions that mimic the ideal Weberian form is often bound to fail" (OECD 2008, 39; cited in Lemay-Hébert and Mathieu 2014, 239). However, as Nicolas Lemay-Hébert and Xavier Mathieu demonstrate, the need for the OECD to operationalize this insight creates a circular argument in which legitimacy is considered both a cause and an effect of state-building processes (OECD 2011, 37; cited in Lemay-Hébert and Mathieu 2014, 241). Indeed, one OECD report notes that including traditional legitimacy in state-building interventions makes it: "difficult to come up with sound, replicable approaches that donors can take in programmes of development assistance" (OECD 2010, 120; cited in Lemay-Hébert and Mathieu 2014, 242). The result is that the OECD reaffirms the institutionalist approach that justifies its organizational mandate as the "provider of expertise on 'good' practices of intervention" (Lemay-Hébert and Mathieu 2014, 242).

The operationalization tensions created by trying to optimize state and peace-building interventions are also apparent in some efforts by academic/practitioner communities of practice to "do development differently" (DDD), and to "think and work politically" (TWP).[17] These approaches (which I have interacted with at the margins) make the important effort to move domestic power politics from the margins of development thinking to the center, at the expense of more formulaic technical approaches to managing violence and service provision that still dominate (World Bank 2017, 271). To do so, they prioritize gathering granular knowledge about local power and resource distribution and the institutions that sustain that distribution—arrangements that are sometimes referred to as a political settlement (Phillips 2016, 631; 2020; see also Laws 2012; Khan 2010; Rocha Menocal 2015).[18]

As a result of the increased sensitivity to local context, the reform of political settlements is now widely seen to hold the key to intractable development problems in fragile states. For example, the *New Deal for Engagement in Fragile States*, which was endorsed by a range of donor and recipient states in 2011, notes that its first peace and state-building goal is "fostering an inclusive political settlement" (International Dialogue on Peacebuilding and Statebuilding 2011, 2). Britain's DFID is one of the biggest institutional supporters of the political settlement concept (though it has also been taken up by the World Bank, the OECD, and other bilateral development agencies). DFID (2010, 23) notes: "The inclusiveness of a settlement, and public perceptions of its fairness, is critical to state legitimacy and the sustainability of the settlement in the long term."

Emerging largely out of practitioner and donor agency-supported research networks, it is not surprising that the political settlements research agenda generally takes a problem-solving rather than a critical approach to thinking about world politics. The research that is produced does not typically attempt, as Robert Cox put it, to "stand apart from the prevailing order of the world and ask how that order came about" (Cox 1980, 129). Rather, it accepts that order and the place of intervention within it, and examines ways of optimizing development assistance (Gulrajani 2011) in fragile states. In so doing, it upholds intervention in the Global South as an inevitable part of the solution to poverty and conflict (see Koddenbrock 2012, 549–50).

The political settlements literature has not engaged systematically with either the possible alternatives to external intervention or, often, with the non-domestic drivers of conflict and division that may make intervention seem necessary.[19] It implicitly constructs external intervention as useful, perfectible, and separated from systemic inequalities that produce the conditions of fragility it seeks to ameliorate. For example, the Political Settlements Research Programme (PSRP—a consortium of five international research institutions, principally funded by DFID) states that its aim is to provide a "better understanding of the formal and informal ways in which elite actors exercise power can help both those within a country and external actors, to intervene more effectively to support a stable and inclusive political settlement" (PSRP n.d.a). More directly, one of the project's three broad research questions is, "How, and with what interventions, can external actors change political settlements?" (PSRP n.d.b). The PRSP's Program Director, Christine Bell, notes that:

> Political settlement analysis as a project should aim to better inform interveners as to how to engage with the reality of political power-balance in the societies in which they intervene, in ways that are smart both to needs to sustain elite consent if change is to be made possible, but are also smart as to how to move beyond permanent elite capture. (Bell 2015, 7)

Others are also explicit about the instrumental goals of the PSRP. Julia Schuenemann and Amanda Lucey (2015, 7) note, for example, that the program is about "transforming political settlements towards open and inclusive settlements." Two tensions flow from the instrumentalism inherent to this endeavor. The first is that it assumes that knowledge of existing conditions has a reasonably linear relationship to the ability to alter them in predictable and desirable ways. That is, that the more fine-grained one's knowledge of local politics is, the more amenable those politics will be to purposeful intervention by the knowledgeable.

Severine Autesserre's influential critique of Western intervention in conflict-affected states (particularly the DRC) calls for peace-builders to better understand and incorporate subnational drivers of conflict in their programs if they want to intervene more effectively (2010; 2012; 2014). This is no doubt important and these points are well made by Autesserre. However, the rise of political settlements analyses, communities of practice like Thinking and Working Politically, Doing Development Differently, and other local context-based approaches (and the laudable nuance that some of this research has produced) suggests that this call has been heard. Moreover, it suggests that it has had an impact on the way that external actors approach at least some aspects of their work. Suda Perera cites a MONUSCO (United Nations Organization Stabilization Mission in the Democratic Republic of Congo) worker: "We've all read Autesserre, we know we need to pay attention to local dynamics, and we are changing our frames" (Perera 2017a, 45). However, this still assumes that knowledge translates into reasonably clean operational objectives within the target state, rather than paradigm-challenging contradictions that require action beyond the domestic realm of that state. That many of the problems associated with intervening in fragile states are well known to, and well documented by, international development actors suggests they often are better informed about local conditions—and the harms and contradictions their actions may entail—than these knowledge-based critiques imply.

This feeds into a second tension, which is that knowledge gaps cannot account for what Patience Kabamba refers to as the "gross cynicism" that local populations often feel for the state, and for the international community's role in propping it up (Kabamba 2012, n.p.). The issue may be less a knowledge deficit than a matter of the power relations inherent to operationalizing that knowledge within parameters that remain defined by the interveners. Questions surrounding the appropriateness of intervention are omitted because the analysis is framed to consider how to manage interventions more effectively. However, as postcolonial and postdevelopment scholars have long pointed out, the quality of an intervention may be less of an issue than the fact that interventions are structured by unequal relationships between interveners and those intervened upon (Mbembe 1992; Escobar 1995; Kothari 2005a, 2005b).

No amount of learning about the local context of a particular state removes the power relationship that intervention inevitably entails. If only the form of intervention is problematized, questions surrounding the broader relationship between recipient states, external actors, and the international order—of which northern donor agencies and governments are generally beneficiaries—are disregarded. These broader factors include issues like the transnational facilitation of elite resource capture, the provision of weapons to local actors, the northern tendency to reinforce repressive regimes, coerced structural adjustments that shift public wealth to private hands, exploitative regimes of debt repayments, toxic waste dumping in unregulated spaces, the lack of transparency in payments made by international extractive industry companies, international trade arrangements that perpetuate structural inequalities, or internationally determined rankings that determine a state's access to affordable global credit (see DiGiuseppe, Barry, and Frank 2012). Complex and intractable though each of these issues are, all have stronger levers for change within the home country of the northern-based donors than within the country being targeted by an intervention. And herein lies the dilemma: broadening the analytical scope to include transnational factors that perpetuate poverty and conflict is to acknowledge the limits of development actors' influence against those factors—at least as that role is currently imagined. More importantly, to accept the significance of drivers beyond domestic level arrangements is to call for a radical overhaul of the practices of development intervention in ways that would threaten the relevance of the intervening organizations.

Outside the Fragile States Discourse

In the critical/postdevelopment and postcolonial literatures, the salience of global power hierarchies on poverty and conflict in the Global South is well established.[20] As the international rules and organizations established after World War II were consolidated and formal colonialism ended, newly independent states entered the modern international system at a profound structural disadvantage to the victors of the war. In addition to the path dependencies (to say nothing of the genocides, violence, and economic devastation) generated by the colonial experience (Mamdani 2001), the states that benefited from colonialism were able to project influence through new the international organizations that set the rules of world order (such as the World Bank, International Monetary Fund, United Nations' Security Council and, later, the World Trade Organization). The rules they imposed calcified postwar power hierarchies in ways suggested by the identity of the five the veto-wielding states in the UN Security Council. Postwar international rules also permitted trade barriers by wealthy states—whether through high tariffs on imports or local subsidies on locally produced goods—while denying similar barriers to states in the Global South.[21]

At the end of the Cold War, the existing international organizations were not radically altered, and neither were major new organizations created, unlike in 1919 and 1945. Instead, organizations like the World Bank, IMF, and United Nations were retooled to focus more on governance, economic liberalization, and deregulation in the south, while maintaining the internal power arrangements that favored G-7 nations, particularly the United States (al-Qaq 2015, 194). A number of recent studies show that tax evasion and other illicit financial transfers by multi/international corporations cost developing countries an enormous amount of revenue each year. Some suggest that the cost is so high that it outweighs what they receive through foreign development assistance, though others dispute this.[22] International tax evasion was at the heart of the G77 negotiations at the Third International Conference on Financing for Development in Addis Ababa (July 2015), where developing countries (many of them designated fragile) pushed for the creation of an international tax body rather than the more exclusive tax reform initiatives dominated by the OECD. Their push was unsuccessful, leading some G77 ministers to decry the process as "bullying," and "a new wave of colonialism under UN auspices" (Shore 2015).

More fundamentally, the rules that were institutionalized in the aftermath of World War II extend the privileges of borrowing money, importing weapons, and selling natural resources to "any person or group exercising effective power in less developed countries" (Pogge 2010, 17). With international sovereign recognition comes access to external sources of funding, legitimacy, and coercion that can help to cushion predatory elites from the repercussions of their actions at home (Bates 2001; Anghie 2004; Englebert 2009). That access to external political and economic buffers also undermines the likelihood that local elites will perceive that their ability to survive rests on their ability to nurture (rather than plunder) the sources of national economic development (Bates 2009, 17; Bates 2001, 86). By focusing on only the local side of this equation, the fragile states discourse is generally silent on the ways that the local is coconstituted with international networks.

Elites in states labelled as fragile tend to spend a disproportionately high percentage of their gross domestic products on military expenditure. This spending helps to embed the collusive patronage networks (Grawert and

Abdul-Magd 2016) that the fragile states discourse identifies as largely responsible for the perpetuation of violence. The global arms trade is a primarily north–south phenomenon, with roughly two-thirds of arms transfers flowing in this direction between 2004 and 2011, and over three-quarters since then (Grimmett and Kerr 2012, 1, cited in Stavrianakis 2015). The relatively easy access to externally produced arms is notably absent from the fragile states discourse, despite its salience to the domestic political economies that it depicts as so problematic, and the role of the industry in corrupting governments in both north and south (see Holden 2016, chapter 5). As conflicts continue in these states, so do the international arms sales and transfers that provide an important means of perpetuating them (see Ayoob 1995, 102). The majority of profits from these sales flows back to companies anchored in wealthy northern states, sometimes with effective state subsidization, so prized is the contribution of those profits to the economy. Of course, not all weapons used in civil wars come from northern states. Russia and China are significant exporters too.[23] However, the absence of international arms proliferation from the discourse about the causes of, and solutions to, state fragility is noteworthy. It suggests that, like other international drivers of conflict and poverty, it is tacitly accepted as one of the immutable, if regrettable, constraints within which international development actors work to build more effective and humane states.

The United States is the world's largest exporter of weapons.[24] Rebecca Thorpe shows that American arms manufacturers have intentionally spread their facilities across most states and congressional districts to maximize the number of constituencies (and thus legislative representatives) that benefit from their profitability (Thorpe 2014, 114). These localized imperatives reduce the likelihood of elected representatives challenging weapons manufacturers on issues related to foreign policy. The US government is also the official vendor for some of the world's largest arms manufacturers, and it applies a surcharge for its involvement, further embedding incentives to promote arms sales abroad (Cockburn 2016). The deputy assistant secretary of the US State Department's Bureau of Political-Military Affairs, Tom Kelly, stated at a Congressional hearing in April 2013 that advocating for American arms exports was:

> an issue that has the attention of every top-level official who's working on foreign policy throughout the government, including the top officials at the State Department. . . . Advocating on behalf of our companies and doing

everything we can to make sure that these sales go through . . . is something that we're doing every day, basically [on] every continent in the world, and we take it very, very seriously and we're constantly thinking of how we can do better. (House of Congress 2013, cited in Hartung 2013)

Weapons are also transferred (as opposed to simply sold) to fragile states, particularly those perceived to be threatened by terrorist groups that also threaten northern states. Those eligible for American Foreign Military Finance (FMF) and Section 1206 Funds programs receive grants from the US government to spend on weapons and support services supplied by American defense contractors.[25] However, these weapons have been shown on a number of occasions to have fallen into the hands of those they were sent to fight, highlighting another dangerous unintended consequence of intervention. A 2016 audit by the US inspector general of the US Department of Defense found that the department did not have "accurate, up-to-date records on the quantity and location of [Iraq Train and Equip Fund] equipment on hand in Kuwait and Iraq . . . for equipment worth over $1 billion" (US-DODIG 2016, i; 10). The US government made a similar admission the previous year in Yemen, stating that it had lost track of more than $500 million worth of military aid provided since 2007, which one had to "assume [was] completely compromised and gone" (Whitlock 2015). In both cases, it was presumed that at least some of those weapons made their way to ISIS (Bacevich 2015) and al-Qa'ida in the Arabian Peninsula, respectively, thereby exacerbating the conditions of violence and fragility that they were intended to ameliorate.

Yet the nature of weapons transfers and the integration of the arms industry into northern political economies are seldom, if ever, referred to as a structural problem facing fragile states by those who produce the discourse about state fragility. The fact that the sale of weapons by northern defense contractors continues to be viewed as a separate issue to that of conflict in fragile states was illustrated with unusual clarity when the UK's International Development Committee framed its position on the humanitarian crisis in Yemen. The Parliamentary Inquiry that it established (December 2015) asked several questions, one of which was: "What more can be done to protect Yemeni civilians?" (UK Commons Select Committee 2015). At that time (and indeed at the time of writing in 2018), Yemeni civilians were facing grave food and medical shortages due to a combination of internal conflicts, a blockade on vital imports imposed by a Saudi-led military coalition, and an airstrike campaign led by the same coalition that had killed thousands of civilians. One-third of those strikes targeted nonmilitary sites (Yemen Data Project 2017). The UK government, along with other Western governments, actively supported the Gulf Cooperation Council's (GCC) military actions and blockade.

In October 2015, Amnesty International argued that prosecution of the GCC's campaign, with its high number of civilian casualties, repeated devastation of civilian infrastructure, and use of internationally banned cluster munitions, provided "damning evidence of war crimes" (Amnesty International 2015). At that time, British companies were the largest supplier of weapons to Saudi Arabia (SIPRI 2015, 2), with the government granting nearly GBP 3 billion worth of arms export licenses to Saudi Arabia since the airstrikes began in March 2015 (Twigg 2016). The British government, along with the United States, also provided decisive political and logistical support for Saudi Arabia's war. This included their military officials having access to airstrike target lists and being present in the command and control room (Graham-Harrison 2016). Neither the UK nor the US governments proactively supported a 2015 proposal that would have "mandated a UN mission to document violations by all sides since September 2014" (Human Rights Watch 2015), and the proposal was dropped after intense opposition from Saudi Arabia and its allies in the GCC. The GCC coalition also maintained a blockade on Yemen's key ports of entry that not only pushed starvation levels toward famine but also prevented the entry of basic anticholera medication during the worst outbreak of the disease in fifty years.

Just one month before the British Parliamentary Inquiry began its work, the UK's Foreign Secretary Philip Hammond was quoted describing the ongoing sale of weapons to Saudi Arabia as creating "British jobs," noting "we'd always like to do more business" (Stone 2015). That the government's own Inquiry so readily detached the humanitarian crisis it investigated from the war it supported illustrates the power relations inscribed in the fragile states discourse. Solutions are changes that occur in the south not those that might follow from changes to the way that the north projects power onto the south.

In August 2018, Britain's DFID continued to actively disconnect Yemen's humanitarian catastrophe from the internationalized war that was preventing food and anticholera medication from reaching civilians in a promotional video announcing its capacity to predict the location of cholera outbreaks. DFID's chief science professor, Charlotte Watts, stated:

> By connecting science and international expertise with the humanitarian response on the ground, we have for the very first time used sophisticated predictions of where the risk of cholera is highest to help aid workers save lives and prevent needless suffering for thousands of Yemenis before it's too late. (quoted in Aid and International Development Forum 2018)

The video showed volunteers teaching Yemeni children to wash their hands to prevent the spread of the disease, creating the impression that cholera was spreading because Yemenis lack basic hygiene practices.[26] The video did not refer to the war or the blockade preventing the entry of basic medicines, and certainly did not mention that many of Yemen's sewage treatment plants, hospitals, and electricity grids had been destroyed in the bombing campaign the British government (of which it is a part) continued to support.

This is a particularly clear example of how the fragile states discourse actively detaches the diagnosis of problems experienced by people in the south from the actions of northern states, or to inequalities within the international system. Instead it remains bounded firmly within the state level units that international donors and lenders are structured to target their work. These states are required to reform themselves under international direction in order to recover from their self-imposed fragility.

I now turn to the unusual structural circumstances faced by Somaliland during its formational years that set it apart from the core assumptions of the fragile states discourse. These assumptions are that external assistance is imperfect but necessarily beneficial for states recovering from civil war; that such assistance is detached from systems that reproduce global inequalities (and is seen to be so by target populations); and that stronger state/state-like governance institutions drive greater peace and prosperity (and can be purposefully established by external actors to this end). The next chapter begins to trace the structural processes by which Somaliland's peace was achieved initially, and has since been maintained, in the absence of significant external intervention.

Chapter 2

Somaliland's Relative Isolation

Somaliland's independence discourse hinges on the fact that its sovereignty is unrecognized even though it has achieved a level of civil order that far exceeds the rest of Somalia. The discourse emphasizes that Somaliland's lack of recognition has contributed to an unusually low (though now rising) level of direct external involvement in Somaliland's financial and political affairs. The resulting isolation is framed as an injustice even though it is sometimes simultaneously referred to as a blessing in disguise,[1] having afforded Somalilanders a level of self-determination in their peace-building process that was closed to other Somalis. This chapter explores how the independence discourse assigns meaning to Somaliland's relative isolation within the international system. To that end, some background is necessary about the kinds of intervention that Somalia has experienced.

Intervention in Somalia

The common contention that Somalia's biggest governance problems are exclusively internal (Mills, Pham, Kilcullen 2013, 306–27) sits uncomfortably with the historical record. The extraordinary level of intervention in Somalia's politics makes it extremely difficult—in fact meaningless—to delineate between domestic or external drivers because Somalia's politics are produced by their intersection. In a globalized world the same could, of course, be said for any state, but it is worth discussing the degree of their entanglement in Somalia.

When the government collapsed in 1991, Somalia was the largest per capita recipient of aid in Africa (excluding tiny states like the Gambia and Djibouti). It had held this position since Siyad Barre swapped from the Soviet to the US side of the Cold War in 1978 (de Waal 1997, 162).[2] As foreign money poured in, the country began to lose its food self-sufficiency, ultimately to the point of famine. This was due to a combination of externally mandated austerity programs, a drought, and the "unintended impact of large-scale annual and often poorly timed delivery of food aid, which depress[ed] prices and [drove] farmers out of agriculture" (UNEP 2005, 30; see also Farzin 1991, 273; Nestle and Dalton 1994, 19).

David Rawson estimates that the total amount of money spent by foreign donors on aid to Somalia between 1980 and 1989 was around $2.5 billion, an extraordinary sum at the time (Rawson 1994, 171). Nevertheless, very little reached the Somali people. USAID was the largest single donor and distributed much of its contribution through cash and commodity grants that were highly susceptible to theft by government officials.[3] The aid, which also included more than $150 million in American military assistance (Rawson 1994, 164), nurtured regime patronage networks, strangled agricultural production systems, and provided the regime with many of the weapons it used to violently repress its citizens. It sustained a widely despised regime beyond its natural life and, in the process, embedded a deep and enduring cynicism about the underlying motives of foreign humanitarian and development assistance (de Waal 1997, 162). Skepticism about the ability of aid to deliver real benefits is still echoed in Somaliland's independence discourse where it emphasizes that the denial of aid fostered people's self-sufficiency and local ownership.

In addition to the economic, food, and military aid that Somalia received from the US and other Western donors, President Barre's tenure was also underpinned by massive loans from the International Monetary Fund (IMF) in exchange for deep structural adjustments. The IMF required that large swathes of the economy be privatized, the currency devalued, and subsistence agriculture shifted toward export crops. These policies proved disastrous and exacerbated a crisis in the agricultural sector that further undermined local food production (Samatar 1993; Webersik 2005). Government repayments fell into arrears and in May 1988 the IMF declared Somalia ineligible for further loans (Kapteijns 2013a, 94), which meant that it could no longer access bilateral Western assistance either (Simons 1995, 77). Somalia (and thus Somaliland) remains ineligible for loans from international financial institutions to this day.

In an effort to recover its money, the IMF imposed further austerity measures and by 1990, Somalia's outstanding foreign debt obligations reached around 277 percent of gross domestic product (GDP) (Mubarak 1996, 16; see also Chossudovsky 2003, 96, 99). It was an impossible task. Even so, interest and late penalties have accrued on this debt ever since that time—something that Somalis are still fighting (Somalia NGO Consortium 2018, 5). As the debt crisis grew, so did unemployment, prices for food, and other basic commodities. Antigovernment insurgencies proliferated and gained momentum across the country.[4] On July 14, 1989, government troops opened fire on civilians in Mogadishu, claiming that they were demonstrators, and sparking two days of heavy street fighting, looting, and further massacres (Simons 1995, 79). The regime endured until the end of the following year, at which point Mogadishu was overturned by violence, first against the regime and then between competing militias (Simons 1995, 93). Siyad Barre fled in January 1991. The expectation of calamitous violence in the capital that built for years was finally a reality. The level of violence in Mogadishu caught up to, and eventually overtook, that experienced in Hargeysa.

There have been two deployments of foreign soldiers in Somalia since 1991, not including the American air strike campaign that has been underway since 2009. The first was carried out by the United Nations between 1992 and 1995 (United Nations Task Force [UNITAF], followed by the United Nations Operation in Somalia [UNOSOM II], with a mandate to initiate nation-building in Somalia).[5] The second deployment of foreign soldiers in Somalia was by the African Union (AU), which was directed by Ethiopia with American support between 2007 and 2008. The AU has since maintained a military presence in Somalia.

UNITAF (1992–1993) was conducted under the leadership of the United States, though it withdrew in the aftermath of casualties sustained by Pakistani and then American peacekeeping forces. The US and UN spent a combined total of around $4 billion on security- and peace-building processes in Somalia during these missions, though neither contributed to such processes in Somaliland (Prunier 1998, 227). With the exception of around $100,000, which was provided by two Western donors (one Swedish, one American) to support Somaliland's Boorama conference in 1993, there was virtually no external funding for any of the conferences that were held in the north between 1991 and 1997, other than from members of the diaspora.[6]

By contrast, there have been at least eighteen internationally sponsored sets of peace talks aimed at achieving national reconciliation in Somalia, most costing many millions of dollars and involving large numbers of delegates.[7] These have been facilitated by the United Nations; the Inter-Governmental Authority on Development; the Arab League; the African Union; the European Union; and the governments of Djibouti, Egypt, Ethiopia, Kenya, Turkey, the United Kingdom, Uganda, Sudan, and Yemen (see Interpeace 2009, 10–23). One such conference in Kenya continued for over two years (2002–2004) and was only brought to a close once the Kenyan authorities held a farewell party as a way of suggesting that it was time for Somalia's delegates leave (Harper 2012, 64).

The UN-brokered conferences that were held during the height of the violence in the 1990s were, on the other hand, hasty affairs with each lasting well under a fortnight (Ahmed and Green 1999, 124). They also tended to sparsely include Somalis. At the meeting to discuss humanitarian intervention in Geneva in 1992, for example, there were 350 delegates from eighty-nine countries, and not a single representative from Somalia (Hussein 1997, 175). Alex de Waal notes that by the time the London Conference on Somalia was held in 2012, there was no longer any "pretense that power was vested anywhere but with the internationals, who provided the money, along with the African 'frontline states', which provided the soldiers" (de Waal 2015, 124).

The power of international actors is clearly illustrated in the Somali budget. At the end of the Transitional Federal Government's (TFG) tenure in 2012, the government relied on the international community to fund around 70 percent of its annual budget (Fartaag 2012; see also ICG 2011, 19). A report by the Federal Government of Somalia (FGS, which succeeded the TFG) noted that this had reduced to about 46 percent by 2018 (Federal

Government of Somalia 2018, 1).[8] Within Somalia's budget one sees not only the persistence of external intervention within core aspects Somalia's state apparatus but also, by extension, the interveners' ongoing mediation of the relationship between the state and society.

While the level of budget support that Somalia receives is high, the proportion of its budget covered by external actors is not uncommon to post-conflict states. In fact, the approach applied to Somalia has strong resonance with that adopted elsewhere, making it an ideal case study for intervention in so-called fragile states. According to 2017 figures from the World Bank, official development assistance (ODA) accounted for 105.2 percent of government revenue in Afghanistan (that is, just over 50 percent of funds in the budget), 260.6 percent in the Central African Republic, 126 percent in Liberia, 143.2 percent in Sierra Leone (World Bank 2017, 268), and was also over 100 percent in the Democratic Republic of Congo's budget between 2003 and 2012 (Autesserre 2010, iv; International Aid Transparency 2012). Other states like Uganda, Benin, Togo, Madagascar, Burkina Faso, Mali, Niger, Sierra Leone, and Ethiopia have all experienced ratios of aid to government expenditure exceeding 75 percent over several years in a row (Deaton 2013, 296). In some countries, these levels have meant that the percentage of GDP supplied by tax revenues actually declined since independence (Collier 2009, 223). Moss, Pettersson and van de Walle (2006, 3) noted in 2006 that thirty-four (of forty-nine) sub-Saharan African states received at least 10 percent of their national income from ODA for at least the last two decades. They point out that even during the Marshall Plan to reconstruct Western Europe after World War II, recipient states never collected more than 3 percent of their GDP in external assistance. Moreover, that funding was only available for a few years. This level of intervention is widely seen within target states as perpetuating the dysfunction that interveners ostensibly seek to undo, a view reflected in Somaliland's independence discourse.

Somalia's clan system is often framed as the "most intractable problem in recent Somali history" (Mills, Pham and Kilcullen 2013, 306–27), supposedly because of the way that "violence is actually endemic in this pervasively bellicose culture" (Lewis 1998, 100). Ioan Lewis even argues that "since, by definition, [Somali kinship] *flows in the blood* and must be taken for granted . . . it is similar to scientific understanding of the biological concept 'race'" (Lewis 2004, 491—italics in the original). Such claims reify clan identity as a natural category that acts in predetermined ways and that need not "be explained in diffusionist terms as a consequence of 'global economics and politics'" (Lewis 1998, 100).[9] As the heated exchange between Catherine Besteman (1996, 1998) and Ioan Lewis (1998) illustrates, it is controversial to ascribe any degree of naturalness to Somalia's clan system.[10] Without rehearsing this debate in detail, my position is that the essentialism of Ioan Lewis and his (many) followers on this point is deeply problematic, and while the Somali clan system underpins many aspects of Somali political life, it does not dictate political life. The clan system is neither monolithic nor static and adapts quickly to environmental changes. Clans transform politics just as they are transformed by politics. For the purposes of this book, the political transformations driven by international intervention receive the most attention.

The clan system (which is discussed in greater detail in chapter 4) is structured, at least in broad terms, by segmentary lineage, which is a branching system of patrilineal descent that was most volubly theorized in the Somali context by Ioan Lewis. Lewis argues that the political ideology of a segmentary system is that "political relations are a function of genealogical distance" (Lewis 1961, 94)—meaning that groups expand and contract on the basis of this distance in relation to in-group conflict or external threats.[11] However, even if one accepts that the structural-functionalism of the clan outweighs other dynamic "cleavages of class, occupation, race, status, and language" (Besteman 1996, 124), the system still allows for many alternative levels of aggregation, vesting it with a great degree of structural flexibility. Being based on male lines of descent, aggregations can conceivably follow as many ancestors as there are males in the line, depending on the salience of those lines to the present circumstances.[12] Women play a crucial role in the structural dynamism of clans, and chapter 3 discusses the often-overlooked importance of maternal descent, which takes on particular salience in times of conflict because (among other reasons) maternal lineage can offer an even greater array of possible aggregations.

External actors contributed to shifts in clan relationships during the UNOSOM II years (1993–1995) by concentrating resources in the major cities and providing an incentive for clan elders to relocate away from their local areas (Little 2003, 47). One effect of this was to alter the connection between the elders and the local communities they claimed to represent. Peter Little notes, for example, that the United Nations and other international nongovernmental organizations (INGOs) tended to hold static conceptions of what the term "clan" meant, which led to a proliferation of Somalis identifying themselves as clan elders. Terms like "indigenous," "clan," and "traditional" were increasingly adopted in written statements by Somalis because they resonated well with external actors who wanted to engage with leaders they believed were both powerful and locally legitimate (Little 2003, 48). As external involvement in southern Somalia grew through the early-to-mid 1990s, international agencies adopted a clan idiom and often insisted on receiving:

> proposals from clan "elders" even when some of these were disguised militia heads. . . . The number of acknowledged clans quickly multiplied in response to such requests and opportunities, and some of these clan leaders were concealed warlords who claimed to have clan support. Approximately 20 separate clan and sub-clan affiliations were represented in one UN-financed peace conference held in Kismayo town during May to June 1994, an astounding number for a limited area. . . . Overall more than 28 separate clan and sub-clan identities had emerged in an area where only seven years earlier I had identified fewer than 10 of any significance. (Little 2003, 47)

Prior to the devastating violence between 1988 and 1992, the clan family (generally the highest level of clan aggregation) did not have military significance, but as the conflict metastasized this changed and the families (Hawiye, Darood, Dir, and, Isaaq) took on that salience.[13] When the US and UN intervened, they mistook these historically contingent and transient formations for a static primordial order and built new structures of authority around them, calcifying them in a protoconstitutional order.[14]

Intervening forces therefore contributed to a morphing of the concept of clan and clan identity by backing their own (mis)understandings of it with power and resources. The practice of tactically emphasizing clan identities to an external audience is a practice that has continued. This was highlighted by a participant at the Second Istanbul Conference on Somalia in 2012, who told me that at the meeting, "people quickly donned the hats of tribal elders because they realized that donors wish to engage with the clans."[15]

Constructing a Self-Sufficient Economy

Somalilanders pointedly distinguish themselves from the external intervention that enveloped the rest of Somalia, widely crediting it as a factor in the success of their peace processes. As Abdirahman Aw Cali Farah, former vice president of Somaliland, maintained in 2011:

> There was no foreign aid, it was our people (Somalilanders) who came to-gether to heal the wounds, it was our people who decided their destiny. All ideas which were raised in the conference were home-grown, there was no foreign influence and I think that was one of the main factors that made the conference successful. (Cited in Arteh and Duale 2011, 4)

Other senior politicians share the vice president's view. For example, in a statement that was typical in the interviews that I conducted (and informal conversations with friends), one minister noted: "We don't have intervention, we are not recognized and that's a good thing. It's a blessing in disguise."[16] This blessing facilitated the creation of a polity that does not conform to the rational institutionalist model imagined in the discourse about fragile states but that has, nevertheless, delivered peace.

Somaliland was already somewhat economically insulated it before it de-clared its independence, and this pre-independence history generates back-ground frames (such as the self-reliance of Somalilanders) that the indepen-dence discourse reflects and reproduces. There were considerable structural differences between the economies of northern and southern Somalia, which shaped different kinds of international connections, too. A first major dif-ference is that in a predominantly pastoral economy like Somaliland's, wealth resides more in livestock than in land. The relative mobility of animal herds makes it difficult for elites to systematically plunder the wealth of farmers (Gellner 2000, 144). The south had a more sedentary agricultural produc-tion base (and decades of higher levels of investment in that base and in its urban infrastructure), which created more resources that could be fought over. Political elites fought over access to productive farmland, port facilities, food storage points, irrigation pumps, and urban real estate not only to en-rich themselves but also to maintain the networks of support and patronage that sustained them politically (Cassanelli 2003, 15). In Somaliland, fewer such assets existed.

A second point of structural differentiation between northern and south-ern Somalia was that the northern economy was in ruins a number of years earlier than was the case in the rest of the country, which was partly due to Siyad Barre's deliberate efforts to curtail development in Isaaq majority areas. One of the tactics that the Barre regime used to this end was restricting the number of business licenses that were available in the north, and even the number of stories that were permitted on new buildings (Carrier and Lochery 2013, 443). A further blow was struck by the termination of the *franco valuta* system, as a condition of the IMF loan in 1981. Franco valuta was an arrangement that allowed Somalis working or trading abroad to invest their foreign capital in consumer goods that were imported and then resold in Somalia. Its abolition was felt most acutely by northerners (who constituted a relatively high proportion of Somalia's international traders) and is believed to have provided an early boost to the Somali National Movement's (SNM) support base (Simons 1995, 54–55). It also offered an early reason for Somalilanders to be suspicious of the conditions placed on loans by international financial institutions, which constitutes a theme in the independence discourse through its emphasis on Somalilanders' preference for autonomy.

Third, Somaliland had escaped the worst effects of the drought that devastated the rain-fed agricultural economy of southern Somalia in the late 1980s. This was partly down to the luck of the weather, but the north's pastoral agricultural production base is also relatively mobile, and so typically more resilient to drought than conventional farming.[17] As a result, the north did not receive the international food aid that flowed to the south, the corrosive impacts of which are well documented (Ahmad 2012). International aid contributions were already disproportionately lower in the north, with only 7 percent of the total foreign aid to Somalia between 1985 and 1990 going to northerners, who were then around 35 percent of the population (Geshekter 2001, 24). This meant that there were also few sources of externally provided aid for SNM leaders to loot had they been so inclined (Bradbury 2008, 69). Any aid organizations remaining in the north-west were evacuated when the Barre regime's assault against the SNM and Isaaq civilians peaked in 1988.

Finally, the dearth of external resources and plunderable domestic assets made the SNM's ability to source funds locally imperative to its ability to survive as an insurgent force. This appears to have reinforced an ethos of economic and political self-reliance from an early stage in the movement's development. Unlike the Somali Salvation Democratic Front (SSDF), insurgency in the north-eastern areas of what now constitutes Puntland, the SNM did not rely on either Ethiopia or Libya to provide funding for a number of geopolitical reasons.[18] The peak of the SNM insurgency also coincided with the end of the Cold War, which further reduced the likelihood of it attracting superpower patronage. Instead, the SNM had to rely on the support of its Isaaq constituency for solvency, legitimacy, and its ability to attract armed men to the struggle (Compagnon 1990/1; Prunier 1990/1; Lewis 1994; Bradbury 2008; Renders 2012). Initially, this reliance was largely contingent on the capacity of the northern Somali diaspora that lived in Saudi Arabia, Europe, and East Africa to send money home. The geographical distances between those funding the SNM and those fighting in its name encouraged the use of a kin-based money transfer system (*abban*) that kept the money bound for the insurgency beyond the control of the Barre regime. The re mittances went through Isaaq financiers, who were based in Ethiopia near the Somali border, from where they sent the money directly to the SNM. This funding model placed Isaaq financiers in a political relationship with SNM leaders, but it did not allow the latter to control the funds, which helped the SNM avoid the southern problem of militia leaders also dominating local businesses and entrenching a conflict economy (Reno 2003, 24).

As the conflict with the Barre regime intensified, the SNM became increasingly dependent on local clan elders to mobilize and organize the fighting. In 1987, General Maxamed Moorgan, known as the Butcher of Hargeysa within Somaliland, wrote that the Barre government sought to "liquidate . . . the Isaaq problem" (cited in Walls 2014, 160). The military's brutality against the civilian population—including through rape and summary executions (Walls 2014, 156)—peaked the following year and further amplified the SNM's call to arms. The SNM lost about half of its forces in 1988 (de Waal 1997, 161) and an estimated 50,000 civilians were killed. Hundreds of thousands of people were also displaced, and the cities of Hargeysa and Burco were levelled. These events are remembered by many Isaaq Somalilanders as an act of genocide against their clan (see Ingiriis 2016).[19] The trauma of the war increased solidarity among the Isaaq as a means of protection against Barre's forces, prompting Gerard Prunier (who spent time with the SNM forces in early 1990) to remark that "in a way, the SNM does not exist: It is simply the Issaq [*sic*] people up in arms" (Prunier 1990/1991, 109).

To supplement the funding from the diaspora for the war effort, the SNM established various forms of taxation, including a requirement that every local household contribute a payment of at least one sheep (or its cash equivalent) to the movement each year and at least one male to serve in its fighting forces (Ahmed and Green 1999, 120). By the late 1980s, most ordinary Isaaq people were contributing both finances and fighters to the SNM, creating a level of dependence on the local communities that made looting those communities a self-defeating prospect. By the time Somaliland declared its independence in 1991 it was, therefore, quite accustomed to international isolation and the need to extract revenues locally for political survival.

Today, Somaliland's government remains detached from most mainstream international funding mechanisms, but, like Somalia, it is the native home of one of the world's most globally dispersed populations, and much of its citizens' wealth is generated externally. Somalilanders benefit from high levels of remittances sent by the diaspora population. The majority of the money is remitted directly to individuals for subsistence without passing through the government. Estimated at around $700–800 million per year (Healy and Sheikh 2009, 4; Government of Somaliland n.d., respectively), this means that remittances are several orders of magnitude above annual government revenues.[20] Thus, while the government does not attract large external rents, a considerable percentage of society (perhaps around 40 percent) survives through the receipt of remittances from friends and relatives abroad. The level of societal dependence on remittances from the diaspora has given its members a strong political voice within Somaliland. When President Silanyo was elected in 2010, for example, half of the twenty-six ministerial positions were given to returned members of the diaspora (Hammond 2012, 175). The primary impact of the remittances has been the provision of subsistence income to ordinary Somalilanders, but the impact of social and knowledge exchange from the diaspora is also undeniable. Driving through the streets of Hargeysa, with its colorful hand-painted shop signs that mimic Western brands or display the owner's "other" home (Ohio Corner Store, Miami Hotel, or England Beauty Salon), one is continually reminded by the city's physical form of its highly globalized population. However, this is not without issues, and tension exists between nondiaspora Somalilanders and the generally wealthier returnees with their sometimes-unwelcome foreign ideas.

While Somaliland is not a traditional rentier state (Luciani and Beblawi 1987), its economy is not centered on the labor-intensive production that gives governments the opportunity to tax physical commodities. Rather, it runs on large amounts of capital accruing directly to the population and circumventing the government. Other than through the pastoral farming industry, which produces livestock for domestic consumption and export, Somaliland (and Somalia more broadly) has a predominantly import-oriented, and service-based economy.[21] Of these services, importing and re-exporting commodities from abroad is one of the biggest sectors, with a plethora of small- and middle-size traders moving goods (sometimes illicitly) across the border to Ethiopia. The primary function of this work is intermediary, and traders generally add little value to the products that they re-export. There is little investment in labor-intensive production like manufacturing or food processing (Helander 2005, 195).

The Somali National Movement's Military Victory

Unlike the other regions in Somalia, the fight against the Barre regime in Somaliland ended in a victory by one party—the SNM (see, for example Drysdale 1992, 24–27; Balthasar 2013). However, by the time that President Barre fled the country in January 1991 the SNM was essentially only a symbolic reference point for the Isaaq clan militias fighting his government (Renders 2012, 80) rather than a united force. Even though the SNM could only claim victory as an umbrella organization, this still gave it a distinct political advantage in the period immediately after the collapse of the government (Phillips 2016, 635).

As a banner organization, the SNM had militarily defeated the minority clans in the northwest (the Dhulbuhante, Warsangeli, and the Gadabursi) that sided with, and were supported by, Siyad Barre. After Barre fell, the SNM's leadership quickly released its prisoners of war and deliberately refrained from taking retribution against those that had collaborated with Barre against them. The SNM leadership seemed well aware that to do otherwise would have extended the war, and its members strongly discouraged acts of revenge by evoking the clan-based norm of *xalaydhalay* (forgiving past wrongs where the losses are so complex or devastating that restitution payments cannot be calculated) (Walls 2009, 387). Instead, the SNM engaged the traditional mediation skills of the clan elders to restore interclan peace in the northwest of the country. By February 1991, SNM leaders had organized a meeting among all of Somaliland's (Isaaq and non-Isaaq) clans in the city of Berbera to negotiate an end to hostilities (Ibrahim and Terlinden 2008, 54). Within two months of the government's collapse, all of the clans in the north had agreed to accept the SNM's political leadership (Drysdale 1992, 13, 24). By this time, the SNM was already riven with internal factional divisions, and its ability to capture the leadership was due to the understanding that there was no viable alternative to it (Ibrahim and Terlinden 2008, 54).

It was not just the victorious Isaaq clans that were keen to mend fences in the north, and key figures from the Dhulbuhante and Gadabursi clans (Garad Abdiqani Garad Jama and Jama Rabileh respectively) had been in talks with the SNM leadership since 1990 (Ibrahim and Terlinden 2008, 54). These relationships were important in establishing the post-Barre ceasefire and moving the reconciliation process ahead under the auspices of the elders, with the understanding that clans would retain a considerable degree of autonomy within their own areas.

The outward military supremacy of the SNM did not last long, and the country quickly descended into violence again, this time between competing Isaaq clan militias. Dominik Balthasar (2013) argues that Somaliland's civil wars tend to be overlooked in narratives of its de facto state formation, often in an apparent attempt to highlight the bottom-up collaborative nature of its political deliberations in the 1990s. He argues that the case of Somaliland provides evidence in support of Charles Tilly's maxim that "war makes states and states make war," despite Tilly's (and others') reservations about the relevance of the observation for contemporary state formation (Balthasar 2013, 219). Balthasar suggests that the civil wars fought during Egal's presidency (and Egal's endeavor to capture the country's most important political and economic levers for an exclusive circle of elites) were a critical driver of Somaliland's state formation (219). As discussed in chapter 3, Egal worked through individuals with established networks in international markets to consolidate his control of a central government apparatus by essentially institutionalizing privileges for this small group. President Egal succeeded in centralizing power and managing violence to a far greater degree than his predecessor President Tuur, but Tilly's original argument also points to the carryover effects of waging war in terms of necessitating the creation of effective bureaucracies that can then extract and administer the finances required for military success (Tilly 1985, 181–83). Here, Somaliland experience's experience diverges from Tilly's analysis as the relationship between the military victories of either the SNM or President Egal, and the nature of Somaliland's governing institutions are not particularly apparent. The latter draw their origins less from military requirements than from a process of deliberative adaptation between existing local and imported institutions. More important than Somaliland's governance institutions to the management of violence is the widespread fear that war could easily reignite should any group defect from the tenuous bargain that was struck. But that very tenuousness has its own counterintuitive stabilizing properties by reifying the need to exercise caution where violence is a plausible outcome—an ideational constraint that nondiscursive analyses miss.

In the south, there was even less martial coherence than in the north, with many militias fighting for power and resources. As the looting and violence in and around Mogadishu spread, the number of actors involved increased exponentially. International food aid agencies became parties to the conflict by paying belligerents for either protection or humanitarian access. They provided "undreamt-of opportunities for extortion" (Compagnon 1998, 86), and not only established food aid as an "alternative currency" for Somalia (Ahmad 2012), but also laid a cornerstone of a pervasive conflict economy. Aisha Ahmad quotes a Somali medical doctor, who worked in humanitarian relief during the crisis: "There is no income except food distribution. Everyone is trying to make money on this food distribution. . . . There is no bank to steal. There is only WFP [World Food Programme]" (Ahmad 2012). Tobias Hagmann (2016, 31) concurs, citing "interviews with dozens of elite business community members and warlords active during UNOSOM [which] reveal [that] 'virtually all of the biggest businesspeople in Mogadishu made their first fortunes from international aid contracts during the UNOSOM mission.'" This point of differentiation around external assistance packages is scored into Somaliland's discourse about how its peace process succeeded where Somalia's failed.

In fact, as Somalilanders struggled to bring the violence in the north under control, UNOSOM II actively played them against one another in an apparent attempt to centralize peace-making efforts in Mogadishu under UN auspices (Renders 2012, 119, 123).[22] To this end, UNOSOM financially supported the political return of Somaliland's first president, Abdirahman Tuur, after he was voted out of office at the Boorama conference in 1993. Rejecting the notion of an independent Somaliland, UNOSOM did not recognize the legitimacy of the Boorama conference—the largest and most significant of Somaliland's peace conferences (discussed in greater detail in chapter 4). After losing the presidency, Tuur had moved south to join General Mohamed

Aideed's self-proclaimed government in Mogadishu instead. There, he re-nounced Somaliland's secession, which he himself had declared just two years earlier. With the assistance of UNOSOM he returned to Somaliland to try to build support for a federal system of government based in Mogadishu.[23] Marleen Renders argues that by sponsoring small fringe conferences in the north, whose participants supported unity with Mogadishu over independence, UNOSOM endangered the larger and more inclusive peace conferences that were still underway (Renders 2012, 123). UNOSOM's sponsorship of an alternative leadership in Somaliland is widely believed to have exacerbated the violence there in the mid-1990s (126; Balthasar 2013, 227). Mohamed Sahnoun, a diplomat who resigned as the UN Special Representative to Somalia just before UNOSOM II was launched in 1993, was a strident critic of the top-down, Mogadishu focused approach that UNOSOM favored, including its insistence that Somaliland be treated as part of a unified Somalia (Bush 1997). The attempts by UNOSOM to disrupt the peace process in Somaliland is one of the clearest enactments of the fragile states discourse, which asserts that centralized state institutions are the most effective and legitimate means of managing violence. The resistance to this notion continues to be reflected within Somaliland via its discourse about the legitimacy of its independence from the rest of Somalia.

Somaliland's Claim of Independence

The Republic of Somaliland is not formally recognized by any state and is derided by most other Somalis in the Federal Republic of Somalia as traitorous. There is, however, fairly broad acceptance that it meets many—some say most—of the formal criteria for such recognition, with caveats surrounding the government's monopoly on the legitimate use of violence and the ongoing territorial disputes in several border areas. *The Economist* noted in 2015, for example, that it "ticks almost all the boxes of statehood" (*The Economist* 2015). Moreover, it is widely considered a more effective state than the rest of Somalia, despite the latter having the benefit of international recognition. While I argue that peace in Somaliland has been maintained without a government that holds (or, even necessarily, seeks to hold) a monopoly on legitimate violence, it is important to discuss the ways in which Somaliland does conform to the conventional definition of a state. Here the independence discourse seems to redeploy elements of the fragile states discourse in order to achieve the objective of recognition. This aspect of the independence discourse reflects an understanding that Somaliland must display the material criteria associated with the conventional definition of statehood to achieve legal independence. Thus, the assertion that Somaliland adheres to the neo-Weberian ideal of statehood forms one aspect of the independence discourse even while it contradicts another core claim: that Somaliland is peaceful because of the identity of its people rather than the capacity of its state institutions.

Supporters of Somaliland's independence point to the Montevideo Convention on the Rights and Duties of States (1933), which gives the only definition of a state in customary international law. It declares that statehood requires: a permanent population, a specified territory, a government capable of maintaining effective control of that territory, and a government that has the capacity to enter into relations with other states. Somaliland has a functioning government, a permanent population, and defined (albeit disputed) territorial borders.[24]

Somaliland has a functioning government, with about 50,000 employees on its payroll, and an undisclosed number of military personnel, making the government the country's largest employer (Iazzolino 2015, 36). It has its own currency (the Somaliland shilling), constitution, police force, armed force, judiciary, national flag, national holidays, national anthem, and car license plates. It issues e-passports,[25] regular development plans, and holds regular elections for three tiers of government (local councils, the House of Representatives, and presidency). It also has the basis of a taxation system,[26] a reasonable level of internal security, provides rudimentary public services,[27] and has additionally seen three peaceful presidential transitions since the civil wars—including once to the opposition. Unlike anywhere else in Somalia, or in neighboring Djibouti (the population of which are ethnically Somali), a member of a minority clan has held the presidency and was returned to office in an election.[28] Matt Bryden argued in 2003 (341) that "There is no longer any reasonable doubt that the desire for independence represents the will of Somaliland's majority." As discussed below, the size of that majority is a matter for debate.

In early 2005, the African Union sent a fact-finding mission to Somaliland to investigate its claim for independence and evaluated it quite positively, finding that Somalilanders have a strong desire not to be reincorporated into a unified Somalia (Hoehne 2011, 335). Apparently buoyed by this appraisal, then President Dahir Rayale Kahin formally presented the case for Somaliland's independence to the African Union in December 2005 (ICG 2006). The claim was based on several factors: some legal, some historical, and others normative. Somaliland's government claims that its case is atypical because an independent Somaliland—the Republic of Somaliland—existed previously for five days in June 1960 and was recognized by thirty-four member states of the United Nations, including the five permanent members of the UN Security Council (Ismail 2006). Support for a single Somali state was high, however, and the new Republic voluntarily united with Italian Somalia to create the Republic of Somalia. These five days have assumed almost legendary status among supporters of independence, who argue that recognition would merely reinstate Somaliland's pre-existing sovereignty without setting a legal precedent for other secessionist entities within Africa (Hastings and Phillips 2018, 20).

On the delicate matter of creating a precedent for secession, the government argues that its declaration of independence in 1991 was never an act of secession but rather a "voluntary dissolution between sovereign states" due to the failure of the union (Bradbury, Abokor, and Yusuf 2003, 457, citing Somaliland's Ministry of Foreign Affairs 2002, 9). Somaliland's foreign minister under President Dahir Rayale argued that several other African states have been permitted to withdraw from voluntary unions—citing Egypt and Syria (1961), and Ethiopia and Eritrea (1993)—and that the same allowances should apply to Somaliland (Ismail, 2006).[29] The government's Recognition Campaign website also argues that the claim is "based primarily on historical title—its separate colonial history, a brief period of independence in 1960, the fact that it voluntarily entered into its unhappy union with Somalia and the questionable legitimacy of the 1960 Act of Union" (Government of Somaliland, n.d.). The problem for Somaliland is that the rest of the Republic of Somalia does not consent to the termination of their union.

Those arguing in favor of Somaliland's independence highlight the haste with which northern Somalis regretted their union with the south and emphasize their good faith in tolerating it despite the violence and repression they endured under Siyad Barre's military regime. When the referendum on the new unitary constitution was held one year after unification in 1961, the vote was widely boycotted in the north (ICG 2003, 5) and of those who did vote, roughly 70 percent of northerners voted against it (Drysdale 1992, 12).

Most importantly for the argument of this book, Somaliland makes a normative claim to sovereignty based on its track record of good governance, particularly that it has adopted a multiparty political system and holds regular elections. President Egal argued in 1999 that Somaliland would not be recognized as a state unless it adopted a multiparty political system (Bradbury, Abokor, and Yusuf 2003, 463) and thereby conformed to Western concepts of an appropriate political system. As Egal expected, Western donors did take notice, and the International Crisis Group (ICG) noted in 2003 that since the approval of the constitution in 2001, which established the multiparty system, "international interest in this would-be state has grown perceptibly" (ICG 2003, 7). However, not all Somalilanders, and particularly those living in the periphery, were convinced of either the necessity or the haste of the transition to multiparty politics from the clan-based model of representation. Some argued that it was unwise to change a system that had held the country together against the odds for the past twelve years (Bradbury, Abokor, and Yusuf 2003, 464).

The case against Somaliland's independence from Somalia is also multifaceted. Some member states of the African Union fear that if the desires of subnational groups to secede from artificial political unions are granted it could open a floodgate of claims and jeopardize stability on the continent. The 1963 charter of the Organisation of African Unity (OAU—replaced by the African Union in 2002) articulates this concern by referring to the "sovereignty and territorial integrity" of its member states three times (cited in ICG 2006, 14). In 1964, the OAU member states adopted a resolution "solemnly declar[ing] that all Member States pledge themselves to respect the borders existing on their achievement of national independence" (OAU, 1964). In this it has been remarkably successful, with full secession being granted to only two independent postcolonial African states since then: Eritrea (from Ethiopia) in 1993 and South Sudan (from Sudan) in 2011. The key difference between these two cases and Somaliland is that both Ethiopia and Sudan agreed to the dissolution of their union, albeit after decades of bloodshed. The Republic of Somalia has, on the other hand, made its unwillingness clear in this regard, at least when it has had a government able to express a view on the matter.

It is important to note that the African Union's (AU) fact-finding mission in 2005 found no cause to assume that granting Somaliland independence would open a Pandora's box and lead to a wave of secession (African Union

Commission 2005, cited in Hoehne 2011, 335). Strong resistance to Somaliland's claim has remained, regardless of this finding. One need not Google far, for example, on Somali websites (even those in English) to find the outrage that Somaliland's claim of independence evokes for many Somalis.

Somalis are one of the more ethnically, linguistically, and religiously homogenous groups in Africa, with a strong sense of shared identity. One of the often-cited ironies of Somalia's collapse is that in a continent riddled with so-called artificial borders binding diverse, and sometimes competing national identities into a single state, it was the relatively homogenous Somali state that experienced one of the most horrific dissolutions.[30] The irony was not lost on the Somaliland's second president, Mohamed Egal, for whom instilling a distinct sense of a Somaliland identity was a fundamental objective.[31]

Within the rest of Somalia (and even in parts of Somaliland), a forceful argument against independence draws on the passionate belief in Somali national unity that dates back to the colonial era. Indeed, it was that ardent sense of nationalism that drove the initial union between Somaliland and the rest of Somalia (then referred to as "Italian Somalia") in 1960. According to Markus Hoehne, the black five-pointed star in the middle of independent Somaliland's national flag articulates the acrimony surrounding its secession, reportedly being intended to symbolize the death of the (never-realized) union of the five regions of greater Somalia within a single state. It is a stark challenge to the lone symbol on the Somali flag—a white five-pointed star—where each point represents one of those five regions (Hoehne 2011, 321). Three of these five regions were lost to neighboring states when the colonial powers withdrew from the Horn of Africa (Djibouti, the Ogaden region in Ethiopia, and the northeastern province of Kenya), and one of the five regions claims independence as Somaliland. The only remaining region that sits within the Federal Republic of Somalia consists of Puntland (an autonomous though nonsecessionist entity within the Republic of Somalia that was established in 1998) and the rest of southern Federal Republic of Somalia. Until the beginning of the Hargeysa conference in 1996, Somaliland had used the SNM flag as its national flag. This flag was white with a green circle in the middle, and "God is great" (*Allahu akbar*) written in Arabic across the top. As will be discussed in chapter 4, the Hargeysa conference was principally intended by President Egal to consolidate the political dominance of the central government over the clan elders. Articulating the strength of the link between Egal's own political dominance and the popularity of independence among the political elite, it was at the Hargeysa conference that Somaliland's new flag was introduced, with the five-pointed black star at its center (Hoehne 2011, 321).

The other main arguments against Somaliland's independence concern its viability as a sovereign state: first, that it does not exercise either military or political control over significant portions of the territory that it claims, and second that its economy is too weak to support independence. As discussed earlier, the matter of economic viability is less convincing, having sustained itself for more than two decades without significant economic support from either Somalia or the international community. The political and military arguments have more substance, as they raise vexing questions about who is included and who is excluded from the idea of an independent state of Somaliland. To those that do not accept Somaliland's claim of independence, Somaliland merely constitutes a territory that has been captured by a separatist and exclusive clan family (the Isaaq) at the expense of marginalized clans in the periphery. As power has been increasingly concentrated in the political center (particularly in Hargeysa), concerns have grown in the periphery that legal independence would further entrench the political and economic dominance of the Isaaq clan (ICG 2015, 4).

As noted in the introduction, it is estimated that perhaps around 20 percent of the total population reject the notion that Somaliland should be independent from Somalia (Hoehne 2011, 323).[32] A former minister—himself a member of the country's elite—underlined the contentious nature of the claim outside of the Isaaq population centers: "There are only two of five regions that want independence, the other three do not."[33] That is, the term "Somaliland" is used almost exclusively by those who support its call for sovereign recognition and who, therefore, produce the independence discourse. This points to the discursive element of marginalization within Somaliland that is discussed at length in chapter 5 and suggests that political inclusion rests on the ideological acceptance of Somaliland's claim of independence from Somalia.

Those who deny the significance of exclusion within Somaliland will often cite the outcome of the 2001 referendum, in which 97.1 percent of voters reportedly favored the new constitution for the nascent independent state.

The process was seen, and actively portrayed by President Egal, as a vote on independence and little else. Four weeks before the referendum, Egal stated "once you have accepted the constitution, you have accepted [an independent] Somaliland" (cited in Walls 2014, 210). However, the fact that the government required voters to place their ballots in either an open white "yes" box or a black "no" box (Initiative & Referendum Institute, 2001: 14) seriously compromised the anonymity of the process. Furthermore, in parts of Sool and Sanaag, the results were quite different, with 45 percent of voters voting against the constitution in the city of Laascaanood (pronounced *Las Anod*) in Sool (Initiative & Referendum Institute 2001, 18). Finally, the turnout figures for the referendum were suspiciously high, leading Michael Walls to conclude that even though the result probably did reflect the will of the majority, it almost certainly demonstrated "levels of enthusiasm that compelled many voters to cast the [*sic*] votes as often as they could" (Walls 2014, 211). Successive government administrations have centralized power and economic development in Hargeysa and its environs. Yet, they have failed to do so in the Sool and Sanaag regions in the east, which are claimed by Puntland and/or Khatumo State, or parts of Awdal on the western areas bordering Djibouti.

Despite the claims of much of the English language literature, Somaliland is not as politically inclusive as is sometimes asserted and appears to have become less so over time. Moreover, the population in the eastern areas of Sool and Sanaag is far less invested in the idea of Somaliland expressed in the independence discourse than the predominantly Isaaq population of middle Somaliland (Phillips 2016, 638).

Puntland is also vehemently opposed to Somaliland's claims of independence. Its government exercises regional autonomy as the Puntland State of Somalia but does not seek outright independence from Somalia. The territorial claims of Somaliland's and Puntland's governments overlap considerably. Somaliland adheres to the old Anglo-Italian colonial boundaries of the British Somaliland Protectorate, while Puntland applies a genealogical claim to the Harti-dominated (Dhulbuhante and Warsangeli) areas of Sool, eastern Sanaag and southern Togdheer (Hoehne 2015, 21). The depth of these competing claims to political authority are apparent even during a bus trip from Hargeysa (Somaliland) to Garoowe (Puntland) through the city of Laascaanood (which is claimed by both Somaliland and Puntland). Markus Hoehne writes:

[The] border starts already in Burco with regard to currency [where passengers exchange their Somaliland Shillings for Somali Shillings]. It continues somewhere in between with changing the number plates [though in Laascaanood cars can use number plates from either Somaliland or Puntland]. In many respects, Laascaanood seems to be part of the Puntland state of Somalia, as indicated by the Somali flag hoisted and painted on walls everywhere, and the issuing of Puntland visas in the local police station. In Garoowe it becomes clear that Laascaanood is perceived as the political periphery and people there are not fully trusted by officials in the capital of Puntland. In this light, the border space between Somaliland and Puntland extends between Garoowe over a distance of circa 300 kilometres. (Hoehne 2010, 104)

Thus, the place at which the various exchanges occur depends on de facto power relations rather than the existence of any one distinct border crossing between Somaliland and Puntland, and thus the Republic of Somalia.

Such indistinct formal boundaries are also apparent in the ways that local businesses organize themselves throughout this politically contested area, as physical control, or at least reliable access, is needed to guarantee the security of a company's physical infrastructure (Iazzolino 2015, 20). For example, Somaliland's largest telecommunications carrier (Telesom) has an agreement with Puntland's largest telecommunications carrier (Golis) over which company is responsible for maintaining infrastructure within various border areas, and whether customers will be treated as roaming or as local subscribers by each company.[34] The city of Laascaanood in Sool is claimed by both Somaliland and Puntland, but Telesom (Somaliland's carrier) views its subscribers there as roaming because Somalilanders cannot reliably gain access to maintain the physical infrastructure and so must use infrastructure that is owned and maintained by Golis (Puntland's carrier) instead. The inability of a Somaliland company to reliably access Laascaanood is a strong indicator that the government of Somaliland, and its attendant claim of independence, are not generally accepted in the area.

Conversely, the city of Ceerigaabo (pronounced *Erigabo*) in Sanaag is also claimed by both Puntland and Somaliland but there Golis (Puntland) treats its subscribers as roaming because technicians from Puntland cannot maintain reliable access to the town and so the company uses Telesom's (Somaliland) network instead. The salience of this de facto control is illustrated by the fact that the same thing has occurred with the Nationlink Telecom company: Nationlink Puntland maintains the network infrastructure in Laascaanood, while Nationlink Somaliland maintains it in Ceerigaabo. The significance of these ambiguous borders vis-à-vis the independence discourse is discussed further in chapter 5.

From Autonomy to Limited Intervention

While the barriers facing Somaliland's quest for revenue are substantial, some of the literature regarding external intervention from about 2000 onwards is misleading. Traditional development assistance is not available to Somaliland's government, but the widely-made suggestions that Somaliland "has never been eligible for foreign assistance" (Eubank 2012, 446), that it receives "little outside assistance" (Kaplan 2008, 147), or that it has not had "the benefit of . . . much foreign development assistance" (Pham 2012, 3) confuse what the government has received with the aid that enters the country overall. These statements may also be assuming that the negligible levels of external involvement in the 1990s remained in subsequent decades. Mark Bradbury notes that by 2004, Somaliland received 37 percent of all aid going to Somalia. The significantly more populous—and more troubled—southern Somalia received only 41 percent (Bradbury 2010, 8).[35]

At least 100 domestic and international NGOs now operate in Somaliland,[36] between them administering over $100 million in funding (Clapham et al. 2011, 16; see also Mills 2015, 579) which, in 2011 when this data was collected, was more than the total operating budget of the Somaliland government.[37] There are eighteen resident UN agencies operating in Somaliland and a further four nonresident agencies. The main streets of Hargeysa are plastered with billboards advertising the presence of the international community in Somaliland, and its two biggest hotels (Maansoor and Ambassador) host an ongoing procession of internationally funded workshops and capacity-building seminars for government departments and local NGOs. The Somaliland Non-State Actors Forum (SONSAF) wrote in 2012 that Somaliland "depends on international donors for most of its development programmes . . . [it] remains dependent on international donors for financing its elections" (SONSAF 2012, 25, 27).[38] It was estimated that donors paid around 75 percent of the $18 million that it cost to hold the 2012 local elections (Africa Research Institute 2013, 16). In the 2017 Presidential elec-

tions, international donors funded 63 percent of the voter registration process and 19 percent of elections materials (Mahmood and Farah 2017, 5).
Somaliland, therefore, does receive international development assistance,
even though in its early formative years (the 1990s) it did not.

Once Somaliland began receiving significant aid, the critical remaining
difference between it and other developing countries (most obviously, the rest
of Somalia) was that no financial assistance went directly to the government
to be spent at its discretion without external approval. Assistance is delivered
as project aid to finance specific projects that are administered by government ministries, local or international NGOs, or UN agencies, and that have
relatively limited objectives. This means that the government has been largely
responsible for extracting the revenue required by the budget—the implied
self-sufficiency of which resonates strongly throughout both the statements
of government officials and of ordinary Somalilanders alike—at least in Isaaq
dominated areas.

The long-awaited Somaliland Development Fund (SDF), which came
into effect in 2014, essentially follows the same model of quarantining overseas money from central government coffers. Established through negotiations between the minister of planning and International Cooperation, and
the British and Danish governments as an alternative model to standard official development assistance, the SDF provides money that is administered
by an external (private, for-profit) fund manager. The fund offers the Somaliland government a channel through which it can apply for external
funds without the money ever going through the central budget.

It is now a growing concern among Somalilanders and donors that the
level of external assistance is creating an expectation of handouts that did not
exist in the 1990s.[39] If the country continues to be drawn into regional geopolitical rivalries, it is likely that such expectations will increase.

Notwithstanding these developments, a core tenet of the independence
discourse remains that the lack of foreign aid and handouts is (still) part of
what separates Somalilanders from other Somalis.

Meanwhile, Somalilanders also widely decry the way that the development interventions that do target the country subvert the local ownership that
is seen to have been so important to establishing peace in the 1990s. Here,
the discontent is not about a supposed clash of values between interveners
and aid recipients (see Sabaratnam 2017, chapter 2) but about power inequalities between interveners and those intervened upon. The controversy over

Somaliland's new NGO act (signed into law in May 2011) is exemplary of these tensions and is worth discussing for the complexities it reveals about the relationship between intervention and independence.

The NGO act directly challenged the UN and other INGOs' lack of accountability, and the inability of Somaliland's government to monitor and manage its own affairs as a result. Article 35(3) of the act stated that "International NGOs shall not become implementers for other International NGOs and UN organisations working in the country," as this was seen to sideline the government and other local organizations. The UN and international (I)NGOs complained that being required to partner with local organizations instead of international organizations would undermine the effectiveness of their programs because, they claimed, local groups lacked the technical expertise to implement them properly (Freedom House 2012). Somaliland's minister for planning and international cooperation countered that the law was intended to build that expertise by giving local organizations "the opportunity to build their capacity and the experience to take on major projects after the international NGOs leave" (cited in IRIN 2011).

The act stipulated that externally funded development agencies must report the amount of money allocated to, and spent on, their programs to the government. It also required that INGOs provide an activity report from the previous year and a reference from its local partner in exchange for the renewal of its registration (Article 34/1), both of which met with resistance from donors. The government's attempt to hold donors to account through the act illustrates the strain between Somalilanders' desire to be treated as a normal state—one that is allowed to receive aid—and the concern that aid undermines the autonomy that partially justifies its independence. This concern is amplified by the fact that the discourse about independence credits its autonomy from international aid as a pillar of the country's peace process.

Three years after the NGO act was issued, Somaliland's minister of planning and international cooperation told me that he still did not have a clear understanding of how much money external actors were spending in the country:

> I don't know exactly. There is a system called DAD—the Development Assistance Database—and all donors are supposed to enter in the amount that they put in, but no one really knows. This year we started to require the UN

and the INGOs to give us their budgets and the balance sheets for the previous year to show what was actually spent. We have been hassling but from 20 March [2013] we have received this from 10 UN agencies (that's about half of them) and 42 INGOs (from a total of about 70). It's an uphill struggle.[40]

When asked an even more general question—whether international agencies were increasing their presence in Somaliland—the minister admitted:

> I don't have a sense of this. I'm not sure. . . . The UN/INGOs come to us at the point of entry but then there are some programs that we are not aware of. In 2010, we passed a law demanding that they give us their previous year's accounts and their projected plans but, as I said, this is not always done.

The inability of the government to determine how much money enters Somaliland is, in part, due to the UN's unwillingness to differentiate between the funds it spends on operations in Somaliland and the funds spent elsewhere in Somalia, because figures are only available for Somalia as a whole.[41] As a senior official in the Ministry of Education complained: "They call us a part of the Somali government. They see us, Puntland, and southern Somalia as one entity, therefore there is money going everywhere and nobody can trace it."[42] The unwillingness to disclose how much money is being spent on operations in Somaliland contributes to the prevalent view that either "the INGOs are more powerful here than the government but there is no accountability for them,"[43] or simply that "the UN is the government here."[44] Putting it even more bluntly, a local researcher working at a Hargeysa-based research institute said, "The truth is that empire is back in a camouflaged way. Governance, democratization, and conflict resolution are all like trusteeships under the UN."[45]

During a meeting at the Ministry of Education about international support for Somaliland's education sector, a senior official said that the international development agencies operating in the country:

> have their own priorities. . . . We have a list of our own priorities (budgets, strategic plans, et cetera) but the donors say: 'this is not in our mandate . . . our mandate is to build 20 schools,' but these schools might be small, and we would rather one good school. . . . They also do training, but we don't need training.[46]

During our discussion, one of the ministry's technical advisors interjected:

> The international community means to do institution building but they un-
> dermine us [in the process]. The blame is, of course, only partly with them
> though. We provide their security and let them operate here. . . . We accept
> their conditions, so it is partly our fault. . . . If we want A and they want B
> we get B. We get abused and we accept it.

Reiterating the lack of influence that locals perceive themselves to have with
the international development agencies, the head of a locally run (though internationally funded) NGO emphasized that: "Donors have their priorities,
and these are sometimes in conflict with your [own organizational] mandate.
For example, if the [European Commission] has a proposal on gender equality and [we] want to do a health project, it will not work."[47]

This person also said that part of their role as the head of a local NGO
was to second-guess donor priorities by crafting proposals that would adhere
to the externally derived mandates of the donor while still meeting local
needs: "I'm not sure how they [the donors] write their plans, but if you're very
clever you can figure it out and pre-empt them." This need to adhere to external priorities regardless of local needs was a complaint often made. The
senior official in the Ministry of Education quoted above noted:

> They bring these ready-made projects. . . . This is one of the biggest prob-
> lems, but we cannot just kick them out. . . . Whatever plan they bring they
> must sit with the government and discuss it. What is applicable to Uganda,
> Tanzania or Kenya is not necessarily applicable here, but they say: "take it or
> leave it."[48]

Two ministers with international portfolios also argued that most of the assistance received by Somaliland has not been particularly useful to its people.
One noted that in 2010 Somaliland received:

> about [US] $80–85 million [in international assistance]. . . . We think that
> maybe between 20–50 percent of that $80–85 million is actually coming into
> Somaliland and the rest is spent in Nairobi, on [international] consultants,
> travel, and security. . . . It's all soft aid here too: capacity building, technical
> assistance. Translated this means "workshops."[49]

For comparison, Somaliland's budget for 2010 was about $51 million, so by the minister's estimate, donors outspent the country's national budget by around 70 percent that year. Another minister argued similarly that for all the aid that was distributed to Somaliland in 2010:

> "There is nothing visible on the ground. The health sector was given [US] $4.5 million and other than vaccines, conferences, foreign experts, and studies with graphs for donors, we never received anything."[50]

As for direct budgetary assistance, he argued: "we can raise it ourselves, we don't want it. . . The aid is not what we desire [because] they decide for us what we need." These comments represent concerns that were widely articulated throughout the research process and endorse the inherent legitimacy of Somaliland's claim that it deserves to be recognized as a sovereign state. They also articulate the self-reliance and exceptionalism that are core threads to the independence discourse, which stands it in resistance to the fragile states discourse, particularly regarding the faith that the latter places in the utility of international intervention.

The unusual nature of Somaliland's relative exclusion from international economic and political structures is reified as a pillar of its ability to establish peace. The absence of intervention during Somaliland's early years energizes a powerful discourse about Somalilanders' exceptionalism, the self-reliance of its people, and the ownership of its institutions, to which the next chapters turn.

Chapter 3

Self-Reliance and Elite Networks

This chapter examines the backgrounds of several elite networks and coalitions that were instrumental to establishing independence and, subsequently, peace in the 1990s, focusing on the relationships, configurations of power, and ideas that they drew on and further embedded. Being denied access to significant external funding or support, these networks were largely dependent upon one another for either their survival as elites or for their prosperity. Their mutual dependence reverberates throughout the independence discourse, building layers of meaning around the idea that Somaliland was forged through the self-reliance of its people, which followed on from the self-reliance demonstrated by earlier civil society movements and the Somali National Movement (SNM) guerilla fighters that took on the Barre dictatorship. This framing of history is not only used to illustrate the authenticity of Somaliland's independence but also the degree to which its experience upends hegemonic assumptions about state fragility and the usefulness of international intervention for correcting it. This chapter explores the ways in which the autonomy of local actors is framed as one of the core elements of Somaliland's peace-building processes.

The story of Somaliland's evolution as an independent entity is, in part, one of a small group of merchants and companies that extended their leverage over a fiscally weak government to entrench their dominance in an unregulated marketplace. Despite the broad political inclusiveness of Somaliland's peace process between 1991 and 1997, the implicit bargain between the political and economic elites that consolidated it was highly exclusive and laid the foundation for the concentration of economic opportunity in the hands of a select few. By the early 2000s the situation (which continues today) prompted Tabea Zierau to observe that the government was so dependent on the loans that it received from a small number of businesses that their withdrawal from the country "would shatter state revenues." Even the threat of withdrawal, Zierau noted, is "usually sufficient to keep the state complacent" (Zierau 2003, 59).[1]

Through its inability (and sometimes unwillingness) to regulate the economy, Somaliland's government has perpetuated a market with limited opportunities for access, placing a ceiling on the prospects for more inclusive development. However, that bargain is still widely seen as preferable to the perceived likely alternative of violence or civil war.[2] The ideational component of this bargain—that economic collusion between elites is preferable to civil war—tends to be glossed over in analyses of Somaliland's political economy, which focus instead on the specifics of the collusion, often in fascinating detail (de Waal 1996; Marchal 1996; Zierau 2003; Balthasar 2013). It is, therefore, with the evolution of those coalitions that this chapter begins, starting with a discussion of the secondary school networks that span a number of them. It then explores the self-help community group (*Uffo*) in the 1980s, SNM, the clan elders and *Guurti*, the business community, and women activists, each of which displayed a strong degree of dependence on other domestic actors.

Secondary School Networks

During the field research for this project, one response stood out when people were asked why Somalilanders were able to establish, and subsequently maintain, peace and relative order: Sheekh Secondary School.[3] Amoud

Secondary School was also often mentioned. Appearing in none of the literature about Somaliland's peace process that I had surveyed, this was not a response that I anticipated. And yet, when I pressed for specifics about the leadership qualities of the key (nonclan based) figures who were active in the 1990s peace processes, answers were often framed in similar terms. The deputy chairman of a prominent civil society organization told me, for example:

> The leaders of the SNM were well educated and it was they who were so influential in the conferences . . . [their secondary education was at] Sheekh and Amoud schools—almost all of them. These were the only two schools that offered GSCs [the General Certificate of Education] in the country.[4]

Along similar lines, a former member of the Uffo self-help group that is discussed below (himself not a member of the school's alumni) also suggested that the leadership qualities of the nonclan elite derived, at least in part, from the fact that:

> Most of the people in positions of influence and power now were educated at Sheekh School, which had British teachers. The people who graduated in the early 1960s are from Sheekh. The best students were sent there and there was no clan element—the principal was from Britain and was very strict that there was to be no clan-based priorities for students. The students from the school refer to themselves as the "Sheekh school boys."[5]

One of the SNM's leaders pointed out that among Somalilanders it is widely accepted that the early SNM leadership was comprised "mostly [of] people from Amoud or Sheekh; secondary schools."[6] One indication of the extent to which these two schools feature in the backgrounds of Somaliland's most influential leaders is that three of Somaliland's five presidents to date attended Sheekh School;[7] the other two, Dahir Rayale Kahin and Musa Bihi, went to Amoud. Three of its vice-presidents also went to Sheekh School, and one (Abdirahman Aw Ali) attended Amoud as well.[8] As part of the research for this project, my research assistant and I compiled a list of the political and technocratic actors (ministers, senior bureaucrats, politicians, and members of civil society) who would be widely accepted within Somaliland as having had a high level of political influence since 1991 (clan elders were listed elsewhere). While an individual's inclusion in the resulting list of fifty-seven people was a subjective judgement, it was one that was made before a person's educational background was known. Of all those for whom educational details could be found (fifty out of fifty-seven), half (twenty-five) had attended Sheekh School. Six had attended Amoud School (in Boorama), and eight Lafoole College near Mogadishu. The remaining number went to local schools (except for one person on the list who appeared to have had no formal education). A similar, though also necessarily subjective, list of politically influential poets revealed that four out of five of them attended Sheekh School, and that one had no formal education. At least six of the twenty imprisoned members of Uffo (the self-help group that spearheaded early resistance to the Barre regime in the 1980s) attended Sheekh School, as did a high proportion of President Egal's first cabinet. As one graduate of the school noted:

> In Egal's cabinet there was a high number of Sheekh graduates. . . . At least seven of the key cabinet members in Egal's first cabinet members were from Sheekh, maybe more, but it was around a third of them—it's always this way, always around a third.[9]

These figures are even more extraordinary when one considers the small number of students that actually attended Sheekh School. The school accepted only fifty students a year for the thirty-one years (1958–1989) before it was destroyed in the war: just 1,550 people over three decades.[10] One graduate noted: "There were only 50 graduates a year, and at least 50 percent of these went abroad."[11]

Sheekh School was a privately funded, merit-based, boarding school that offered free tuition to the top male students in Somaliland—women were not admitted. It had a strong emphasis on extracurricular activities including debating, dramatic productions, competitive sports, a house system, and provided for students to elect individuals from among their number to lead some of the school's administrative functions. Sheekh School was built by the British Protectorate administration and received its first intake of students in 1958, which was a group that had been transferred from Amoud School (the first secondary school in Somaliland, which was also built by the colonial administration).[12] This first group of students graduated in 1960. At that time, Sheekh and Amoud were the only two boarding schools in Somaliland, and were, as mentioned above, the only schools to offer the GSE (the British General Certificate of Education, or O-levels). The first headmaster of the school was Richard Darlington, who fought in Burma in World War II as the commander of the Somaliland Protectorate's contingent and remained as headmaster until Siyad Barre ordered his departure in 1971. Darlington was, according to a number of graduates, a dedicated teacher who worked to train students in leadership and critical thought. One graduate reflected:

> Sheekh School had a major influence on Somaliland. Its practice was to train national leaders. . . . There was a democratic culture there with an emphasis on the rule of law, and there was a strong committee system for each form—each form was responsible for one committee and positions on them were highly competitive. People aspired and campaigned to become part of the school committee, which was the committee run by the Forth Form and it practically ran the school. . . . We had debates; there was a culture of open debate and we used to vote . . . it was an institutionalized culture, a well-disciplined culture, where there was the rule of law. The students had a high quality of analysis, organization and management skills. . . . Elite leadership was trained in us there.[13]

A more critical graduate highlighted the colonial aspects of the education offered at the school, suggesting that Sheekh students were trained to project the values of British colonial power in their subsequent positions of leadership and, presumably, cultivate sympathy with empire:

> In hindsight, we were being groomed to lead, to become the elite. Despite the consciousness sweeping the developing world as colonialism ended we were being trained to pray in the direction of Britain—to be Britain's black people. We were trained in this and, unconsciously, we became this. We were disciplined and internalized the idea that we were the elite and had the right to lead people.[14]

These comments highlight the complex ambivalence of Somaliland's colonial experience within the construction of Somaliland as an independent political entity. On one hand, the independence discourse frames independence as legitimate because it reinstates the colonial borders that were internationally recognized for five days in 1960. The government bases part of its claim to independence from Somalia on the fact that the two have a "separate colonial history" (Government of Somaliland, n.d.). It is also widely claimed that the British style of indirect rule left Somaliland's clan structures and institutions intact and thus capable of shaping the peace process in the 1990s. This is contrasted to the devastating legacy of the Italian colonial administration's direct rule in the south (ICG 2003, 3; Dua 2011). On the other hand, Somalilanders' autonomy from the international system animates the discourse about the validity of its independence. Somaliland's independence is variously framed as a product of the country's entanglement in, and its autonomy from, global politics of domination.

Sheekh was a selective school that offered entry on the basis of students' exam marks though Darlington was reportedly adamant that the student body should be inclusive of all clans (albeit only their male members). According to one graduate, preferential entry was offered to some students from the marginalized (and non-Isaaq) eastern regions of Sool and Sanaag, but "for everyone else it was on grades."[15] In addition to the training in leadership and critical thought that Sheekh students reported to have received, alumni pointed to the importance of their educational experiences in building and consolidating networks of trust among the student cohort that were, in some cases, maintained decades later. One graduate referred to the networks that have emerged from the school as functioning "like a secondary tribe" because of the level of trust that was built by the shared experience of being a student at Sheekh.[16]

During the time that Sheekh was run by Darlington (1958–1971), students had the opportunity to compete for tertiary education scholarships abroad: "Before the military regime the top ten students got to go to the UK, others would go to Sudan or Uganda [and elsewhere]. After the military regime, the school became more local, so no more scholarships."[17] One of the older graduates said that he had raised this issue with donors:

> We used to say to the international community [that] all we need is three Sheekh Schools. . . . The international community is fixated on primary education and on literacy, which is obviously important but there is no focus on educating the elite. We tried to convince them in another way, saying that whatever happens in a country is a product of its people. . . . We all know what they think is important, and that that is short-term training programs. These are not futile, but they also are lacking in many areas.
>
>   This kind of thing should be the job of the UNDP [United Nations Development Programme] but they focus on important but intangible things, like the rule of law. A school is something that you have to sustain over time. It's the whole approach—their focus is short-term and is about rehabilitation and security.[18]

The minister of planning noted that while donors have funded some build-ings for secondary schools there has been no investment in the quality of the education provided: "We have quantity but not quality."[19]

Educational networks like those that have emerged out of Sheekh are not uncommon. In a number of African countries, a small selection of second-ary schools is conspicuous in the educational backgrounds of the national leadership.[20] Deborah Brautigam and Tania Diolle found that in Mauritius an "unusually high number of people who were stakeholders and decision-makers at independence were graduates of the island's elite, meritocratic government-run secondary school, Royal College" (Braugtigam and Diolle 2009, 32). David Sebudubudu (2009, 29) shows that in Botswana, "many of the elite studied together in institutions outside the country and/or in a few elite schools within the country, [where] they developed a common political and social value system." In Ghana too, the backgrounds of key reformist leaders suggest the importance of networks built at elite meritocratic second-ary schools, particularly Achimota, where around one-quarter of the coun-try's most significant developmental elite studied (Jones, Jones, and Ndaruhutse 2014, 43). Likewise in Singapore, the alumni of the Raffles Institution (also a secondary school) have dominated senior government positions, including the prime ministership and presidency. Perhaps not surprisingly, this is also a phenomenon in Britain, the colonizer of each of these states. Twenty of the UK's fifty-five prime ministers (and one from Northern Ireland) were educated at Eton College, while a further seven were educated at Harrow School, and six attended Westminster School.

The prominence of Sheekh School graduates in Somaliland's early lead-ership positions and bureaucracy, and the way that their prominence was repeatedly framed in interviews, illuminates the self-reliance that Somalil-anders perceive to have guided the transition from conflict. Those who sought to build an independent state were able to draw from a pool of relatively well-educated Somalilanders to staff a nascent bureaucracy, many of whom also operated in an existing, albeit exclusive, network of trust from their school days. Rather than needing (or being expected) to rely on outsourced inter-national technical expertise, as is often the case in donor-funded state-building programs, Somalilanders emphasize their self-sufficiency. The history of the networks formed at Sheekh School form part of the basis for this emphasis.

The Self-Help Group Uffo

The self-help group Uffo ("Whirlwind," also known as the Hargeysa Group) was critical in galvanizing Somalilanders' resistance to the Barre government in the early 1980s and in instituting the relatively inward-looking modes of political organization that are generated and reproduced in the independence discourse.

Following Somalia's humiliating defeat by Ethiopia in the 1977–1978 Ogaden War, and the subsequent economic crisis, Siyad Barre declared a state of emergency in 1980 and further concentrated political control within a narrow inner circle of family and clan members. Its members were principally from the Marehan, Ogaden, and Dhulbahante clans of which Barre, his mother, and his powerful son-in-law (also head of the national security service), respectively, were members. This small cluster was known locally as the MOD (Marehan, Ogaden, and Dhulbahante) alliance. The exclusive and clan-based nature of Barre's powerbase was darkly ironic considering that his scientific socialism doctrine so vehemently disavowed tribalism as a dangerous anachronism.

As public services in the north were being ground to a halt in the early 1980s, a group of young urban professionals (mostly teachers, doctors, and engineers) who had returned relatively recently to the north from Mogadishu or abroad (Bradbury 2008, 55) formed a self-help group. The group intended to revive long-neglected social services, starting with the Hargeysa Hospital. According to Mark Bradbury, the hospital improved to such an extent within a year that it was once again one of the best in the country—a reputation it had not enjoyed since the British colonial era (Bradbury 2008, 55). The group also tried to mobilize people by using the government-owned radio station to raise awareness about the importance of public health issues (Jama 2003, 21)—a service that often contained political undertones. Their activities attracted public support, funding from local businesses, and also from the international NGO German Emergency Doctors, which raised around two million German Marks for Uffo's refurbishment of Hargeysa Hospital (Jama 2003, 21–22). The group branched out and began working on projects such as the provision of mother and child healthcare services, the Hargeysa Nursing School, and free teaching services. Uffo's local popularity did not go unnoticed by the Barre regime, and sensing its political challenge, the security services began to build a legal case against its members.

The timing of Uffo's work coincided with the emergence of the Somali National Movement (SNM) in London and the publication of its monthly newspaper, *Somalia Uncensored*. In late 1981, twenty-nine members of Uffo were arrested. Four months after their arrest, on February 19, 1982, all those arrested were charged with high treason for belonging to an illegal organization. The crime carried a mandatory death sentence. On February 24, students took to the streets in protest and were met with tanks and heavy gunfire. Several people were killed, and many others were wounded and/or radicalized. Around four hundred students were also arrested and imprisoned (Jama 2003, 39). Meanwhile, Barre redeclared the state of emergency in the north (Renders 2012, 63), imposing a curfew on Hargeysa and other urban centers, and giving extraordinary powers to the military and police against the Isaaq population. Africa Watch reported that "the arrest in December 1981 and the trial in February 1982 . . . (of the Hargeisa Group [Uffo]) . . . was one of the most important events that triggered the politically explosive situation in the northern region" (cited in Jama 2003, 32). The government's response to the student protests are remembered within Somaliland as marking the beginning of the Somali civil war (Bradbury 2008, 3) and under Barre students marked the anniversary each year with further protests (Jama 2003, 62). Northern civil servants and military personnel soon began to rebel and eleven officials were summarily executed, including the military commander of the Berbera zone (Renders 2012, 63). From this point, the actions of the state became widely perceived as Barre's attempt to destroy the entire Isaaq population (Bakonyi 2009, 439) and the idea that only a separation from the unitary state of Somalia could prevent this began to gain more traction.

The arrests of Uffo members and the subsequent protests proved critical for galvanizing the population in the north against the Barre regime and helped to provide an ideational link between the SNM—at this point still an elite diaspora movement—and grassroots dissent. However, the SNM's ability to move from its elite support base and find support, and local legitimacy, among the lower urban strata and peasantry was more difficult than just articulating an ideational link between its aspirations and those of local communities (Bakonyi 2009, 438). As discussed below, this required the organization to work politically to gain the support of the clan leaders.

All defendants from Uffo pleaded not guilty. The trial for the twenty-nine men took only ten hours (Jama 2003, 51) and while none were sentenced to death, their prison sentences ranged from between three and thirty years. Nine of the accused were acquitted due to a lack of evidence. The twenty prisoners were put into solitary confinement, where some of the men spent the next six-and-a-half years (Jama 2003, 53) before their release in 1989.

Why was this self-help group formed? The answer that is usually offered is that its members, who had recently returned to the north, were appalled by the state of health and education services in the north-west of Somalia and believed that they could do something about it. A closer look at their backgrounds reveals another factor, however. Jama Musse Jama, who has written the most comprehensive account of the group, notes: "Members of [Uffo] . . . were all acquainted with each other form [sic] childhood and they all went to schools in the region" (Jama 2003, 21). Of the twenty men who were imprisoned, the majority were from Hargeysa, which is not surprising considering that it is the demographic center of the north-west. At least six of the twenty men also went to the same secondary school—Sheekh.

Therefore, not only did these people know and trust each other—many of them since childhood—but a high proportion of them had access to some of the best secondary education in the country. At least one-quarter of them had attended tertiary education abroad as well, including in the United Kingdom, Germany, India, Yemen, Poland, and Czechoslovakia. International connections within Hargeysa were also leveraged to gain funding for their work—something with which its members were presumably comfortable and familiar with. Uffo's leaders had strong personal ties of trust between them, international experiences with which to compare their experiences at home, and were disproportionately well educated. In fact, for nineteen out of the twenty members about whom information was uncovered in this research, all had attended secondary school—an unusually high proportion. These links were widely underscored in the interviews with local elites cited above, who reported their frustration that external actors continue to overlook the salience of existing local capacity in favor of interventions that uphold their own existing organizational mandates and structures.

The Somali National Movement

By the early 1980s, Somalilanders were already a globally diffuse, though still well-connected population. Many people were forced to relocate abroad during the drought and famine that affected the north in 1974–1975 or by the repercussions of Somalia's war against Ethiopia in 1977–1978, which brought an influx of Ogadeni (Darood clan) and Oromo refugees from Ethiopia into Somaliland (Lewis 1994, 179).

The SNM was officially established in London in April 1981, having grown out of three different groups: two in the diaspora (one based in the United Kingdom and one based in Saudi Arabia) and one group based in Somalia. The latter primarily provided people for the fight against the Barre government and was largely led by officers who had received their military training in the Soviet Union.[21] The Saudi group first began their collaboration in 1977, but the individuals involved failed to decide what sort of organization they should form—a political party or something less formally defined (Lewis 1994, 181). After several false starts, its members were able to gather some money from their supporters and by 1980 were transferring finances to London to help fund the monthly newspaper *Somalia Uncensored*, which launched in June 1981 (182). In 1980, the key leaders in the Saudi group determined that London provided a more favorable political climate for operating an international dissident group, and several people relocated to London to work full time with the movement. Those who left Saudi Arabia were from the Isaaq clan, although the group had made an earlier effort to incorporate members from other north-western clans (the Dhulbuhante and Gadabursi) without much success (182). While these early groups—that were later to become the SNM—remained wary of the influence of the Issaq clan in the organization, attempts at greater inclusiveness proved difficult (190).

As Ioan Lewis describes it, the London group had similarly small-scale origins and emerged from the weekly meetings of a few young Isaaq intellectuals at a pub next to London University (Lewis 1994, 184). This younger group found common cause with a group of retired Isaaq Somali officers from the British Merchant Navy "who formed the backbone of the Somali community in the United Kingdom" (185) and functioned as elders of the Somali community there. Their union was sparked when the Somali embassy in London announced that it was increasing the cost of renewing a Somali passport to GBP £71. The dramatically increased fee posed a problem for both the younger students (who had now formed the Somali National Party—SNUP) and the retired officers, both of whom needed a current passport to either work in the UK or return home. The two groups combined, along with the Somali Student Union to form the Somali–London Association, and organized a meeting with the Somali ambassador to discuss the new charges—although their opposition to the Barre government went deeper than the passport renewal fee. Again, according to Lewis, who offers the most detailed account of the early diaspora activist groups that became the SNM, the ambassador advised members of the Somali–London Association from the Darood clan not to attend the meeting. They complied, and when only Isaaq members showed up the ambassador accused the association of being tribalist (187) in a successful effort to drive a clan-based wedge into the group. Shortly after the meeting some of the non-Isaaq members of the association's central committee denounced the group for being too anti-government and too dominated by the Isaaq. The association responded by announcing that it would be celebrating the anniversary of the five days that Somaliland's independence was internationally recognized in June 1960 (187). In so doing, the association added to the—technically incorrect—impression that it was an exclusively Isaaq nationalist movement seeking to partition Isaaq clan territories from the rest of Somalia (193).[22] In reality, the desirability of, and mechanisms for, achieving cross-clan collaboration in the UK-based anti-Barre movement was always a point of tension, and it persisted throughout the life of the movement. The clans provided networks of political leadership but simultaneously generated other hurdles, at times fueling the fighting. Such complexities underline the broader argument that clan norms and structures do not predict outcomes in any straightforward way.

In these early iterations of what became a strong insurgent force, it is possible to identify some of the core issues that later bedeviled the organization: tensions over whether or not the organization should be an Isaaq nationalist movement or become more inclusive of other clans and questions over how to effectively incorporate clan elders into the political leadership. As with the members of Uffo—and political movements more generally—personal relationships were critical to the contours of the group. According to one of the SNM's early leaders, and an avid historian of the movement, of the three initial core groups (those in Saudi Arabia, Somalia, and the UK):

> Everyone knew each other through personal relationships and depended on verbal messages because of fears that they could be captured. . . . [They knew each other] through schools, or work in the ministries. . . . They were mostly people from Amoud or Sheekh [secondary schools].[23]

Therefore, like the members of Uffo that were critical to catalyzing political change in Somaliland, Sheekh and Amoud schools also formed an important influence in the lives of the SNM's founders.

When the SNM held its first conference in October 1981, it issued a press release entitled "A Better Alternative," which stated that any Somali was welcome to join the movement as long as they believed in the SNM's principles (Lewis 1994, 198). The intention was to emphasize that the SNM was not an exclusively Isaaq movement. These principles explicitly placed clan structures and institutions at the core of its political vision marking it as unique among Somali opposition groups. The press release also stated that the SNM sought to combine "the advantages of Somali democracy and egalitarianism with the benefits of modern national government" by using traditional institutions such as *xeer* (customary mediation within and between kinship groups) at the national level (cited in Lewis 1998, 199). The clan system had been so maligned by Siyad Barre (at least rhetorically) that the idea that it should form the basis of the political system was quite radical (Bradbury 2008, 63). So too was the notion that the clan system could be incorporated into modern national government institutions. However, beyond its belief in the fundamental importance of (somehow) maintaining Somali cultural values, the SNM did not adhere to any unifying ideology (Bradbury 2008, 64).

As time went on, and despite the ongoing efforts of some members to become more inclusive of other clans, the SNM became an increasingly Isaaq movement. This was largely because the movement had become reliant on the clan elders for access to logistics, fighting power, supplies, and a support base. The SNM could not fight a war against the Barre regime without devolving military, and thus political, control to the clan-based guerrilla forces that were fighting under the SNM banner in their local areas.[24] The SNM leaders also used clan-based norms to access greater support for the insurgency by directing its members to go to their local subclan areas and remind people of their obligation to support clan members in distress; a traditional concept known as *qaran* (Bakonyi 2009, 439).

These modes of engagement transplanted traditional pastoral-nomadic ethics into the cities (Bakonyi 2009, 439) and further helped to transform the clan elders from local notables into leaders on a much larger geographical and ideational scale, something that proved crucial to the shape that Somaliland's postindependence political landscape took.

Even before the Barre regime's devastating military campaign against the Isaaq civilian population in 1988, the representation of non-Isaaq members within the SNM central committee was small and declining. In an illustration of that clanism, fighters from non-Isaaq clans that had been dispersed within various SNM units were redeployed in a separate fighting unit—the SNM Southern Front—and relocated to fight from within "their-own" clan areas (Bakonyi 2009, 440). Within the Isaaq units, clan and subclan affiliation also become an increasingly important determinant of who fought in which militia units and in which locations those units fought—a symptom of the amplified military salience to clan identities throughout the country. Having ever-tighter control over the day-to-day activities of the fighting forces, the Isaaq clan elders rendered the original political cadres a minority group within the movement (Compagnon 1998, 77). By the time Barre was ousted, the clan elders held de facto, if not de jure, power within the SNM.

What began as an elite movement across diaspora communities to address political grievances with Mogadishu was thus transformed—by the circumstances of violent conflict, access to resources, and ideas about what was at stake—into a grassroots guerrilla movement led largely by clan actors that controlled local constituencies. Structurally weak, the SNM was subordinated to the influence of the clan elders that had delivered the military victory. This took the traditional political authority of some clan leaders beyond the local level and turned them into actors with a stake in the wider geographical territory that would be claimed as Somaliland. In fact, it was the SNM leaders that were reluctantly carried along by the clan elders in the decision to secede. Many of the (nonelder) SNM leaders were against the idea of secession, believing that the north was too weakened by war to be self-sustaining (Walls 2014, 166). The SNM's preference was for greater autonomy in a federal system of government with the national capital remaining in Mogadishu. In June 1989, the *Indian Ocean Newsletter* reported, for example, that the SNM was "actively preparing to take over government in Mogadishu" (cited in Simons 1995, 76).

However, as the violence in the north continued, the idea of an independent Somaliland gained tremendous grassroots popularity in the Isaaq areas and was well entrenched by the time that Barre fled the country in January 1991 (APD 2002, 17). When the SNM met in Borco in May 1991, the leaders did not intend to declare independence from Somalia. Rather, they were strong-armed into this by some of the clan actors present (Samatar and Samatar 2005, 118) who were representing the strongly proindependence sentiments that had become entrenched among their grassroots constituents. The difference between the two groups on the issue of independence is a clear indicator of the degree to which the clan elders—and those they represented— were politically dominant.

Clan Leaders and the Guurti

The House of Clan Elders, or Guurti, is widely recognized within and outside of Somaliland as having been the most important group of actors in the postindependence peace-building process (1991–1997), although it has since been significantly marginalized in favor of the central government.

When Siyad Barre fell the SNM became the main political party in Somaliland. As discussed in chapter 2, this was a result of a number of factors, including its military victory; its insistence that revenge not be sought against its battlefield opponents; and the successful clan-based peace talks that were carried out by members of the SNM-Guurti in its name. At the time of the first peace conference in Borco in 1991, the Guurti was officially a consultative body to the SNM, but by the Boorama conference in 1993 the Guurti was in control of the peace process (Renders 2012, 100). Between these two conferences, momentum had built for the Guurti to be transformed into a more formal political institution—something that had been a particular demand of a group of female activists and is discussed later in this chapter.

The clan actors at Boorama established the new institutional framework for Somaliland in the National Charter, the details of which are discussed in greater detail in chapter 4. Suffice it to say here that the new framework formalized the role of the Guurti within the government. It became responsible for ratifying, rejecting, or opposing amendments to laws passed by the House of Representatives (other than those dealing with state finances) on the basis of their compliance with Somaliland's traditions, religious beliefs, and security (Lindeman and Hansen, 2003) of which its members were now the guardians. However, despite the formalization of the Guurti's responsibilities, membership remained somewhat fluid, with kinsmen often filling in for members who were absent from meetings (Farah and Lewis 1993, 19).

The evolution of the Guurti into a national institution began when the first nationally-focused Guurti was formed in early 1989 after a meeting in Ethiopia to address the growing influence of clan leaders within the SNM and their dissatisfaction with the political leadership of the movement (Renders 2012, 81). According to Markus Hoehne, it consisted of nearly fifty traditional authority figures (Hoehne 2013, 202). However, a member of the SNM's leadership who was present at the time claimed that the clan leaders in the original SNM-Guurti were not all elders in the traditional sense that they represented pastoral constituencies on the basis of local consensus for their leadership. Rather, they "were just men who happened to be around. They dyed their beards with henna and put on some traditional clothes and that was it" (cited in Renders 2012, 81). In other words, at least some members of the first SNM-Guurti were already a different type of leader—people that emerged from clan structures and used clan idioms but who were politically ambitious beyond a grassroots pastoral context and who had existing urban networks to draw upon as a new political landscape emerged. This is not to say that the leaders in the Guurti were urban pretenders to clan authority but rather that they exercised influence in a political environment that was neither entirely pastoral nor defined by a strong state apparatus.

The members of the Guurti (some of whom were urban-based professionals) represented their clan-based constituencies but did so through new and sometimes novel means. One example of the innovations of the earlier inter-clan Guurtis was the form that the peace negotiations took, most of which adopted "modern conference techniques" such as chairmen and technical committees—that were comprised of professionals, bureaucrats, and military officers (Farah and Lewis 1993, 17)—and the recording of minutes (Renders 2007, 445). They were also conducted on a much larger scale than a traditional pastoral *shir* (deliberative meeting)—which were generally held under a tree between clan elders within a subclan or a descent group (Renders 2007, 445)—involving instead a large and diverse group of actors from across the country. The role of the national Guurti also extended far beyond their traditional functions of reactively stopping violence and crime, a function that was sometimes referred to by elders as *dab damin*, or "extinguishing fire" (Farah and Lewis 1997, 369). In this, and in the urban base of many of its members, the Guurti was a reflection of the shifts in Somaliland's social fabric since the colonial period, where power had slowly transitioned from rural nomadic groups to leaders based in more urban trade centers (Farah and Lewis 1993, 19).

The Boorama conference formalized the role of a certain type of clan leader in Somaliland's political system—one that was willing and able to be detached from a pastoral context—and it also formalized their responsibilities beyond clan leaders' traditional functions as mediators and peacemakers (Lewis 2010, 147). The formalization of the Guurti moved its members to the frontlines of national political confrontations where they did not have natural reserves of social capital to draw from and where they were often physically detached from the communities they were ostensibly representing. The politicization of traditional positions transformed the nature of the leaders' legitimacy and made them vulnerable to accusations of corruption and political self-preservation—something that successive presidents have exploited as a means of increasing their own power vis-à-vis the Guurti. The members of the Guurti have done little collectively to assuage such criticism by accepting patronage, repeatedly extending their own terms, engaging in acts of graft, and siding with the government of the day on unpopular matters (Hoehne 2013, 204). The conference at Boorama represented the pinnacle of the Guurti's political power (Renders 2012, 100), but the tension between political authority derived from grassroots contexts and political authority derived from proximity to the apparatus of the state has since undermined its moral authority.

Like the members of Uffo and the SNM, many of the clan leaders active at Boorama, and within the Guurti more broadly, had pre-existing personal relationships with one another. Unlike the other groups, however, such relationships were generally forged through previous interclan mediation sessions, not in nonclan-based settings like school or places of employment. It is an expectation that clan elders, particularly those in close geographical proximity to one another, are well acquainted in order to facilitate their mediatory capacity. Also, unlike Uffo and the SNM, it appears that very few of them attended secondary school. In fact, few of the key clan actors at Boorama had formal education beyond studies in religion, which the vast majority of them appear to have received.[25] Those individuals with a religious education but no experience of formal education are more likely to be able to read Arabic (the language of the Qur'an) but not necessarily Somali—due to Arabic being taught at primary school. Somali was not a written language until the 1970s and illiteracy is not necessarily a significant limitation for a Somali clan leader. Somalia and Somaliland maintain a very aural culture and the ability to speak persuasively generally trumps the ability to read and write in the skill set required for effective leadership.

The Boorama conference was hosted by the (non-Isaaq) Gadabursi clan, which took responsibility for much of the organization and logistics for the nearly five-month-long conference held in their territory. The level of cross-clan inclusion was high, and participation extended well beyond the Isaaq clans—something that was less apparent within Uffo and the SNM. There were 150 official delegates from the national Guurti active at the conference, but it was also attended by a total of around two thousand other participants (only seventeen of whom were women) and observers, again from across the spectrum of north-western clans. The chair of the SNM Guurti, Sheekh Ibrahim Sheekh Yusuf Sheekh Madar, wanted the conference to include representatives from all of the major northern clans and formed a cross-clan preparatory committee to ensure it would be as inclusive as possible (Interpeace 2008, 49). The high level of inclusivity was critical to the establishment of Somaliland's first robust national peace settlement at Boorama. Therefore, while the political space in this period was notable for its high levels of horizontal and, to a lesser degree, vertical inclusion, this was not reflected in the economic sphere, which became increasingly exclusive as the peace process progressed. That exclusivity is discursively reproduced as evidence of the self-sufficiency upon which Somaliland's peace and independence stands.

President Egal and the Business Elite

When Somaliland's first president, Abdirahman Ali Tuur, went to the Boorama conference in 1993, he expected the Guurti to endorse him for another term as president. Much to his surprise, he received only one-third of the votes and was replaced by Mohamed Haji Ibrahim Egal. Egal was Somalia's last civilian prime minister before Siyad Barre's military coup in 1969 and had championed Somaliland's union with Somalia in 1960. The hasty termination of his predecessor's presidency probably meant that Egal began his own term in office with a clear understanding of the threat to a president's longevity that clan-based negotiations and arrangements contained (Renders 2012, 146).

Egal's first major accomplishment was to substantially demobilize the clan militias, which was achieved with the help of loans received from business-men that were predominantly from his Habar Awal clan. Egal bought peace by co-opting clan elders whom he believed capable of demobilizing local clan-based militias and maintaining public order, and thus he drew these elders close to the political center practically and in the eyes of their followers (Renders and Terlinden 2010, 742). As clan authorities were subsumed under the rubric of the central government, they lost much of the perceived neutrality that had played such an important role in their initial political legitimacy. The more the clan elders were drawn towards the center, the less willing and/or able they were to provide independent oversight of the presidential executive. An often-cited example is that in 2006 the Guurti voted in favor of a presidential decree to extend its own term by four years despite constitutional stipulations against this. The Guurti's mandate has continued to be extended without an election. It was initially set to expire in 2003, which was then pushed to 2009, 2011, 2013, 2018, and is, at the time of writing, set for 2020. By the time this expires some members of the Guurti will have served for twenty-seven years instead of the constitutionally mandated six.[26] For these reasons (which are discussed further in chapter 5) the politically active elders of the Guurti have become widely perceived as serving their own interests over those of their clans. The declining legitimacy of the Guurti has embedded the sense that Somaliland's traditional institutions do not have the capacity to prevent violence that they did in the early independence period— something that is reflected in the discursive caution surrounding the weakness of Somaliland's institutions.

President Egal wanted to marginalize the power of the clan elders in political life but was not averse to relying on his own clan members to secure resources and political support. To finance his state-building plans he quickly secured loans of around $6 million from a small group of eight Isaaq traders,[27] most of whom were based in Djibouti, and six of whom were from his own Habar Awal clan (a subclan within the Isaaq). While thumbing through the official papers documenting the tax concessions given to these traders in exchange for the loans, the director of planning and statistics at the Ministry of Finance exclaimed: "These pieces of paper show how Somaliland was created; these are the founders of the country. . . . It cost six million dollars to start the government."[28] By offering these traders extremely generous tax exemptions on the goods they transported through Berbera port, Egal pro-

vided the Isaaq/Habar Awal commercial elite with opportunities to monopolize business in the north without the risk of needing to re-enter the violent
turbulence of Mogadishu. These merchants became—and remain—some of
the most powerful within Somaliland's economy.[29]

As the son of a well-respected and affluent real estate developer, Egal was
already independently wealthy. He owned considerable land and personally
vouched for some of the money he received in loans. According to an official
in the Ministry of Finance who worked under Egal at the time, his family's
business reputation, combined with Egal's personal charisma, was critical to
the level of trust that he was able to command within the business community, as none of those who supplied him with the early loans appeared to have
known him personally. This lack of a pre-existing connection is unusual
among the other elite networks discussed in this chapter. As further proof
of the esteem with which Egal was held by the business community, his successor, Dahir Rayale Kahin, "never received any money from the business
community because they did not trust him," according to the director of planning and statistics at Somaliland's Ministry of Finance, who served under
each of Somaliland's presidents.[30] As a result, when Dahir Rayale was voted
out of office in 2010, he left a debt of $22 million to the government of Pres-
ident Silanyo that succeeded him. President Egal was not averse to being seen
with wealthy international patrons, travelling to Libya in 2000 to meet with
then President Mu'ammar Qaddafi, who reportedly gave him $40 million.
Qaddafi tried to convince Egal to lead a future united Somali government
(Reliefweb 2000), which Egal refused upon his return to Hargeysa to nation-
alistic fanfare.

However, more important for Egal's ability to secure the loans than his
personal charisma and family connections were the commercial opportunities
presented by the possibility of a more stable—and virtually unregulated—
business environment, particularly once Mogadishu became so tragically
insecure. Egal used the loans to fund the demobilization of militias and consolidate control over Berbera Port, which had been claimed by members of
Egal's Isaaq/Habar Awal/Issa Musa clan (which reside around the port)
during a conflict with his predecessor, President Tuur (Ciabarri 2010, 79).
Some of the income that the central government brought in by gaining control over the Berbera Port Authority in 1993 was diverted from the port directly to the president's office, providing Egal with around $10–$15 million
per year to spend at his discretion (Balthasar 2013, 223). Much of Somaliland's

relative stability has been attributed to the commercial and clan-based arrangements that were established in 1993 under President Egal, in which the government gained access to Berbera Port and secured revenue through tariffs (Ciabarri 2010, 79; De Waal 1996). These vertically exclusive arrangements helped to lay the foundation for the monopolistic practices that have become entrenched in Somaliland's domestic economy (Ciabarri 2010, 80; see also Buh 2010).

In 1994 Egal delivered another benefit to his Habar Awal financial creditors.[31] This time he borrowed $1.4 million to have a new national currency—the Somaliland shilling—printed in London. It was introduced as legal tender in September 1994 in an act laden with the symbolism of Somaliland's proclaimed independence.[32] But it also filled Egal's immediate financial needs. Trading with the old Somali shilling was banned quickly—by January of the following year—but instead of destroying the recalled Somali shillings, Egal sold them to his creditors at a heavily reduced rate for hard currency. His creditors were able simply to transfer the old (and now cheap) Somali shillings to the south, where it remained the national currency (Renders 2012, 134–5). By investing in the outward appearance of a sovereign state, Egal gained legitimacy as a champion of Somaliland's independence while the traders that gave him loans made a lot of money. Egal used the windfall to fight the clan militias that were trying to gain control over Hargeysa airport in 1995 and to fund the demobilization of other clan-based militias.[33]

Through the combination of exclusive business practices and somewhat greater control over the means of coercion, Egal and his backers edged out their economic competitors to dominate the economy. Egal emerged in a financial position to centralize patronage networks and diminish the political dominance of the clan elders while simultaneously grafting grassroots support for independence to his own political ambitions. Collusive business deals for a highly select elite were thus enmeshed with major security dividends for the wider population. Exclusive though the arrangements were, Egal's use of the loans to demobilize the militias remains widely accepted by most Somalilanders as a legitimate use of public funds. The fact that this remains legitimate is in large part a function of the ongoing popular support for independence and the consolidation of peace that made Somaliland's de facto independence possible. Egal's actions are widely remembered as critical to both of these outcomes.

Egal's veneration as the founding father of an independent Somaliland is on clear display throughout the parts of the country that support its secession from Somalia. His portrait hangs prominently in government offices and Hargeysa's international airport was renamed after him, in an apparent nod to the role he played wresting the site from the militias in the mid-1990s, which was a major milestone in the peacebuilding process (Gandrup 2016, 11—the conflict over the airport is discussed in chapter 4).

In addition to the money Egal acquired from loans, the tariffs on goods transiting through Berbera Port, and from the currency deals, Egal also swiftly levied tariffs on *qaat* (a plant that has a mild stimulant effect) imports to increase government revenue by a further 10 percent. Again, Egal relied on supportive clan factions to achieve this, as qaat was chiefly imported through a town (Tog Wajaale) that was largely under the control of Habar Awal militias that supported Egal (Balthasar 2013, 223). While Egal benefited from support within his clan, he resented his reliance on clan leaders for access to revenue and so reshuffled individuals in control of the customs checkpoints to undermine their level of direct control over the income being extracted from within their areas (223–24).

Egal was also successful at changing the language used to frame the conflicts with which he was contending, removing the protagonists' clan as a reference point. Instead of referring to the clan identity of combatants, Egal referred to them as either nationalists (those fighting for an independent Somaliland—and supporting Egal) or federalists (those fighting to preserve the union with the south—and opposing Egal) (229). This helped him to both gain legitimacy among the many Somalilanders who supported independence and to divert attention from his own personal history as an architect of the union with Somalia back in 1960. It also shifted the vocabulary of political contestation at the clan level to one that reproduced the righteousness and viability of Somaliland's sovereign independence.

President Egal pursued a deliberate strategy to increase the influence of Hargeysa-based politicians relative to that of the clan leaders through a combination of co-optation (assisted by increased government revenue) and by rejecting calls for further clan-based negotiations. He used his authority as president to disrupt local peace negotiations and community self-help projects, asserting that such processes were the responsibility of the central government and not the clan leadership (Balthasar 2013, 229). Marleen Renders

recounts, for example, a clan-based peace meeting that was organized between the Habar Yunis and the Habar Awal/Issa Musa clans in the town of
Mandera in August 1996 to try to end an ongoing conflict between them.
Egal managed to convince the elders from his clan (the Issa Musa) to termi-
nate their participation, which infuriated the Habar Yunis elders and scut-
tled the prospects of a deal between them (Renders 2012, 147–48). The following month, he sabotaged another deal, this time between the Habar Yunis
and the Habar Jalo clans in the town of Beer, by first (unsuccessfully) attempting to prevent the release of Habar Yunis prisoners of war. After the prisoners were released, Egal changed tact and invited the would-be participants
from a peace conference in Beer to attend the Hargeysa conference instead.
The Hargeysa conference was held under the auspices of the central government rather than the clan leaders (Renders 2012, 148). Egal offered money
and political offices to those prepared to attend the government-sponsored
Hargeysa conference over the clan-based Beer conference. He ultimately prevailed by depriving the Beer conference of so many participants that there
was little option other than for them to go to Hargeysa as well (Renders 2012,
148–49). Egal also undermined a number of community-based service provision initiatives in order to emphasize that Hargeysa was the political capital of an independent Somaliland. Local NGOs in the city of Boorama had
established connections with international NGOs to carry out development
projects, but Egal threatened that if the international agencies did not shift
their headquarters to Hargeysa they would lose their right to work anywhere
within Somaliland (Renders and Terlinden 2010, 733).

Egal was a savvy politician who understood how to work with and against
clan-based institutions in order to limit widespread violence, build state
organizations, and thereby consolidate his own power. He did so with the
support of several important backers and beneficiaries from within his clan.
He and the coalition surrounding him shifted the structures in which they
operated using a combination of coercion and centralized patronage, and by
adhering to an already popular local discourse about the legitimacy and
viability of an independent Somaliland. As is discussed in chapter 4, Egal
attempted to consolidate his power against the clan elders by establishing a
multiparty system as an alternative institutional framework to clan-based
representation.

One of the most discussed aspects of Somaliland's peace process in the
English-language literature is its inclusivity, which is widely credited for its

success (Bradbury, Abokor and Yusuf 2003, 473; Kibble and Walls 2010, 46; Pham 2012, 31; Paice and Gibson 2013, 55).[34] The literature highlights the egalitarian and consultative aspects of clan-based institutions as fundamental to that success (Boege et al. 2009, 609–11; Jama 2010, 89–90; Ibrahim and Terlinden 2010, 76–79). However, while the conferences that established the rules for Somaliland's demobilization and peace (discussed in detail in chapter 4) were politically and socially inclusive, the funding model behind them after Egal came to power was not. Thus while Somaliland's peace process is typically seen through a lens of inclusivity, it was sustained by economic exclusion.

The maintenance of peace is the issue around which all other political and economic considerations orbit and on this basis, peace has been exchanged for restricted access to the key drivers of economic growth. However, as is discussed in chapter 5, this has prompted some observers to describe Somalilanders as "hostages to peace" (Bryden 2003, 363; Stremlau 2013) because pushing for greater economic inclusivity is seen to risk the peaceful relations that the exclusivity underpins. Thus far, the exchange has been broadly acceptable within the parts of Somaliland that support independence.

Female Activists

In order to understand how important women were in the peace process, some background information about prevailing clan norms is helpful. Most women unofficially hold dual-clan identities. When women marry, they remain members of their father's clan but are considered to be affiliated with their husband's clan. A common Somali phrase says that "a woman's clan is the clan she will marry into" (*gabadhi qabiilkeedu waa reerka ay u dhaxdo*)—a belief that tends to reinforce the marginalization of women within their paternal (birth) clans (Dini 2008, 91). Their dual-clan identity—still that of their father, but also that of their husband—means that men may not trust the women in their clan to be unswerving defenders of the clan's interests in the way that men (whose clans do not change with marriage) are. On the one hand, women's dual-identities exacerbate men's unwillingness to include them in decision-making processes for fear that they might share information or manipulate outcomes in favor of their other clan. On the other hand, these norms position women as messengers in times of crisis because they can move between clans to gather or share information and other resources. Most importantly, they mobilize their own relationships to facilitate negotiations between clans. For this reason, women are sometimes referred to as "clan ambassadors" (Lewis 2010, 164). Cross-clan marriage is an important means of building alliances and ensuring that lines of communication remain open in times of conflict or resource deprivation. This positions women as structural circuit breakers in times of conflict because each clan can choose to ensure that they have a legitimate, face-saving means of connecting with other clans.

The ability of women to cross clan lines played a facilitating role in the clan-based conferences that consolidated the rules for building and maintaining peace. A group of activists organized a large protest in late 1992 in order to remonstrate the failure to finalize the Sheekh ceasefire agreement that had been drafted in October of that year. While these women were excluded from the conference proceedings, they hung microphones in the room and listened in, waiting outside the venue and applying pressure that none of the men leave until all of the issues had been resolved (Interpeace 2009, 20). One of the instigators of the protest, Shukri Harir Ismail says that the clan elders had sat in Hargeysa

> for one week and didn't sign anything so women organized the largest demonstration ever in Somaliland in front of the Ministry of Internal Affairs. . . . We wrote nine articles saying that we would not go home until they signed. Four ladies took the letter with the nine articles to the elders. The main points were to sign the peace agreement without delay, to establish a police force, to stop UNOSOM from entering Somaliland (we did not want any foreign troops coming here), clean water for Hargeysa (back then the water was very bad), and for the clan elders to go back to their clans and to demobilize their militias.[35]

In keeping with the discursive foundations of an independent Somaliland, one of their principal demands was that the elders communicate to the United Nations that UNOSOM must not deploy its forces in Somaliland—a communiqué that was delivered in March 1993 after the Boorama conference.

Women provided logistical support for the conferences, such as raising money, cooking, and cleaning, but they also helped to create the political space within which negotiations occurred in a variety of innovative ways, including the public composition of poems urging men not to exclude them from the peace process (Rayale 2011, 12–13). The leaders involved in the process discuss their ability to draw upon their moral authority within the private sphere when persuading male family or clan members to work towards peace:

> Women were also talking to the media, organizing demonstrations and pushing the elders to stop the war and make peace. . . . We wanted to make a big conference from all regions to formalize the peace. . . . The women were pushing for [the clan conference in] Boorama.[36]

Women also drew upon their power in the home in less subtle ways to call for peace, reportedly by threatening to abstain from cooking for, or sleeping with, their husbands until a deal was made. Clan structures can thus afford women the space to work politically within family and clan units which can, at times, be translated into the public sphere, although the translation process is often performed by men. Shukri Harir Ismail noted:

> When men are discussing issues, they accept input from their wives. When they need solutions, they come to women for ideas but then when they get the solutions they deny our contribution. . . . When the problems are solved, the women are out again.[37]

Like everyone, women were traumatized by the war against Siyad Barre, and a large number of them were left as the sole heads of households after the deaths of their husbands. A group of about fifteen women, most of whom, again, knew each other personally from experiences during the war, mobilized using established clan mechanisms that overlapped with the new institutional norms that were emerging from the peace conferences. They pushed for the Guurti to be formalized in Somaliland's political system and also wrote a first draft of a policing act for the new country. One of the women involved reported that, despite their efforts, men took the credit for both initiatives.[38] Women have thus largely, though not exclusively, worked around public processes that are dominated by men to exercise influence. Their level of influence is considerable, and activists feel a strong sense of ownership in the success of Somaliland's peace process: "In Somaliland women struggled during the war and we made the peace."[39]

For Somaliland, less external involvement meant a greater need for people to depend on one another and to generate political space for locally legitimate solutions to emerge. A relatively high percentage of those who formed the early technocratic backbone of Somaliland were educated at Sheekh Secondary School. Testimony from graduates highlights the degree to which the critical thought and leadership skills were prioritized. From the activities that graduates later participated in, many reflected the skill of being able to incorporate norms and institutions that were locally legitimate with those that were being adapted from elsewhere. This is particularly visible within the Uffo group and the SNM, both of which combined elements of community and clan-based institutions with aspects of formal political systems found elsewhere. The other key (male) partners to the peace process were the clan-based leadership who clearly understood local needs and were able to work politically with the technocrats to establish viable arrangements to both end and continue to manage violence. The clan system further played a role in helping President Egal to gain access to and then foster and strengthen a network of business elites who funded much of the demobilization process. Women were also important figures in the peace process, albeit mostly behind the scenes. The critical role they played was both facilitated by and heightened by to the cross-clan mutually supportive activist networks they created both during the war and during the peace process. The next chapter moves to discuss the rules of the game within which these actors moved and altered as a result.

Chapter 4

LOCAL OWNERSHIP AND THE RULES
OF THE GAME

The discourse about fragile statehood frames the possibilities for violence almost exclusively through the lens of institutional constraint. It asserts that without state institutions (or, sometimes, their informal "functional equivalents"—Börzel and Risse 2016, 150) providing effective disincentives to violence, the risk of it increases. But this assumption extends well beyond the fragile states discourse and can be seen in most work concerning political institutions more generally (including some of my own on Somaliland's transition from conflict—Phillips 2013). Somaliland's relative stability is thus almost invariably seen through the lens of its clan-based institutions, its formal government apparatus (Hansen 2009, 30; Bahadur 2011, 39; Balthasar and Grzybowski 2012, 159; World Bank 2013, 147; Schäferhoff 2014, 680), or, most often, the country's innovative blending of the two (Bradbury 2008; Renders 2012; Harper 2012, 140; Walls 2014, 27; Richards 2015; for critique, see Campos 2016, 5; Phillips 2019b). This chapter shows how Somaliland's institutions have, in fact, helped to facilitate both war and peace, which is reflected in the way that the independence discourse emphasizes that peace is never guaranteed and so must be actively nurtured.

Somaliland's governance institutions are sometimes used as an example of how states escape fragility. The World Bank mentions the country in the opening pages of its 2017 *World Development Report*, stating that Somalilanders' commitment "to renounce violence and endow the state with a monopoly on the legitimate use of force . . . has been achieved by establishing institutional arrangements that provide sufficient incentives for all key groups to work within the rules" (World Bank 2017, 5). This claim is instructive for its presumption that peaceful cohabitation in Somaliland derives from a state that successfully claims a monopoly on the legitimate use of force. I suggest that the state-based argument is as limited as those that attribute direct causal force to Somaliland's clan-based or hybrid institutions. To do so, I show that the *inability* of any of these institutions to offer a reliable a security guarantee has indirectly stabilized peaceful cohabitation by reproducing two important ideas. One idea is that war is always possible, and the other is that mobilizing for political violence would dissolve the differences that separate Somaliland from its Somali other.

This chapter charts the evolution of the governance institutions that structured key aspects of Somaliland's recovery between 1991 and 1997, contextualizing their role in ending the violence and in the subsequent maintenance of peace. It emphasizes the contested nature of their emergence and the degree to which their contingency diminishes the notion that there is a "basic set of tools emerging from experience" (World Bank 2011, 16) that can be applied to post-conflict situations. After illustrating the complexity of the rules of the game that were iteratively established over several years and across dozens of the clan-based conferences, I zoom in to examine the government's institutional capacity to enforce rules that are not directly related to either to violence or civil order: the payment of tax. I argue that the government's inability to compel people to pay tax has actually helped to produce a limited measure of taxation compliance. This resonates with the broader argument of the book that the meanings ascribed to institutions are more important than their ability to reliably enforce rules. Lacking strong coercive power, the ability of Somaliland's institutions to manage violence is contingent upon widespread fears about the re-emergence of violence as a result of that very weakness.

The interclan conferences that took place in Somaliland between 1991 and 1997 were the most important forums in which north-western elites negotiated the rules of Somaliland's formal political system. There was a total of thirty-two major reconciliation conferences during that period (Jimcaale 2005, 64), but the four that are discussed here—Borco, Sheekh, Boorama, and Hargeysa—were by far the most significant from a national perspective. It was at these conferences that the frameworks for national security, political representation, and the constitution were established. The actors at the conferences drew on existing rules and norms such as: proportional representation for the clans (*beel*); *xeer* (customary law and mediation practices); seeking consensus over majority voting; *xalaydhalay* (forgiving injustices where the losses are so complex or catastrophic that blood payments cannot be calculated) (Walls 2009, 387); and each clan having considerable autonomy within, and responsibility for, events occurring within its territory. However, they did so in new ways, creating innovative structures of authority. Underpinning each of the conferences was the overriding belief that extracting Somalilanders from the violence overtaking the rest of Somalia was the main objective. Everything else was subordinate to that goal. This chapter first discusses the clan-based institutions that provided an important underpinning for the peace conferences before moving on to discuss the processes at the conferences in greater detail.

Clan-Based Representation (*beel*)

Somaliland's political system rests on an underlying acknowledgement that the complete exclusion of any politically significant clan/subclan group will undermine the stability of the political system and make violence more likely. This resonates with the broader risk of one clan group becoming empowered to violently dominate others, something that caused so much suffering to Isaaq clan members under Siyad Barre. Some caveats exist regarding the degree of political significance attributed to each group, as this is not necessarily based on population (which all parties have an incentive to exaggerate), but on power, resources, center–periphery relations, and, in the contemporary context, a group's ideological acceptance of Somaliland's claims to independence. This latter factor further excludes the eastern Harti clans (the Dhulbuhante and Warsangeli) in Sool and Sanaag from power in Hargeysa.

The beel system is essentially one of clan-based representation that theoretically aims to express and maintain a relative balance of power between the clans/subclans of Somaliland, although some—namely the subclans of the Isaaq—are often more equal than others in practice. As Jimcaale (2005, 83) writes:

> every beel [clan group] is actually represented in the current Parliament—an important concession to peacebuilding. But few beel, if any, are satisfied with their allocation. . . . Powerful clans want more seats and less powerful or powerless clans are deprived and unable to obtain their political rights.

In the aftermath of the Somali National Movement (SNM) insurgency against the Barre regime, the Isaaq clan (from which the SNM was almost exclusively derived) drew on the principal of *xalaydhalay* (forgetting injustices where the losses are so complex that appropriate restitution is incalculable—Walls 2009, 387) when it announced that there must be no reprisals against the clans that had fought on Barre's side if Somaliland was to become peaceful. There was the clear recognition that Somaliland could not afford to define itself as an Isaaq state if it were to survive, and that accommodation with the non-Isaaq inhabitants of Somaliland was essential to ending the violence. Within the SNM, clan affiliation also drove representation within the leadership, and each clan was given a fair share in the power structure, although the definition of fairness was fraught (Renders 2012, 68).

Somaliland's first president, Abdirahman Ahmed Ali Tuur, was scrupulous in ensuring that there was balanced representation between the major clans within his first cabinet, and it was generally accepted that he achieved this (Drysdale 1992, 8), having given six of eighteen positions to non-Isaaq members (APD 2002, 17). Likewise, President Egal was conscious of the need to achieve a balanced representation of Somaliland's clans among his cabinet members. He used his first speech as president (May 1993) to declare his intention to "set up a very small cabinet, but efficient. I promise to form a cabinet which is not more than twelve ministers" (cited in APD 2002, 30). However, the requirements of the beel system for balance between the clan representatives soon undid this promise, and by 2001 Egal's cabinet had increased to twenty-six members as a result of his need to include, and weight, more groups than a mere twelve positions would allow. In an attempt to justify this inflation, Egal later argued: "There is not a single minister I have appointed who was not recommended to me by a clan or sub-clan head. I am not selective about the cabinet, what matters is the solution. . . . They may not be the best but they are the solution" (cited in APD 2002, 30). Even despite Egal's clear desire to undermine the role of the clan elders in political life, he did not believe himself at liberty to make decisions about who to include in his cabinet without their direction.

In successive governments, cabinet members and senior government officials have been spread quite widely across the clan/subclan groups (at least numerically if not in terms of their actual power) to ensure that each has a reasonable level of formal representation within the government.[1] Isaaq subclans have not held the presidency exclusively either and Dahir Rayale Kahin, who succeeded President Egal upon his death in 2002 (and was returned to office in the 2003 elections), was from the minority Gada-bursi clan.

The beel system is sometimes credited for helping to maintain peace in Somaliland (ICG 2003, 10; Inigiriis 2017, 118) but it also has significant problems, one of the most important being the calculations over the level of representation that each clan ought to receive. The Boorama Charter of 1993 kept roughly to the allocations for the House of Representatives used in the 1960 council despite widespread disagreement, and while minor adjustments were eventually made, these were to nobody's great satisfaction (Jim-caale 2005, 83). The charter allocated the major clans of Habar Jalo, Habar Awal, Garhajis, Gadabursi, and Dhulbuhante ten parliamentary seats each (Renders 2012, 136), with the smaller clans receiving less in accordance with the formula. The Garhajis confederation (the Habar Yunis and the Idagale) felt the most aggrieved by the arrangements reached at the Boorama conference, which stipulated that they be counted as one clan rather than two. Having just lost the presidency to a member of the clan that they had been fighting (Mohamed Ibrahim Egal of the Habar Awal) they believed they were also being slighted within the House of Representatives.

Similarly, the Harti clans (Dhulbuhante and Warsangeli) felt that the newly formalized beel system undermined their historical level of influence. Under British colonial rule, the Harti clans were considered second only to the Isaaq in terms of population and influence. The settlement at Boorama, however, gave the vice presidency to a member of the Gadabursi clan, while the Dhulbuhante was allocated the less prestigious position of parliamentary speaker. The Harti clans approved the agreements reached at Boorama, but the feeling that they were being sidelined in an independent Somaliland deepened (ICG 2003, 11).

The beel system also does not consider the geographical location of the clans and so clan representatives can be selected disproportionately from one region, which can disenfranchise those clan members residing in other areas (Renders 2012, 136). Members of the Harti clans residing in in the middle corridor of Somaliland (which includes the cities of Hargeysa, Berbera, and Borco), therefore, tend to be more likely to be selected for office than those living in the east. Government and civil service positions are not publicly advertised and so potential applicants only know about vacancies or other opportunities through personal or clan connections, which makes proximity to Hargeysa a significant factor in finding government employment. Perhaps most significantly, the system has been criticized for prioritizing a balance of power between the clans over both issue-based policies and the greater inclusion of minorities.

The beel system of balanced representation is straining under its weight, particularly now that it acts in conjunction with regular competitive elections, where political parties have an incentive to use clan-based categories to mobilize voters. Mohamed Ingiriis argues that in the lead up to the 2017 presidential elections, the overt use of clans to rally support left the country's "relative peace . . . hanging in the balance for the first time" (Ingiriis 2017, 118). After detailing what he describes as a "toxic attitude and destructive clan mentality" (121) pervading Somaliland's politics, Ingiriis makes the passing observation that, "the repercussions of the armed conflict are still clearly visible in people's psyche and whenever violence is on the offing, the recent wars between various rival clans [1991–1996] were cited as an example of the destructive legacies of the war" (126). Here again, the likelihood that clan-based institutions could spark violence appears to heighten the fear of war and reflexively limit the conditions under which violence might be realized.

Xeer

Inter-clan relationships are guided by *xeer* (pronounced in English roughly as "hair" or "hayr"). *Xeer* refers to an evolving set of rules and obligations intended to mediate competitive relationships between clans and subclans. During deliberations, precedents are evoked, and future precedents set, which makes the parties conscious of the potential implications of any decisions reached (Collins 2009, 53). Some aspects of xeer relate to quite specific contractual agreements between neighboring clans while others relate more broadly to the interclan relations across all of Somalia (Le Sage 2005, 32). The aspects that are common across all clans include: the collective payment of blood compensation (*diya*); maintaining the protection of socially respected groups like women, religious figures, and the elderly; entering into negotiations with peace emissaries in good faith; adherence to family obligations such as dowries and inheritances; and economic relations regarding the use of common resources like water and pasture (Le Sage 2005, 32–3).

The outcomes of xeer deliberations are binding on participants. Being an oral tradition, xeer is open to interpretation, and is thus best understood as a series of principles to guide interclan relations in which the perceived power of the parties to enforce decisions also plays a part—though not necessarily the dominant part (Le Sage 2005, 16). While clan institutions are critical to Somali life, they rely more on negotiation and persuasion than coercion, and they are weak at imposing order upon those that disregard the system (Leonard and Samantar 2011, 569). Like all institutions, their ability to provide order is only as strong as the regard its adherents have for that ability.

Revisiting a discussion in chapter 2, another aspect of the clan system that affords individuals agency is affiliation practices, which can also be dynamic, with divisions and unions resulting from violence, personal conflicts, business disputes, or resource scarcity. Divisions can exist on a large scale or at the household level. Polygamous families may choose, for example, to emphasize their attachment to the lineage of one maternal clan over another as a means of connecting to, or disconnecting from, other clans (Hesse 2010, 249). Genealogical links between clans can be discovered to facilitate new cross-clan alliances, and clans that live in border areas can make use of identities on both sides of the border for pragmatic reasons like accessing resources. In the case of Somaliland, this is particularly prevalent in the Sool and Sanaag areas that are claimed by both Somaliland and Puntland, where residents engage with—and attempt to extract resources from—both government administrations. The shared lineages that the clan system is based on are, to some extent, constructed and imagined lineages of patrilineal descent that can change over time and in response to other factors. Joakim Gundel (2009) writes that "it is almost impossible to draw an entirely correct chart of all the clan families, because they form a living organism, and it is difficult to keep track of the constant developments." One Somali analyst remarked along similar lines: "if someone tells you they're an expert in clan

politics they're lying. Not even we can completely track it; it's always changing."[2] In this sense the genealogical maps that one finds in the opening pages
of so many books about Somalia should be taken as indicative only because
the structures they represent are dynamic, shaped by the interplay of agency
and circumstance. This is not to say that the clan system cannot also be
highly static in many circumstances, only that being explicitly agential as
well, clan structures can morph in response to perceptions of threats and
opportunities—including those created by the international community. As
was discussed in chapter 2, the corrosive impact of this has been more visible
in southern Somalia than in Somaliland due to the far higher level of international involvement in the south.

Having established the role of agency within Somalia's traditional institutions, I now move to discuss their norms with respect to the evolution of
the peace conferences. In so doing, I examine the nature of Somaliland's wars
(and the complexities of clan relationships within them), emphasizing the
ways that Somalilanders narrate their ownership of the institutional innovations that helped to end the violence.

The Borco Clan Conference (April–May 1991)

Siyad Barre fled Somalia in late January 1991, and the largely Isaaq clan guerrilla groups fighting under the SNM banner achieved victory against the
non-Isaaq clan guerrilla movements that Barre had supported in the northwest. In February, the SNM leadership engaged the clan elders to negotiate
a ceasefire with the other north-western clans, and their acquiescence to the
SNM's political leadership. A meeting in Berbera laid the foundations for a
much larger conference that was held in the city of Borco two months later—a
city in which prosecessionist attitudes ran particularly high. The Grand Conference of Northern Clans was convened from April 27—May 18, 1991 and
took place in conjunction with the meeting of the SNM's central committee. After tense (some, like Samatar and Samatar 2005, 118, say outright coercive) negotiations, the SNM and the clan leaders agreed that the territory
of the British Somaliland Protectorate that had been recognized as a sovereign entity for five days in 1960 was withdrawing from its union with the
former Italian Somalia (APD 2002, 17–18). In its place, the Republic of Somaliland was announced and the Chairman of the SNM, Abdirahman Ali

Tuur, became the first president of the new republic for a transitional period of two years.

While delegates at the Borco conference had agreed to continue working towards establishing peace and agreeing to "a common political program" (Renders 2012, 91), a framework for how this should occur was far from ready. When independence was suddenly announced, the security situation in the northwest was extremely precarious and conflict resumed shortly after the Borco conference. Some groups had spontaneously demobilized, but many had not, and armed young men with combat experience returned to devastated communities where some sought to earn a living through coercion (APD 2002, 17). Some militia groups established checkpoints along trade routes to extort passersby and others took control of key public infrastructure, particularly ports and airports, within their clan territory as a means of extracting revenue. By 1993, the government estimated that there were some 50,000 armed clan militia members in the country (APD 2002, 17). The cohesion amongst the Isaaq clans that had helped the SNM defeat Barre's forces had fallen away, and President Tuur was proving incapable of reigning in the militias that were competing for control over public resources, particularly the lucrative port in Berbera and Hargeysa airport. The already problematic factional splits within the SNM also deepened, and President Tuur was accused of siding against one faction, the *Alan As*[3] (or Red Flag), (APD 2002, 18–19) in a bid to cement his own power. The fight over resources became increasingly characterized in clan terms as elites on both sides mobilized support from within their clans—in turn helping to spread the conflict to clan areas farther afield. The Garhajis clan confederation (comprised of President Tuur's Habar Yunis subclan and the Idagale subclan) lined up against the clan base of the Alan As faction of the SNM, which was largely comprised of the Habar Jalo and Habar Awal subclans. Each of the clans that were drawn into the dispute happened to inhabit parts of Borco city and the Berbera port area. Both sides could additionally call on clan-based alliances within the city of Hargeysa itself, an issue that would become significant during Egal's presidency.

Before continuing, it is worth explaining the clan geographies that were drawn into this conflict, as they illuminate the intra-Isaaq civil wars that plagued Somaliland until late 1996. This explanation also illustrates why the common clan-based explanation for Somaliland's relative peace and stability—that Somalilanders are mostly from the same clan family and therefore less likely to fight—is misleading. It also demonstrates the length of time that the peace process took and the nonlinear way that it progressed, with conflicts re-erupting, and negotiations being required to start again. What is striking throughout is the degree to which participants appeared to be aware that there were no alternative options to ending the violence than to dealing with each other directly, a narrative that has come to be embedded within the independence discourse.

The Habar Yunis and the Idagale clans are genealogically close, both being descendants of one of Sheekh Isaaq's eight sons (Garhajis) and the two are often referred to collectively as Garhajis. Being lumped together as a singular Garhajis clan means that the confederation is counted as one entity rather than two under systems of clan-based representation. Its members dispute this, arguing that such a classification undercuts their rightful level of representation. The Habar Yunis clan principally resides in parts of Berbera, Hargeysa, Borco, and Ceerigaabo (Sanaag), while the Idagale resides in the southern parts of Hargeysa and in small parts of Borco. President Tuur was a member of the Habar Yunis clan. Habar Yunis has had longstanding historical disputes with the Habar Jalo clan, and these two subclans are often rivals at a national level.[4] Conflicts between the two groups have also tended to spread to other areas where these clans are also based.

Habar Jalo is geographically interconnected with the Habar Awal/Issa Musa subclan, and the two have maintained largely friendly relations at the national level. Members of Habar Jalo reside in parts of Berbera and Borco, while Habar Awal/Issa Musa members reside largely in parts of Berbera, Borco, and the eastern parts of Hargeysa. President Egal (Tuur's successor) was a member of the Habar Awal/Issa Musa subclan that was aligned with the Alan As faction of the SNM, and so was on the opposite side of the Borco-, Berbera-, and Hargeysa-based conflicts (1992; 1992; and 1994–1996 respectively) to that of his predecessor, Abdirahman Tuur. Despite this, it is important to reiterate that clan membership is not always a predictor of alliance or conflict on either an individual level or within larger coalitions, but it does provide a historical background against which it is possible to frame alliances or conflicts if this is perceived as desirable. Returning to the importance of agency in these matters, it is possible to understand contemporary political and economic conflicts as potentially energized or deflated by being grafted onto so-called traditional pastoral and clan rivalries (Renders 2012, 96).

In January 1992, a conflict broke out between the Habar Yunis (Garhajis) and Habar Awal/Issa Musa militias in Borco after President Tuur attempted to organize a national military force to disarm the militias in the area—a move that was seen by the Alan As faction as partisan maneuvering against them by the president. A group of clan elders successfully mediated the concerns of local parties to stem the violence, but the conflict set a precedent of fighting between the two groups over the control of public assets and of the government's relative powerlessness to intervene. President Tuur needed money if he was to fund demobilization, and to get that money he needed access to public assets, the most lucrative of which was Berbera Port. Problematically for Tuur, the port was under the shared control of his Habar Yunis subclan, which was native to the region, but also to Commander Ibrahim Degaweyn, a member of both the Alan As and the Habar Awal/Issa Musa subclan (Renders 2012, 95) that was in alliance with the Habar Jalo. A violent power struggle ensued, with each side evoking the "traditional" rivalry between the Habar Yunis and the Issa Musa.

Unlike the incident in Borco two months earlier, clan elders were unable to negotiate an end to the violence in Berbera, which flared intermittently for six months and was eventually overcome by the antigovernment (Habar Jalo and Habar Yunis) forces (APD 2002, 19). Elders from a non-Isaaq clan, the Gadabursi, volunteered to leverage their independence and attempt to mediate an end to the underlying cause of the conflict, namely the control of public assets. They succeeded in achieving a ceasefire, which formed the basis of the next major clan conference in the town of Sheekh, to be attended by all clans of Somaliland in the hope of solidifying the peace between the clans in Berbera (APD 2002, 20).

The Sheekh Clan Conference (October 1992)

While the primary aim of the conference at Sheekh was to consolidate the ceasefire between combatants in Berbera, the participants had also hoped to agree to more generalizable principles that could be employed at the next major conference scheduled in Boorama. At Sheekh, Gadabursi clan mediators again took the lead and focused on the wording of a previous peace agreement with which the antigovernment group (the Habar Awal/Issa Musa) had taken issue. The original agreement stated:

> Public facilities and state properties *that are found in Berbera*, like the port,
> fuel depots, airport, government factories, roads, etc. are public properties and
> their access should not be denied to the people of "Somaliland." Their man-
> agement and control is the responsibility of the central authority. (Cited in
> Farah and Lewis 1993, 54—emphasis added).

By changing the word "Berbera" to "Somaliland," the agreement referred
to *all* public assets, as opposed to those located in Berbera alone. The Gadabursi elders were thereby able to obtain agreement from the opposition Habar
Awal/Issa Musa militia that all public facilities should now be under the control of the government (Renders 2012, 98). This alteration meant that the
Habar Yunis and Idagale clan militia (together Garhajis) with whom Habar
Awal was fighting in Berbera would have to give up their claim to Hargeysa
airport under the same agreement. However, when Mohamed Egal became
president in 1993 he did permit the Habar Awal/Issa Musa militia that controlled Berbera a further six months (to December 1993) to continue extracting revenue through the port before it was converted into the national asset
mandated by this agreement (Balthasar 2012, 172), prompting claims that he
was favoring the interests of his own clan.

The conference made important progress towards formalizing principles
for the management and resolution of violent conflict under the understanding of "*ama dalkaa qab, ama dadkaa qab*," translated as: "either you have your
land or you have your people," and which in context implies that "each clan
is responsible for whatever is committed in their territory" (Interpeace 2008,
48). This principle had been applied in local contexts previously, but this was
the first time that it was adapted to serve as a general principle for future
negotiations towards reconciliation across all of Somaliland (48). The communities represented at Sheekh also agreed to recall militias to their clan territory, to return fixed assets seized during the war to their owners, exchange
prisoners of war, and to clear all roads of militia so that traffic could pass
unimpeded (APD 2002, 20). The Sheekh conference thus established a
framework—expanded at Boorama the following year—through which the
clan leaders would participate in key governance issues in a more formalized
manner and that formally designated clan leaders as the primary authorities
for ensuring security in their local areas.

The Boorama Clan Conference (January–May 1993)

The principles agreed to at Sheekh served as the basis for deliberations at the Boorama conference and were consolidated as a Peace Charter and National Charter for Somaliland, both of which further enmeshed the clan leaders in the fabric of national governance. The National Charter served as a working constitution for Somaliland until the new provisional constitution was introduced at the Hargeysa conference in 1997 (APD 2002, 20).

The National Charter set out a system of clan-based proportional representation (*beel*) for Somaliland that was to be combined with some Western-style formal institutions. The formula for clan-based proportional representation was based on similar formulas used in earlier national bodies[5] with slight amendments due to disagreements over relative clan populations. Eventually, each subclan was allotted a number of votes as a proportion of the 150 voting delegates (Interpeace 2008, 51): the Isaaq subclans were allocated 90 of the 150 votes (down from their original 95); the Harti subclans (Dhulbuhante and Warsangeli) received 34 votes; and the Dir subclans (Gadabursi and Issa) were given 26 votes (Interpeace 2008, 51).

The charter established a two-tier legislature with an elected House of Representatives, a nonelected House of Elders (the *Guurti*), an elected presidential executive, and an independent judiciary. The parliament was to be the main institution through which to express the beel system of representation, the formality of which offered greater flexibility in determining positions of influence within both the executive and the civil service (ICG 2003, 10)—even though the executive was theoretically still supposed to be subject to beel calculations (APD 2002, 30). In the civil service, the beel system was conceived to apply only to the positions of minister, vice minister, and director general (the three most powerful positions in a ministry), and not to ordinary bureaucrats. There is, however, an informal presumption that individuals allocated positions on the basis of the beel system will employ people largely from within their own clans, effectively institutionalizing clan-based representation.

The charter also established a hierarchy of appeal in which community elders were made formally responsible for meditating disputes within local Guurtis, and higher Guurtis were to be responsible for disputes that involved more segments of the "clan chain" (Interpeace 2008, 53). The charter established the executive committee of the national Guurti (Grand Committee of

Elders of Somaliland) as the highest body for dispute resolution, thereby formalizing the role of the national Guurti for the first time (Interpeace 2008, 53).[6] There were seventy-five positions in the first national Guurti and membership was driven by clan-based selection. The Guurti was charged with the protection of national security by managing conflicts, and the protection of Somaliland's customary law and Islamic values (APD 2002, 32). Its first order of business was to demobilize the clan militias, affected on the basis of the Somaliland Communities Security and Peace Charter. Under the peace charter it was agreed that all militias must be stood down and all weapons surrendered to the government. Each community was to take responsibility for banditry occurring in its territory and to establish a local security council and clan-based police force, with the intent that these forces would eventually be incorporated into a national police force. All communities also agreed to resist any incursions by outsiders into the territory claimed as Somaliland (Interpeace 2008, 52–53). It was intended that security would later become the responsibility of the government after demobilization had been completed, thereby paving the way for the creation of a national army (Renders 2012, 101).

The conference at Boorama saw the transition from the SNM to a civilian administration, and nearly two-thirds of the 150 official delegates at Boorama voted President Abdirahman Ali Tuur (an SNM leader) out of office. Mohamed Haji Ibrahim Egal (Habar Awal/Issa Musa) became Somaliland's second president with Abdirahman Aw Ali (Gadabursi) selected to serve as vice president in a transitional government with Egal. This arrangement was only initially intended to last for two years but was extended until 1997 due to the declaration of a state of emergency during the civil war and a parliamentary extension (ICG 2003, 11). Abdirahman Tuur's clan (Habar Yunis of the Garhajis confederation) felt that they were not adequately compensated for losing the presidency, which was a grievance that continued to fester. In November 1994, tensions boiled over when President Egal attempted to gain control of Hargeysa airport by force from an Idagale clan militia (the other member of the Garhajis confederation slighted by Tuur's loss of the presidency). The fighting was so intense that it amounted to a second civil war, with fighting spreading from Hargeysa and into Borco, where Garhajis-Habar Awal tensions were also high (ICG 2003, 11).

Local Ownership at Boorama

The local (Gadabursi clan) community was overwhelmingly responsible for funding the Boorama conference. This constituted a considerable financial burden for them as hosts, as they were obliged to provide food and shelter for some two thousand participants over a five-month period.[7] However, the participants were quite aware of the imposition being placed on their hosts and of the fact that, unlike international donors, that reciprocation that would likely be expected of them. The local funding of the conference helped to remind participants that time and resources could not be wasted. Decisions at the Boorama conference were almost always taken on the basis of consensus being reached between parties rather than as the result of a majority vote. This was time consuming—the conference lasted more than five months— but it was felt by participants that consensus was more likely to achieve a legitimate and durable result. When seemingly intractable issues arose, parties were given deadlines (sometimes repeatedly) in order to reach an agreement that was acceptable to all rather than putting the issue to a vote. One of the elders present purportedly explained that the general view at the conference was that "voting is fighting; let's opt for consensus" (cited in Interpeace 2008, 52). Interpeace notes that at times the chairman would "fall ill" when an important agreement remained out of reach in order to allow further time for discussion (52) and, presumably, a face-saving outcome for those involved.

Much of the activity also occurred outside the formal sessions and involved delegates meeting socially and without the immediate pressures of finalizing outcomes. Deliberation, mediation, and a purposeful lack of haste were all critical rules of engagement that allowed substantive issues to be creatively brokered. The inclusion of the non-Isaaq clans was also crucial to the success of the conference, not only for the wider legitimacy of the outcomes (and helping to allay fears that Somaliland was simply an Isaaq nationalist project) but also for their ability to mediate between the numerically dominant but divided Isaaq subclans (Interpeace 2008, 55). The principle of maintaining a balance of power between the clans, seen through the use of the beel system of proportional representation at the conference that was discussed above, continues to cut across many of Somaliland's political and economic arrangements.

It goes without saying that achieving success at these conferences made considerable demands of the participants and required extraordinary willpower. It was an exercise in determination to reach an agreement that all clans in the northwest could (at least for the most part) accept—with some caveats surrounding the difficulties in eastern Sool and Sanaag. The way that these three conferences were conducted point to the fact that those involved had strong motives to find ways to cooperate with one another. It is hard to escape the conclusion that one of the most powerful of these was the agonizing failure to end the violence in the south—something that found greater expression once the peace in Somaliland was consolidated. It is equally clear that the lack of attention Somaliland received from international donors during its formative years helped to keep the eyes of political elites fixed on one another rather than on outsiders as a means of securing the revenue required to formalize a peace settlement. Moreover, the fluidity of the timeframes allowed local actors to deliberate and find consensus, without being pressured to simply put key issues to a vote in order to finalize proceedings and declare a successful outcome.

Therefore, unlike many states targeted by international state-building initiatives, the agreements that limited large-scale violence in Somaliland evolved without explicit externally driven expectations, schedules, or technical indicators of success (Bradbury 2008, 246–47). As Farah and Lewis (1997, 373) explain:

> The Boorama conference was set to start in January [1993] but was delayed until February. To discredit the government, which was against it, the elders declared it open on February 24th with virtually no preparation. It was opened with seven days devoted to reciting the Koran so as to give time to effect [*sic*] arrangements. The actual business started on March 3rd.

In other words, the Boorama conference reflected highly local power struggles without the need to respond to timeframes or benchmarks of those not intimately connected to the process. It is worth briefly comparing this to the 2012 UN-led roadmap for Somalia, which is exemplary of the cookie-cutter approach that prevails in contemporary state-building exercises. As the Transitional Federal Government (TFG) prepared to hand over to the new Federal Government of Somalia in 2012, the UN Political Office for Somalia set out a timetable in which participants could scarcely draw breath as they raced to establish a new institutional framework for the country. The roadmap required:

Somali "stakeholders" to finalize a provisional constitution (by April 2012), create a 1,000-person national constituent assembly (by May 2012), hold a vote by the constituent assembly on the provisional constitution (by May 22), select a new 225-person parliament (by June 15), and have the new parliament elect a speaker (by July 20) and a president (August 20). (Menkhaus 2012, 170)

Once this was achieved, the president would be required to establish a new government to run the country for four years, after which a full election would be held. That is, the roadmap set out to achieve in five months what the previous government had not done in seven years—with many Somalis fearing (rightly, it seems) that the arbitrary and hasty timing was likely to sacrifice the new government's chance to gain popular legitimacy (Menkhaus 2012, 170). It is the stark differences like these in the levels of local ownership that Somaliland's independence discourse affords so much importance to.

The Centralization of Power at the Hargeysa Conference (October 1996–February 1997)

With the return of former president Abdirahman Tuur (now a senior official in General Mohamed Farah Aideed's government in the south and backed by UNOSOM II) to Somaliland's political landscape, clashes over public resources erupted again. In a mirror image of the Berbera conflict in 1992 (in which the Habar Awal defied the government by claiming Berbera as its territory), members of Tuur's clan confederation (the Idagale of the Garhajis confederation) began agitating for control of Hargeysa airport in 1994. Initially, the majority of the Idagale disparaged the militia's moves, but when government troops ousted them from the airport, causing a number of casualties, the conflict escalated. More combatants became involved, and so too did more clan alliances, particularly from Hargeysa and Borco where violence also became acute (Renders 2012, 130–31).

Despite the conflicts in Hargeysa and Borco between 1994 and 1996, President Egal made strides towards demobilization shortly after taking office in 1993. By 1995, he had established an army of around five thousand people, largely from the militias that had been disarmed using the funding secured from some of Somaliland's wealthiest merchants (discussed in chapter 3) and the increased capacity to extract income from the points of entry (APD

2002, 22). Despite this success, there were still some ten thousand militia members yet to be demobilized, and the conflict around Hargeysa airport facilitated a wider remobilization along clan lines (Balthasar 2013, 225).

The differences between the Boorama conference and the Hargeysa conference three-and-a-half years later were stark. Whereas Boorama was almost entirely funded by the local communities,[8] the Egal administration organized and funded the Hargeysa conference using loans from the business elite (and did so also as a means of undermining other local peace initiatives that were occurring outside of the government's auspices). As such, there was a clearer and more centralized political agenda expressed at Hargeysa, with some critics decrying the process as being overly dominated by the president and his largely Isaaq/Habar Awal inner circle (APD 2002, 25). The loans from local businesses that funded the conference furthered the symbiosis of the Somaliland government (though principally President Egal) and the country's wealthiest merchants. The former increased the centralization of its power while the latter made large profits a in virtually unregulated and— when compared to Mogadishu—relatively stable business environment.

Unlike the conference at Boorama, where the incumbent president (Abdirahman Tuur) was unseated, the Hargeysa conference reinstated both President Egal and the Parliament (APD 2002, 25). It also increased the number of Guurti members from seventy-five to eighty-two. The original members had been selected by their clans, but the additional seven people were reportedly hand-picked by President Egal, to the disappointment of some of those the appointees were supposed to represent (Hoehne 2013, 203–4). However, even those members that were nominated by their clans for the Guurti and the House of Representatives were not selected in a transparent manner. Somaliland's Academy for Peace and Development (APD) reports that the nomination process did not occur through wide grassroots consultations, but rather via "urban-based clan leaders and . . . powerful associates of clan leaders—Af-miinshaaro (self-appointed 'political brokers' or 'spin doctors')" (APD 2002, 39). The APD concluded that this process served to alienate constituencies, making elite authority dependent on a small group of "kingmakers" rather than their grassroots communities (39). Egal also changed the name of the conference from the usual clan conference (*shir beleed*) to a national conference (*shir qameed*), ostensibly because there was now a legitimate civilian government in place but also to undermine the centrality of clan elders to the political process that Egal sought to dominate. Egal also changed the rules for presidential candidature in order to remove other actors with presidential ambitions. The presidency became available only to candidates that were married to Muslim women, thus disqualifying the chairman of the Guurti, Saleban Gaal, who was married to a non-Muslim. To this, Egal added that prospective candidates must have spent the past five years in Somaliland, thereby eliminating several other hopefuls from the race. The International Crisis Group notes that Egal also successfully lobbied to increase the number of nonclan delegates at the conference by insisting that half the delegates be members of Parliament, which helped to further dislodge the notion that the clan-elders lay at the heart of Somaliland's political processes (ICG 2003, 11). The Hargeysa conference, therefore, marks a significant turning point in Somaliland's political history, and was the point at which the influence of the clan elders began to lose its potency against the central government.

The New Constitution

The Hargeysa conference also replaced the national charter from Boorama with a provisional constitution that was ratified by referendum in 2001. The document, which Egal sold to the public as a referendum on independence, introduced an electoral multiparty system, stipulating that elections would be held during the first term of the new administration. The language of the new constitution was that of international best practices and good governance—something intended to elicit a positive response from Western donors. Particularly noteworthy was the stipulation that Somaliland's electoral system would be based on universal suffrage for Somalilanders over the age of sixteen. Steve Kibble and Michael Walls (2010, 41) note that despite this no women were actually consulted in the process of drafting the constitution, despite the demands of a number of women activists for inclusion.[9] The apparent recognition of women's political empowerment seemed, therefore, to be more about fitting to an established international template of contemporary state-building than providing women with substantially increased space for political activity. This is revealing because it underscores the ways in which the rules of the game had changed between the Boorama and Hargeysa conferences (1993 and 1996–1997, respectively). Now, there was an increased emphasis on pre-empting external perceptions of Somaliland and

on trying to highlight its modern state attributes to generate external support for its independence from Somalia. As discussed in chapter 5, it appears
that this shift consisted of a strategic redeployment of the fragile states discourse as a means of creating space through which to achieve Somaliland's
goal of independence. I consider these developments to mark the end of Somaliland's foundational period.

As Somaliland's outward political focus increased, some elements of the
earlier, and more horizontally inclusive, political arrangements were dis-
carded. For example, clan elders were strategically drawn into centralized
state patronage networks, placed on the government payroll,[10] and detached
from their grassroots constituencies. Elite economic monopolies also became
more entrenched, as discussed in chapter 3. The eastern areas of Sool and
Sanaag were increasingly marginalized in the vision of an independent Somaliland among the Hargeysa-based elite, and political activity also took on
a more liberal democratic vocabulary as the political elite sought international
recognition more assertively. Finally, foreign development agencies began to
outspend the government by a significant margin on development projects.

Of course, Somaliland's government was constrained by having neither
sovereign recognition nor the possibility of reintegration with a peaceful,
functioning state in the south. Feeling the constraints of nonrecognition, the
Somaliland government redoubled its efforts to persuade the international
community that it had more attributes of statehood than its southern neigh-
bor, despite the massive amounts of international funding received by the latter. These efforts also served to reinforce the discourse about independence
that had long held sway with grassroots Isaaq communities.

Elections and the Multiparty System

The introduction of the multiparty system was part of President Egal's attempt to formalize state structures (and thus the power of the central government that he led) at the expense of the clan elders. It also served to provide legitimacy to Somaliland's desire for recognition through the provision
of good governance, or at least a form of governance that was more familiar
to external observers. The design of the multiparty system was ostensibly intended to limit the role of clans in the public's political affiliations but has
ironically had the opposite effect in several ways. In an attempt to incentiv-

ize cross-clan electoral collaboration and national political platforms, only three political parties are constitutionally permitted to contest parliamentary or presidential elections. The three parties are given legal status on the basis of their performance in the local council elections across Somaliland's six electoral regions, where they must receive a minimum of 20 percent of the votes. These top three parties are then mandated to compete in parliamentary and presidential elections for the next ten years, after which the selection process should be repeated. The outcome of this system has been, however, that elections have demonstrated the political salience of clan networks in candidate selection and voter mobilization, and they have tended to entrench both parochialism and the principle of clan-based representation within elected government institutions.[11] In the first parliamentary elections held in 2005, the representation of the Isaaq clan increased by nine seats, to a total of fifty-seven out of eighty-two (around 70 percent), and the Gadabursi increased their representation from eleven to thirteen seats. These increases came at the expense of the Harti (Dhulbuhante and Warsangeli) people, whose representation declined from fourteen to ten seats, something that has not helped to reverse their sense of marginalization within Somaliland (Abokor et al. 2006, 20).

Since the multiparty system was formally introduced in 2001 there has also been an increasing tendency for parties to call on clan affiliations to gain votes, as politicians often explicitly rely on traditional elders to select local candidates. For example, in the local elections of 2012, each party worked through local clan elders to determine the candidates that they would support in the district, usually by being provided with a list of names by the clan leader/s, presumably in exchange for payment or other benefits. In the lead up to the elections it was common to hear people ask: "Who is your family supporting?" (*reekow kii bu wata?*), or "Who are we voting for?" (*ayaanu doraana?*) both of which essentially acknowledge that each clan should support candidates collectively so as not to split their votes and lose seats in the local councils.[12] This meant that aspiring candidates who did not have the support of the clan elders working with the parties were unlikely to be selected. It also meant that clan affiliation was by far the most important factor for achieving a nomination to run for office. For example, in the capital city of Hargeysa, no party nominated a member from either the Gadabursi or Habar Jalo clans (with one partial exception)[13] because they are not numerically significant within the city, and were not, therefore, expected to mobilize clan-based support for their candidacy. A local council consists of twenty-five seats and each party fielded the full twenty-five candidates in Hargeysa, where the possibility for national political influence is the highest. Parties favored the Hussein Abokor subclan (Habar Awal/Saad Musa) but each also made sure to have candidates from the Arab, Habar Yunis and Garhajis tribes that reside in the city in order to have the best chance of victory. Similarly, in the nearby district of Gabiley, no party nominated any candidates from the neighboring Gadabursi clan because it was believed that the majority clan (Habar Awal/Saad Musa) would not vote for them, even though in the previous local council there had been one member from the Gadabursi clan. It appeared that the party leaders did not want to risk a defeat by being seen to go against the recommendations of the clan elders.

With the partial exception of the ruling Kulmiye Party, the political parties had limited resources to spend on their candidates' campaigns, making the candidates further dependent on their clans for financing and thereby increasing, as in previous elections, the expectation that candidates promote clan rather than party agendas (Renders 2012, 251–52). However, there was also a level of individual pragmatism to the electoral process, and a vote-economy was apparent throughout the country. Somalilanders spoke of going rates to travel to various parts of the country to cast their vote(s), seemingly for financial more than clan-based reasons, though a combination of motivations is likely. Anecdotal observations suggest that Berbera fetched the highest rate (around $60) even though Ceerigaabo (reportedly only valued at $30) was further away and required travel along a more dangerous stretch of road.

It was also common to hear people ask on election day not whether they had voted but rather how many times they had exercised that right. Large groups gathered openly outside the polling centers to wash the supposedly indelible ink from their fingers with bleach, and some people happily demonstrated to international observers how effective the chemicals were at removing the ink from their fingers, allowing them to vote repeatedly. The widespread occurrence of multiple voting raised the question of whether it was being done at the behest of one party (or coalition of parties), or whether it was more a case of equal opportunity in which the ability to transgress the system was not the particular privilege of one group over another, and a commitment to victory was all that was required to win. In most cases that I observed, there was not a strong sense that this was something to hide, which again added to the question of whether people felt that they were adhering to widely legitimate (if informal and strictly illegal) rules in order to get their preferred candidate over the line—if everyone agrees to transgress the formal system in a roughly equitable and widely accepted manner, is it really a transgression? It appeared that the more important principles guiding behavior on the day were that participation should be both highly inclusive and in the service of one's clan-based loyalties. Despite the procedural problems throughout polling day and in the lead-up to the election, there was a clear sense that there was something to play for and that victory in the election was worthwhile.[14]

Somaliland's New Institutions and Political Order

As noted in chapter 1, many scholars have emphasized that there are no rigid lines demarcating formal and informal institutions as they necessarily overlap and interact with one another (Helmke and Levitsky 2004; Menkhaus 2006/2007; Boege et al. 2009; Doornbos 2010; Hagmann and Péclard 2011; Hastings and Phillips 2015). All political and economic systems entail elements of hybridity because all mix rational-legal (formal state) institutions with an array of informal customs, conventions, and norms, including those in the Organisation for Economic Cooperation and Development (OECD) that are usually held up as examples of full Weberian statehood. Regardless of this ubiquity, institutional forms only tend to be referred to as hybrid when they occur in the south, to refer to the ways in which formal and informal spheres cannot be meaningfully seen as distinct categories of authority.

In Somaliland, these forms of authority are so "connected, intermingled, and interpenetrated" (Renders 2012, 28) that the fluidity between informality and formality is a defining feature of the way that power is practiced. A generic example would be a clan leader who is popularly elected to serve in a national legislature. As an elected leader, their authority draws upon, but simultaneously alters, their status as a traditional clan leader to reflect a new form of power. The leader does not generally switch between being a clan leader in some instances and a parliamentarian in others but draws power from being both simultaneously. In this sense, the term "hybrid" that is so often applied to Somaliland's system is something of a misnomer: the barriers between the formal and informal spheres are permeable and fluid to the point that they are easily meaningless. They change according to time, place, and as a function of political and economic expedience. To insist on their hybridity is to uphold a binary that ratifies a divide between the normal (apparently nonhybrid) institutions that are familiar in northern political systems and those that incorporate "tradition" and are found in the south. For this reason, they are better understood as institutional formations that reflect "*new* forms of political rule and statehood" (Hameiri 2011, 197—emphasis in original).

Somaliland's government authorities perform some typical state functions, but others are outsourced to (or performed by) nonstate entities, such as clans or other armed neighborhood watch groups. Most people report that they would still turn to their community elders over the police for protection in the event of violence, and the government's statutory courts remain the least trusted institution available for resolving criminal matters, behind clan elders, religious elders, and the police (Observatory of Conflict and Violence Prevention 2015, 30–33, see also Stremlau and Osman 2015, 8).[15] The police usually only intervene in conflicts once they have been requested by clan elders to do so (Hills 2014, 90). If a government soldier kills a civilian in the line of duty, it is not the government that is responsible for providing restitution but the soldier's clan.[16] Marleen Renders gives an account of the way the police and lower courts in the municipality of Borco (Somaliland) handle theft and petty crimes but transfer crimes involving murder to the clans to negotiate the terms of blood money payments (Renders 2007, 450). These lines are fluid, and clan elders are often involved in helping to resolve more minor crimes and disputes (Renders 2007, 450) just as government authorities are sometimes involved in resolving and punishing perpetrators of major crimes (Balthasar and Grzybowski 2012, 166).

These dynamics are illustrated by a conflict that occurred between the Issa and Gadabursi clans in the town of Xarirad, shortly after the 2012 local elections. A member of the Issa clan was accused of killing a member of the Gadabursi clan, but the Issa clan elders either did not try to, or did not succeed in, capturing the suspect—a customary requirement for interclan negotiations to commence. This created a deadlock, and a revenge-killing by the victim's clan (the Gadabursi) was likely. The minister of internal affairs attempted to break the deadlock by issuing an ultimatum to the suspected offender's (Issa) clan elders: capture the offender or be arrested collectively. At no time did the minister suggest that government forces would attempt to intervene to investigate or arrest the suspect. The suspect remained free and the minister arrested more than ten elders from the Issa clan. The elders were detained for a short period and upon their release were addressed by the minister, who explained that they had been arrested to both persuade the victim's clan members to delay their revenge and because it was the elders' responsibility to prosecute the crime. The minister told the elders that the condition of their release was that they negotiate a solution to the problem as their customary responsibilities required.[17]

In this incident, therefore, the government authorities played a mediating role, using their coercive capacity to detain the elders and cajole them into negotiating a solution outside of the government's judicial institutions. The use of coercion by the government (the arrest) was intended to prompt clan mechanisms that had, for whatever reason, stalled. The government did not attempt to divert the dispute to its own jurisdiction, seeking only to remind the clan elders that local security matters were their responsibility. The role of the government was to ensure that the two parties came together so that this process could run its course within the clan system. This anecdote reveals that the government has not established the monopoly on legitimate force that the World Bank (2017, 5) and others presume it to, but, more importantly, that it is not necessarily actively sought by the government either.

There are international constraints to the government's ability to assert itself physically as well. The ongoing United Nations embargo on Somalia (of which Somaliland is still formally a part) means that the government of Somaliland cannot legally purchase weapons for its military or police force and so remains reliant on refurbishing old Soviet-era weapons and illegal imports (Hussein 2011). All members of the police force are thus still required to use privately owned weapons in the line of duty (Balthasar and Grzybowski 2012, 164), as the government cannot issue weapons. The Somaliland Police Force (SLPF) has an estimated six thousand employees, but that figure is believed to include a high number of ghost employees who receive salaries without performing active duty.

The Aborted Effort to Establish Taxation Institutions

Some of the key claims in this book rest on the argument that Somaliland's governance institutions have a poor ability to compel compliance but that this has been indirectly harnessed as a source of order. So far, it has principally focused on institutions associated with security and the rule of law—a discussion that is developed further in chapter 5. However, the government's largely-aborted attempt to wrest greater tax revenue from the country's most lucrative businesses offers a complementary window into this lack of capacity and the discourse about independence and self-reliance that it underpins. This is explored in some detail in order to support the broader contention that Somaliland's ability to maintain peace and relative stability cannot be boiled down simply to the widely made claim that it has "a functioning regional government [that] maintains public order [and] . . . enforces stability and security through over 17,000 police and security forces" (Schäferhoff 2014, 680).

As with the control of violence, the struggle to institutionalize control over central finances was a core aspect of European state formation. Margaret Levi's seminal contribution, *Of Rule and Revenue*, makes the influential claim that "[the] history of state revenue production is the history of the evolution of the state" (Levi 1988, 1). While this, like Charles Tilly's arguments about the centralization of violence, may be less applicable to states that receive large amounts of external budgetary assistance, as is widely the case in postcolonial states, the collective action problem that Levi highlights governing the payment of tax can be seen in Somaliland. This is because, unlike many so-called fragile states, the government of Somaliland's access to external revenue is tightly constrained, making inland revenue a more pressing need for its continued existence.

Levi argues that paying tax is a quasi-voluntary activity, where people choose to either pay or not pay on the basis of the services that they expect to receive. Compliance levels are based on perceptions of fairness in the rate that is charged and on the ability of the ruler to coerce, compel, or otherwise persuade tax payers into payment (Levi 1988, 52–55). The collective action problem comes from the fact that each side generally wants the other to bear the costs upfront, even if they perceive the likely mutual benefits of cooperation in the longer term.

A member of Somaliland's telecommunications association who was deeply involved in the government's efforts to assert greater control over the industry between 2010 and 2011 summed up the sector's position: "We need [the government] to enforce the rules. We don't have [real] police or courts. We need a real enforcer."[18] He was arguing, therefore, that if the government cannot or will not enforce the rule of law in the first instance, it cannot legitimately demand higher taxes from business. Elsewhere, the general manager of Jubba Airlines (a Somali company) highlighted this dilemma to a team of local researchers studying state-business relations, saying that his business has to pay for its own security because it cannot rely on Somaliland's government to do so: "We provide money to the guards of the airports, we also give them mattresses and food because above all they are guarding our planes, and if there is no security in the airports then our businesses are over" (cited in Arteh and Dualeh 2011, 6). That is, without an entity that can consistently enforce the rule of law and provide security, businesses can legitimately argue that they must spend the money they would otherwise spend on tax protecting their interests independently of the government.

A closer look at the early days of the Silanyo administration (2010–2017) illustrates the dynamics of this contestation and the inconsistent efforts of the government to assert control in the area of domestic revenue collection. In 2010, Silanyo's then minister of finance, Mohamed Hashi Elmi, signaled his intention to improve public services and increase civil servants' salaries by imposing more stringent taxation requirements on local businesses. In what was partly an attempt to sideline the perception that the government was beholden to the big businesses that had funded its electoral campaign, and partly an attempt to pay back the $22 million debt it had inherited from the previous government, the minister raised taxes almost across the board. This was unprecedented. However, the Silanyo government remained stretched for funding and soon approached the business community for further loans. That year, it received nearly $3 million from the business elite and in early 2012 it received a further $500,000 from Telesom (Somaliland's largest telecommunications company), all of which further blurred the lines between the government and private interests.[19]

Unlike the loans that were extended to President Egal in the 1990s, the arrangement was that the government would pay its creditors back with money, not tax exemptions. By July 2012, the government had paid everything back, including the $22 million of debt that it had inherited from the previous administration.[20] Again this was unprecedented, and it appeared that the new government was effectively working to reduce the concentration of wealth in the country and improve its own hand against the companies that monopolize the country's key business sectors. By the time the

budget for fiscal year 2012 was drafted, the government's projected revenue was $106 million, up from less than half that amount under the previ-
ous government just two years earlier. The increase was due partly to tax
increases but also due to the end of the live export ban that had strangled
the economy between 2000 and 2009.[21]

However, despite these areas of progress, the only line item in the budget
that was not targeted for tax increases between 2009 and 2012 was business
profit tax. In fact, taxes on business profits fell by 31 percent during that period (Somaliland Ministry of Finance, 2013), representing a major loss in
potential earnings. Profits are inherently difficult to establish where goods
are not readily visible, because this relies on accurate accounting records being either voluntarily or coercively obtained from the companies, which
makes it a deeply political exercise. Gathering this information is particularly challenging in the service sector, which is the major player in the
Somaliland economy. As a result, the government still collects around
80 percent of its tax revenues through customs tariffs at the point of entry/
exit, and it essentially accepts that collection will be minimal after that
point. This means that service providers (like telecommunications and
finance companies), which are not reliant on importing or exporting goods,
are largely exempt from paying tax.

To put this into perspective, Somaliland's budget for 2011 was around $81
million,[22] while the combined income of its two largest domestic companies
(Telesom and Dahaabshiil) was informally estimated to have been around
$66 million.[23] According to an official within the Ministry of Finance, the
ministry calculated that Telesom should probably have paid about $7 million
in taxes based on its estimated profits for 2011, but the government only
requested $500,000. He explained:

> The figure [of $500,000] was made up because they didn't know a figure, they
> just guessed. . . . In 2012 they paid the same, and it was in the budget. This
> year [2013] it was $670,000, even though everyone knows [Telesom] should
> pay more than that."[24]

For ministry officials negotiating for a percentage of profits rather than a flat
rate, the problem remained: "we don't know what they earn,"[25] and the government lacked the ability to compel businesses to divulge that information
accurately. The governor of the Bank of Somaliland concurred in 2014: "Tele-

som is out of our reach: we don't know how much money it makes and how to levy taxes [on it]" (cited in Iazzolino 2015, 35). A member of the ruling party's parliamentary block said that there were informal sanctions within his party against pushing too hard to regulate Telesom: "we can't—they're too powerful."[26] A lawyer working to help draft tax legislation for a local NGO commented on the political dilemma entailed by pushing too assertively for tax increases: "Everyone wants Dahabshiil and the telecoms companies to pay equal taxes [to everyone else but] it's hard to tax someone who put you into office."[27] The World Bank reported that applying even a levy of 10–15 percent on the estimated profits of the telecommunications sector would contribute from $40–60 million dollars annually (cited in ICG 2015, 6) to a budget that was just $106 million in 2012. The budget has climbed steadily from $125 million in 2013, to $152 million in 2014 (Mills 2015, 479), and $353 million approved for 2019 (SomTribune 2018).

In April 2011, the government tabled an ambitious but controversial piece of legislation that aimed, in part, to extract more revenue from the country's largest and least regulated industry: telecommunications. However, the Telecommunications Act was not only controversial for its attempt to wrest more tax from telecommunications companies but because it simultaneously included a clause sanctioning a monopoly for a single company (Somcable) to provide all fiber optic services in Somaliland for the next twenty-five years. The exclusive rights awarded to Somcable in this clause created further controversy over the fact that its owner, Mohamed Said Guedi (Isaaq/Habar Awal), had supported President Silanyo financially in the elections and that Silanyo's wife, the first lady, was a shareholder in the company (*Indian Ocean Newsletter* 2016). That landmark piece of legislation starkly revealed the ambiguity of the government's relationship with the telecoms sector and with big business more generally. On the one hand, the law represented a considerable technocratic effort to generate more revenue; while on the other, it scarified that revenue by handing an extremely lucrative contract to one of its largest funders without a tendering process.

The contradictions within the Telecommunications Act also highlighted the splits within the government over the issue of taxation. The act had many different stakeholders with competing interests: Somcable and its supporters sought to monopolize the fiber optics industry, some members of the government saw an opportunity to increase taxation in the telecommunications sector, and Somtel (owned by Dahabshiil—of President Silanyo's Habar Jalo clan) sought to gain the long-desired ability for its customers to be able to call Telesom customers for a price that was to be set by the Ministry of Telecommunications. The government's inability to compel compliance was writ large over the entire process. It was either unwilling or unable (though perhaps both) to require that the market leader, Telesom, allow its subscribers to call or transfer money to subscribers with competing networks. The impact of this was that most people had multiple many sim cards, so they could make and receive calls from other (cheaper) service providers.[28] The government's apparent inability to compel Telesom to operate its extremely lucrative money transfer service, Zaad, in the Somaliland shilling rather than the dollar (Iazzolino 2015, 35) is another widely cited example of the government's regulatory weakness in this area.

In the end, the Telecommunications Act was undone by its contradictions. It was passed by both the parliament and the Guurti, but President Silanyo never signed it into law. The government remained unable to access the companies' revenue sheets that would allow it to calculate their profits (Iazzolino 2015, 24). There were no significant further moves under the Silanyo administration to try to increase the amount of tax paid by the telecommunications companies.[29] In the view of a former telecommunications minister, Telesom had been very effective in selectively offering shares to politically influential figures both within the government and beyond in order to maintain the its virtual monopoly:

> It's really incredible. The government wants the international community and the UN's help [in setting taxation policy] but they don't really. They could have very good income from the telecoms companies but some people in the government just don't want this. Telesom's minimum profit last year [for shareholders] was 125 percent, which means that if one share is $10,000 every year you make $12,500 profit. There is no taxation, no competition. It's not good. The government could have made a lot of money.[30]

The efforts of the former finance minister, Mohamed Hashi Elmi, to extract greater tax revenues brought dissent from traders on a number of occasions, and some even stopped importing essential foods, causing inflation in local markets. This was seen by some as a deliberate tactic to pressure President Silanyo to reign in the finance minister's campaign to bring big business under greater government control. The president arranged for an alternative company (Dahaabshiil) to import the food, which furthered popular perceptions that the government was beholden to Dahaabshiil, whose head is from the president's clan and is widely believed to have paid $420,000 to lavishly refurbish Silanyo's house when he won office in 2010.[31]

In continuing to push for significantly increased tax revenues, including from those who had financially supported the government's electoral victory, the minister of finance was deemed to have acted too assertively, and he was ousted in a cabinet reshuffle in March 2012. President Silanyo named the deputy speaker of Parliament, Abdulaziz Mohamed Samaale, as the new minister of finance. Members of the business community (particularly middle-sized importers) invited the new minister to a public conference at the Ambassador Hotel, in an apparent demonstration of their appreciation of his predecessor's removal. According to one of the people who attended the conference, the businesspeople conveyed the message to the officials from the ministry present that they expected a new relationship between the ministry and the business community.[32] By continuing to push for significantly increased tax revenues, including from those who had helped to support the government's electoral victory, like Dahabshiil and Telesom, the minister of finance threatened the protection of elite economic privilege that was established under President Egal, and which remains an important component of the arrangements that keep the country's political elite in power. One of Somaliland's smaller commodity importers expressed the conundrum facing the government as follows:

> All tariffs are fixed, on food, on cosmetics, on everything, but this depends on who you are. [Jama] Omar [Saeed] imports but pays a lot less. He gives rice to the government to give as rations for the military and the police, so the government really relies on him. The government will not pressure him. . . . This is quite common. Bahsane [Red Sea Distribution Company] imports car engines, tires, engine oil, lubricants. He is also big in real estate [and] the government borrows from him. Red Sea Petroleum Company also gives petroleum to the government. . . . It's always been like this. The government can't do without these companies. They can stop the government from operating quite quickly.[33]

The rise and fall of the finance minister, Mohamed Hashi Elmi, illustrates the government's inability to compel financial disclosure from companies operating within its borders. A senior official in the Ministry of Education summed up the government's dilemma: "The government has little to offer other than an appeal to patriotism. For the big businesses, this is not enough. They feel that they are already paying for their own land, electricity, water, security: what is the government offering them?"[34] The government was thus reduced to trying to persuade businesses to honestly declare their profits and, on that basis, to pay more tax in exchange for the promise of better legal protections and infrastructure in the longer term. These were, however, protections and infrastructure that the government was not yet capable of, or consistently willing to provide. A serving minister emphasized in an interview that the government does provide services, but he ultimately conceded that the willingness of businesses to pay tax is something that they need to be persuaded of:

> Without us [the government] they [the telecommunications companies] would have to hire their own army; they need a skilled workforce [and the government is responsible for education] and they need roads. . . . We are *appealing* to them to abide by the laws like people who earn much less.[35]

However, despite the financial dominance of big businesses over the government, they have not been able, or perhaps willing, to entirely ignore the calls of some within the government for more formalized requirements for the payment of tax. The political negotiations between the government and the telecoms sector surrounding the Telecommunications Act were intense but they underlined that at least some members of both groups believed that if peace is not maintained, the business community cannot survive in the long-term. In interviews with business leaders and government officials, both widely reproduced the popular discourse about independence, wherein the primary goal of all Somalilanders is to maintain peace, which is often offered as a justification for the apparent malaise on other political or economic issues. A senior executive at Telesom told me, for example: "We have to understand that the government needs tax to maintain peace and the functionality of the government, and we are willing to cooperate."[36] Emphasizing such willingness—and particularly the place of big business in helping to maintain peace through this willingness—has become an important part of public relations within the telecommunications sector. This in itself represents a shift from assertions that the sector already contributed to society in other ways and that requests for taxation constitute an unreasonable additional burden. Throughout this period, the underlying narrative that both sides returned to in their public rhetoric was that maintaining peace outweighs all other political and economic calculation and that neither wants to push the other too hard to achieve their goals. This is, of course, a key thread of the independence discourse. A clan elder and former member of parliament articulated this thinking to a team of local researchers exploring state-business relations in the country:

> The business community is closely tied to peace-building efforts. The economy would be destroyed if there was conflict. Businesses need peace. Even the suspicion of instability is very bad for business. We don't have foreign money invested here; everything has been built upon the little resources we have, and only because of the peace we have. Peace and the willingness of locals is what business is built upon. There was nothing before 1997. (cited in Arteh and Dualeh 2011, 5)

As some government actors, particularly the finance minister, became more assertive in their efforts to increase domestic revenues from taxation, it was clear that some of the finer details of state-business relations had changed since Egal's time, where tax was either captured at the point of entry/exit or not at all. However, the substance remained familiar, with profits remaining untaxed, and the wealthiest merchants and businesses continuing to receive exclusive access to some of the country's most lucrative commercial opportunities.

The issue of tax is essentially a chicken and egg problem: At what point does one side trust the other enough to invest in its success? In a sense, Somaliland's government has little to offer other than to reproduce the independence discourse, particularly its emphasis on the precarity of peace, in its efforts to achieve greater compliance to taxation legislation. The government lacks the institutional capacity (and often the willingness) to compel the business community to pay substantial tax, but it puts considerable effort into framing taxation as part of the broader discourse about Somaliland's viability as an independent sovereign entity. The government thereby frames its inability to compel compliance as the reason that people ought to comply anyway. That is, the government's lack of institutional capacity to enforce its own rules is, somewhat counterintuitively, harnessed as a justification for people to adhere to them.

Chapter 5

WAR AND PEACE IN THE INDEPENDENCE DISCOURSE

In the popular understandings of Somalia and Somaliland, political outcomes are almost always characterized as resulting from either the quality of institutions that monopolize violence, the endurance of clanism in political life, or thirdly from the stabilizing influence of hybridity, in which the apparently inevitable logics of state and clan are fruitfully entwined (Campos 2016, 5). This closes the door to seeing how discourse structures the conditions of possibility, which is the subject of this chapter.

The most common account of Somaliland's relative stability suggests that its in/formal governance institutions, while weak, are still strong *enough* to maintain relative peace and civil order (Bahadur 2011: 39; Hansen 2009, 30; World Bank 2013, 147; Schäferhoff 2014, 680; Walls 2014). This chapter demonstrates that many local elites report to doubt this, highlighting instead that the security services lack the capacity to protect the population against serious threats, and that civil order is more a function of Somalilanders' identity—and even of the very weakness of Somaliland's state/state-like institutions.

Mary Harper (2012, 137) cites "a senior official in Somaliland's security department" who stated the military and police are too corrupt and weak to tackle any serious security threats: "the law here is fifty US dollars." This was a commonly articulated sentiment in my own interviews. For example, Somaliland's counterpiracy authorities, discussed in greater detail later in this chapter, routinely noted their inability to curtail piracy through their formal institutional capacity, signaling instead the degree to which they rely on ordinary people reporting possible operations to them. The Somaliland Police Force is also widely seen as ineffective and faces significant "challenges in winning respect from the citizenry" (UNDP 2010; cited in Balthasar and Grzybowski 2012, 164). The Observatory of Conflict and Violence Prevention (2015, 30–33) showed that of the eight hundred households surveyed in Borco, most respondents reported that they preferred the protection from violence provided by community elders to that of the police (see also Stremlau and Osman 2015, 8).[1] That lack of confidence in the police exists within the force itself; a high-ranking official from the Somaliland Police Force's regional administration reportedly announced at a community meeting in Hargeysa: "We have the responsibility of protecting you, but we cannot do it without you—it is you [who] protect yourselves" (cited in Balthasar and Grzybowski 2012, 164).

However, even the clan institutions (particularly those at a national level) that were once lauded by Somalilanders as pillars of peace are also increasingly seen as adding to, rather than reducing, insecurity (Hoehne 2013, 206). The consultative council of clan elders (*Guurti*) is now widely seen as "threaten[ing] to undermine the polity's stability" due to the corruption and parochialism of its members (Renders and Terlinden 2010, 742). The research director at a local institute argued in an interview in 2013 that "the Guurti hangs around like a monstrosity. . . . In times past, elders had weight. They had gravitas, circumspection, and dignity. Now they are cynically maneuvering like an oily lawyer."[2] One member of parliament suggested that the Guurti's local popularity was so depleted that it was largely sustained by international donors, who tend to uncritically romanticize customary institutions as inherently legitimate despite the changing views of Somalilanders.[3] He also suggested that there was another reason for this support: "International NGOs prefer to work with the Guurti because they don't ask the hard questions [to the international community] because they are elders, and most of them are illiterate."[4]

These widely stated doubts in the ability of the government to deter violence point to the importance of the noncoercive means by which political violence is excluded from the range of actions that are considered possible. This chapter argues that the independence discourse sets broadly respected limits for collective behavior—or rather, it excludes certain behaviors from obvious consideration—in ways that Somaliland's formal and traditional governance institutions do not. That is, the discourse has helped to prevent people from mobilizing on a large scale to violently affect politics.

Somalilanders had experienced a decade and a half of conflict and displacement by the time its leaders had formalized an end to the destructive interclan violence in early 1997. The trauma of this violence forms a baseline narrative that runs through Somaliland's discourse about the legitimacy of its independence from the rest of Somalia. A survey by the International Republican Institute about public attitudes in Hargeysa captures the pervasive sense that violence is ever possible: "95 per cent of respondents [reported that they] feel very safe, *but chief among their fears is conflict or civil war*" (IRI 2011, emphasis added). The independence discourse frames Somalilanders as unified in their desire to avoid repeating this outcome at all costs, stemming also from a fear of returning to their own violent past—whether from the persecution they faced from the Barre regime or the internal wars that followed. This is purported to not only differentiate Somalilanders from other Somalis but also to justify their permanent legal separation from the Republic of Somalia. The intermingling of these two narratives—Somalilanders' supposedly exceptional ability to maintain peace and civil order without significant external assistance and the notion that this legitimizes their claim of independence— is essential to understanding how this trauma was channeled into a discourse that has, to date, helped prevent violence from re-emerging.

This chapter analyses a number of key events that reshaped Somaliland, showing how actors emphasized the tenets of the independence discourse as a means of delegitimizing political violence or civil disorder. However, as explained in the introduction, this is not to argue that there is a simple causal relationship between the independence discourse and peace, wherein more discourse about peace invariably brings more peace. Ideas have causal power but not in any predictable manner because they are coproduced with the nonideational institutions that enact them. Rather, the argument is that the discourse organizes and stabilizes Somaliland's peace in ways that its other institutions and circumstances do not.

There are two key mechanisms that act to maintain order embedded within the discourse about Somaliland's legitimate independence from Somalia. At its most basic level, the discourse frames the maintenance of peace and civil order as the linchpin of Somaliland's normative case for a permanent legal separation from Somalia. This aspect casts certain behaviors, particularly civil violence and maritime piracy, as incongruent to the identity of Somaliland as an orderly member of international society. It draws a sharp distinction here between Somalilanders who (according to the discourse) thrived on the autonomy that the lack of external intervention afforded them, and other Somalis. These other Somalis are framed as having demonstrated that they "don't want peace" by their ready acceptance of intervention and its offer of material benefits at the expense of social cohesion.[5] At a deeper level, though, the stabilizing influence of this discourse rests on its expression of peace/war and order/disorder as coconstitutive (see Barkawi 2016), accentuating the frightening ease with which the former becomes the latter, and the inherent uncertainty over where the separation between them lies at any given moment. Of particular importance is its emphasis on the weakness of the country's institutional protections against the re-emergence of violence and civil war.

At a public discussion about the drivers of peace in Somaliland, a former minister argued: "the peace in Somaliland holds not because of strong institutions and forces . . . it's something that has grown out of the common collective will of the people. . . . We wish it to be stable."[6] The mayor of Berbera also pointed to the agential, rather than institutional, nature of the Somaliland's sustained peacefulness: "You can walk around (Berbera) at any time day or night, and this isn't due to an army enforcing the peace. Peace has become one of the most important dynamics. People have worked tirelessly to keep the peace'" (cited in Arteh and Duale 2011, 4). A senior opposition leader put it slightly differently in an interview with me, though still emphasizing the primacy of agency over institutions in maintaining peace: "In Somaliland our peace is not based on legal enforcement but on social responsibility. The government is not willing to formalize the institutions to enforce peace."[7] Such doubts in the ability of the country's governance institutions to deter violence point to the importance of the noncoercive means by which political violence seems to be excluded from the range of actions that are considered possible by a critical mass of Somalilanders.

In these comments (which are representative of sentiments that were widely expressed to me), the *weakness* and unreliability of its institutions has shaped Somalilanders' identity as one that is inherently peaceful and self-reliant. That is, Somalilanders have responded to institutional weakness by discursively compensating for it on the level of identity and by asserting their ability to maintain peace without strong institutions on the basis of that identity. Of course institutional weakness is also part of the identity that is expressed, and this creates a tension in which institutions may need to remain weak (and external intervention minimal) lest what it means to be a Somalilander be threatened. The 2003 elections offer a useful window onto the constraints that the discursive prioritization of civil order has historically placed on people's behavior, particularly on those with the capacity to mobilize others for political violence.

Fears of Violence and a Peaceful Election

The stakes of Somaliland's 2003 presidential election were particularly pronounced because the parliamentary elections that were meant to occur simultaneously were cancelled at the last minute. This meant that whichever party won the presidential election would run the country without the participation of the other parties, leading to fears that Somaliland was effectively becoming a single-party state (Renders 2012, 241–42). The election was an incredibly close race in which the incumbent, President Dahir Rayale Kahin, maintained power over his main challenger, Ahmed Silanyo, by an initial margin of just eighty (of the 498,000) votes cast, despite Silanyo having initially declared victory. The Supreme Court later revised the margin to 217 votes, but it was still clear that a missing ballot box (of which there were many) could have been sufficient to reverse the outcome. Yet the dispute was handled peacefully. Observers reported that while the poll itself was "tolerably fair" (ICG 2003, 23), the tabulation process for the count was highly problematic and lacked transparency, which meant that there was no way of independently verifying the outcome (Lindeman and Hansen 2003). The International Crisis Group concluded that "there are excellent grounds on which to question the authenticity of the result" (ICG 2003, 26). Lindeman and Hansen note that members of the Guurti and of the (ultimately victorious) UDUB (United Democratic People's Party—*Ururka Dimuqraadiga Ummadda Bahawday*) both applied considerable pressure to the members of the National Electoral Commission to tabulate the results in a manner favorable to President Dahir Rayale. They conclude that there was nothing to suggest that the procedural errors were part of a systematic attempt "to reach a particular result or in other ways trying to influence the outcome of the elections" (Lindeman and Hansen 2003, 41). The formal count was, however, deeply uncertain and open to dispute—and the weakness of the formal institutional capacity of the National Electoral Commission and the Supreme Court were plainly apparent.

Faced with a brewing crisis, many expected violence (Bradbury, Abokor, and Yusuf 2003, 471; Daud 2003), based partly on Somaliland's recent history and structural similarities to Somalia, and partly on the lack of robust institutional deterrents to violence. The ICG (2003, 25) wrote shortly after the event that "Somalilanders at home and abroad held their breath, fearful of the worst." However, people were acutely aware of the seriousness of the situation, which was widely articulated through the example of how violence spiraled out of control elsewhere in Somalia with a fearsome velocity. As the defeated candidate Ahmed Silanyo stated, he had no intention of dragging Somaliland down the same path that Mogadishu had so painfully travelled and that he was, therefore, committed to peacefully resolving the crisis: "Some of my supporters say 'Why don't you just form a [parallel] government?' But I won't go down that road, because no one can guarantee that we won't end up like Mogadishu" (ICG 2003, 31). He also noted: "We don't want bad things to happen to the country and the population . . . we declared that there was an injustice against us [but] bearing in mind the interests of the nation and the people . . . we have accepted the results" (BBC Somali Service 2003). Silanyo's Kulmiye Party spokesman, Mohamed Iid Dimbiil, used a similar justification for not challenging the results:

> We as the Kulmiye party and its supporters should avoid what can bring unrest. It is good for us to keep the peace and search for what we want through a peaceful way. They [the government] usually say, as propaganda, that Kulmiye is against the peace, and acts in ways that can cause violence and instability but Kulmiye cares for peace more than anyone else.[8]

In this statement, it is clear that the desire to maintain peace was central to politicians' claims of legitimacy—and central to how they sought to deny legitimacy to their competitors. The other defeated candidate, Faisal Ali Warabe, made a comparable point about the results and the fragile peace that they threatened: "I'm requesting that the population and the political parties, including the [challenger Ahmed Silanyo's] Kulmiye Party, accept the results of the election, which state that UDUB [President Dahir Rayale's party] won the election, and keep the peace."[9] Here, Warabe was implicitly referencing the notion that peace is tenuous and that its maintenance trumps partisan politics.

In the 2017 presidential electoral campaign, there was a stronger sense of political brinkmanship, particularly from some (opposition) Waddani Party officials, one reportedly saying, "We have to win these elections and if [this] doesn't happen, we need to do something about it" (cited in Elder 2019, 151). However, this kind of rhetoric was challenged from within the party. A former statesman suggested that such statements were made by diaspora members who were "unfamiliar with the political arrangements in place" (Elder 2019, 151)—an apparent reference to the norms of nonviolent contestation coded within the independence discourse. Claire Elder cites an interview with a Waddani Party supporter:

> I told Waddani's advisor that it was selfish, so what if you lose power, threatening this peace is not worth it. . . . I've heard from 8/9 people from both sides, "if our camp doesn't win, there will be no deal"—such rhetoric has not happened in the last 20 years. Kulmiye in 2003 lost by 80 votes, didn't challenge or anything, but conceded defeat. (Elder 2019, chap. 5)

In the aftermath of the elections, the defeated candidate, Abdirahman Irro (Waddani Party), cited electoral irregularities during his concession speech but again underlined the danger to peace should he choose a forceful response:

> I've decided to concede defeat for the sake of maintaining unity and peace in Somaliland—not because [president elect] Musa and Kulmiye won. . . . I will not destroy this country for my own personal ambitions, nor will I allow my people to drop blood for me—but I am still fearful that Kulmiye will destroy this country under their rule. (Cited in *The National*, 2017)

Despite the brinkmanship that colored aspects of the 2017 campaign, the idea endured that peace and stability must be maintained no matter the electoral outcome.

Somaliland's closely contested elections—though particularly the 2003 campaign—offer clear examples of the way that the independence discourse, the various strands of which emerged out of the exclusion and brutality that Somalilanders endured from the 1980s, has shaped the preferences of key elites. These elites might otherwise have had a reason to believe that they could do well out of civil war, as predicted by Collier (2000) and other scholars who argue that violence tends to occur where structural opportunities permit (Fearon and Laitin 2003, 88; Hironaka 2005, 149–52; Walter 2015, 23). The peaceful way in which the appeal process was handled was not an indicator of the strength of the country's formal or clan-based institutions per se, though the latter played a more constructive role than the former. In fact, the peaceful resolution demonstrated the way that institutional weakness, and the proximity of violence that this weakness permits, has been repurposed as a justification for de-escalating crises. That is, the crisis was not resolved *despite* the weakness of Somaliland's institutions, but because there was something about that weakness that helped facilitate a peaceful resolution.

The National Electoral Commission was quite powerless to alter a matter of such magnitude, and the Supreme Court's final verdict was taken to have confused matters further (ICG 2003, 27). The resolution of the crisis was, therefore, an expression of stakeholders' understanding of the popular ideas that constitute the independence discourse about the ready susceptibility of peace to war—and of the likely costs of failing to enact them. Some of this was expressed through formal institutions such as the National Electoral Commission and the Supreme Court, some by the mediation offered by members of the Guurti, and some through unofficial wrangling out of the public eye; but as a whole, the process was buttressed by the paramount desire to prevent violence, regardless of the electoral outcome. Here, it is clear that people do not just receive the content of a discourse and then hold it internally as an idea, but they also speak it, circulate it, and thereby rereproduce the behavioral constraints that it frames as integral to the Somalilander identity.

The literature referring to these elections tends to focus on Somaliland's hybrid institutional capacity to the exclusion of the ideas or discourses that underpin those institutions. For example, Rebecca Richards (2015, 16) attributes the peaceful outcome of the 2003 electoral crisis to the Guurti's ability to "negotiate . . . the concession of the runner-up candidate." Marleen

Renders also credits Somaliland's governance institutions: "The clash between Somaliland's two chief politicians turned into a major test of Somaliland's institutions. The test was passed, but only just narrowly" (Renders 2012, 241). She notes later that "more than anything, people wanted peace" (248) but does not expand on the implications of this desire for the fact that peace prevailed. Michael Walls (2014, 232) highlights a more agential (albeit individual) component, stating: "It is to [Silanyo's] credit as a leader, that he eventually did declare that, in the interests of peace, he would accept the results." Thus, for both Renders and Walls, an ideational component sits in the background, but it is institutional capacity and agency (respectively) that is directly credited for the success in avoiding violence.

Had Silanyo not accepted defeat he would have contravened the linchpin of the independence discourse: that the maintenance of peace is what sets Somaliland apart from Somalia. It is unlikely that Silanyo's acceptance was motivated purely by individual altruism but rather by an understanding that to challenge the result, and thus be seen to risk violence, would have been seen as illegitimate by ordinary Somalilanders. Such an action would have contravened the way that the Somalilander identity is coconstituted with action in the discourse, wherein Somalilanders are peaceful and so should not contest the results—and that not contesting the results demonstrates that one is a genuine Somalilander, who is peaceful. Thus, the Kulmiye spokesperson cited above emphasized that the government accuses the party of being "against the peace." This illustrates that portraying opponents in this way is seen as a potent means of discrediting them. That it occurred when the stakes were so high also shows the power of the discourse within the speaker's target audience. In this instance, therefore, the common understanding that peace is too precious and too fragile to gamble with apparently underwrote his decision not to continue with a legally justifiable challenge to the results. Silanyo won the subsequent presidential election in 2010.

The Independence Discourse and Civil Order

The independence discourse sets clear and broadly respected limits for collective behavior. It constructs an essentialized identity that emphasizes the supposedly inherent predisposition that Somalilanders have for peace and orderly conduct, while also accentuating the fragility of peace in such a way that urges cautious action. I will take these in turn, starting with the differences constructed between Somalis and Somalilanders regarding their alleged proclivities to violence and order, respectively. Somaliland's independence discourse constructs the Somaliland identity via the creation of binary oppositions/radical difference (see Connolly 1991; Campbell 1992; Doty 1996) that casts peaceful Somalilanders against a violent or otherwise menacing Somali other. On this basis, it defines those who partake in violent or criminal activity as being "from the south; not Somalilanders."[10] This particular phrasing was used by a senior official in the Ministry of Justice to refer to the national origins of maritime pirates, but it is representative of the way that many interviewees reported to understand Somaliland's achievements principally through the prism of Somalia's purported dysfunction. For example, when I asked one political analyst why Somalilanders had been able to establish and maintain peace, he answered: "we are like a flower growing out of a pile of garbage."[11] Another answered with reference to his daily routine, which he contrasted to the bloodlust he believed was rampant in Somalia: "Here in Somaliland, I can walk anywhere I want but in the south [southern and central Somalia] they enjoy killing people and you cannot move at all."[12]

A minister told me in 2012 about a lost-and-found service provided by Radio Hargeysa, where people call in to say, "I have found some money—maybe five or ten thousand dollars—or some gold. Call me if you have lost it." An intrigued phone call to the radio station confirmed that people do regularly use this service but that the amounts were smaller than the minister had stated, and were usually in the range of $100–$200.[13] While not the extravagant sums suggested by the minister, it still represents a sizeable amount of money considering that the average annual income per capita was then (very) roughly estimated to be around $350 (Clapham et al. 2011, 12). Other senior government figures told me—the foreign researcher—that they do not lock their houses when they go overseas or that they often leave cash lying around without concern, usually with pointed reference to the theft that such carelessness would provoke in southern Somalia:

> In Somaliland, there's the question of honour but in Somalia it is dishonourable not to steal; in Somalia if you can't steal you are stupid or you are not a man. Here in Somaliland it is the will of the people to abide by the law; it's a choice, it's the will of the people.[14]

The visible locks on front doors, the broken glass cemented into fences to prevent intruders, and the presence of security guards at businesses all highlight the exaggerations in these claims but their factual veracity is not the point. The point is to communicate the idea that Somalilanders are exceptional in their predisposition towards peace and civil order. The independence discourse frames Somaliland as both separate to, and more orderly than, other Somali territories—a separation that is used to support its call for formal independence to the international community. In so doing, it essentializes the Somalilander identity as uniformly pro-independence and uniformly peaceful. Of course, such uniformity is not always upheld. For example, the speed with which the country's first president, Abdirahman Tuur, abandoned independence in favor of federalism after losing the presidency (as discussed in chapter 2), and the other prominent Isaaq political figures that have served in southern governments (Bradbury 2008, 250), belie the strict uniformity of this claim, even among the Isaaq elite. However, such a self-representation of political consensus supports the strategic goal of having Somaliland's independence internationally recognized.

Another of Somaliland's ministers portrayed the country's success in maintaining peace as resulting from the fact that: "We never had any of our [peace] conferences in five star hotels like in the south. . . . We were sending money to Boorama [where the first major clan conference was held] and there was no foreign money there—thank God Ethiopia was too poor then."[15] The lack of external intervention is a strong thread in the independence discourse, which was demonstrated starkly during a public talk that I gave in Hargeysa in 2015. In a research paper that I had published previously, there was a footnote provided for the previous quote, which noted that the minister's statement about the absence of foreign money was: "not technically correct, as there was a very small amount (around $US100,000) of donor funding at the Borama Conference" (Phillips 2013, 50, footnote 63). A journalist in the audience took issue with the suggestion that there was any external funding at all:

> You wrote that the difference between the Booroma conference and the Hargeysa conference was that Boorama was almost entirely funded by local communities but in the footnote, you wrote that there was a $100,000 contribution [for the Boorama conference] from various donors. We don't know those donors. Where did you get that from?[16]

Before I answered, another member of the audience offered an alternative explanation of where the figure of $100,000 might have come from. Like the original quote from the minister that I cited earlier, in which Somaliland is fortunate that Ethiopia was "too poor" to intervene, the next explanation from the audience also underscored the autonomy of Somaliland's peace. This was specifically contrasted to Somalis' purported acceptance of external intervention despite (perhaps even because of) its likely negative consequences:

> You probably heard 100,000 "something." Well, I know of 100,000 bags of rice that was donated by France , , , so that "100,000" alone was donated to the Boorama conference. I don't know if anybody else donated anything else or not. . . . But in Somalia, the more that is given, the less likely it is that Somalia will have peace . . . because peace [is of] no interest to [Somalis].[17]

Somaliland and Somalia are conjoined in the independence discourse: one good and free of external interference, the other bad and either unwilling or unable to reject that interference despite its harmful consequences. However, the Somaliland depicted in the independence discourse does not exist without its other, which serves as a reminder that the violence in the south (actual and imagined) is never far away, and that it could re-emerge with little provocation.

To some, however, there is a further menace contained in Somaliland's proximity to the violence in Mogadishu: that if that violence ends, the political, economic, and ideational basis upon which Somaliland has been built will be overturned. A local researcher and consultant from Hargeysa articulated this fear when we discussed what he saw as the major threats facing Somaliland in 2013:

> I'm afraid that if the south becomes more stable and the government [in Somalia] begins to function, then what binds the people together here will be reduced. *What binds us together now is that there is no other option.* I don't see anything that can bind us together if there is peace in the south.[18]

Not only is Somaliland's peace constructed against a backdrop of Mogadishu's violence, but peace in Mogadishu is suggested here to pose a threat to peace in Somaliland. Another Hargeysa-based researcher highlighted this concern from a different angle, invoking less the fragility of Somaliland's peace and more the contingency of its claim to sovereign independence on violence levels in the south:

> Now that progress is being made against al-Shabaab in Mogadishu, many Somalilanders are worried that this will mean that more of the head offices of UN agencies and INGOs dealing with Somalia (and therefore Somaliland) will move from Nairobi to Mogadishu, which will anger many people here. Somaliland will protest that [move] because it will have to deal with them through Mogadishu. Somaliland realizes that this might happen soon and that once the head offices are in Mogadishu everything will shift there instead of Nairobi—and all of the decision makers will be in Mogadishu. It will create real problems in Somaliland.[19]

Both comments illustrate that Somaliland's peace and independence rest on a discursive base of the dysfunction of its Somali other. If that dysfunction subsides, the independence discourse may lose traction, posing a direct threat to Somaliland's own peace and stability.

A member of the Guurti requested that when I return home I "tell the international community that they must support us and our peace, and we will then support our Somali brothers . . . we can negotiate peace [in southern Somalia] in our own way."[20] This possibility constitutes a common refrain from Somaliland's politicians, President Egal noting in a 1998 speech: "We hope that international community will understand that Somaliland could be the solution for Somalia's problem. If we get recognition and build our country we can be an example for the other Somalis" (cited in Qoti 2013, 69).

At least within the capital of Hargeysa, the belief that Somaliland deserves recognition on the basis of its ability to maintain peace and its adherence to international norms of good governance is projected at foreigners with an apparent sense of routine and purpose. Voters in the 2012 local elections were, for example, keen to narrate their participation in the poll to international observers as behavior that warranted the conferral of statehood: "I've been standing in line since 2:00 a.m.—Somaliland should be recognized."[21]

The Present Absence of Piracy

The fact that piracy has not been a significant problem off Somaliland's coastline is used as further evidence of the exceptional ability of Somalilanders to maintain peace and order in the absence of formal constraints, again in pointed distinction to other Somalis.[22] During my interviews about Somaliland's general lack of piracy, people often affirmed the difference that this marked between Somalilanders and other Somalis: "All the pirates are from the south; [they are] not Somalilanders."[23] The divergence was sometimes explained with reference to Britain's colonial practices which left Somaliland's indigenous social and political structures relatively intact, while the Italian administration in the rest of Somalia intentionally decimated them as a means of asserting control. In one former minister's view, Britain's rule left "us to negotiate our own affairs, ethics, styles of mediation, and ways of living with our neighbors. The other side of this equation is Somalia. . . . Italian colonialism destroyed them."[24] While this explanation brushes over the complexity and brutalities of the colonial period, Jatin Dua (2011) suggests that its purpose may be to cast Somalilanders as holding a British sense of respect for law and order. Meanwhile, it casts other Somalis as being historically predisposed towards the mafia-like violence and criminality that maritime piracy entails. In the words of one senior official in the Ministry of Foreign Affairs, Somaliland is exceptional for not succumbing to the temptations of piracy despite the strong incentives to join in: "90 percent of the pirates are from Puntland and yet Puntland has gained about 95 percent of the international resources available. . . . The more peace you make, the less resources you receive."[25] This framing seems intended to suggest that Somalilanders even though Somalilanders might benefit materially from engaging in piracy they cannot because of their 'inherent' (according to the discourse) predisposition towards peace and orderly conduct. This quote—made by an official in the Ministry of Foreign Affairs to a foreign researcher—also suggests that Somalilanders are eager to be seen by foreigners as being actively engaged in international efforts against piracy, which demonstrates Somaliland's sense of moral responsibility to international security. A local analyst working for an international non-governmental organization suggested that this sentiment was one that was felt outside of the ministries whose job it is to promote Somaliland's national interests to the international community:

> The key thing for the [local] community is recognition, and anything that will get in the way of recognition—whether it's piracy or extremist ideology, anything—I think the population is alert to what the international community needs to see to recognize Somaliland. They want to protect that.[26]

Somaliland's House of Representatives, Abdirahman Abdillahi, highlighted the connection between Somaliland's actions against piracy and the legitimacy of its claims to statehood in an interview with Reuters News Agency: "The passing of these [antipiracy] laws proves that we are willing to cooperate with the international community" (Anderson 2012). Similarly, in a number of conversations with officials in the Ministry of Justice about an agreement to transfer convicted pirates from the Seychelles to Somaliland, the officials emphasized their hope that there would be more prisoners transferred in the future.[27] Such a hope highlights that Somaliland's engagement on piracy is also marshalled as evidence of Somaliland's commitment to helping the international community contain the problems caused by the violence and instability in Somalia. This serves to reinforce the reasonableness of Somaliland's desire to formalize its independence from Somalia by achieving international recognition (Hastings and Phillips 2018, 21).

Somaliland's foreign minister, Mohamed Abdulahi Omar, told me in an interview that:

> None of those captured [for piracy] are Somalilanders. Somaliland's interest is to work with the international community to fight something that is damaging its economic interests. . . . The pirates are mainly from Puntland and southern Somalia. We will keep them [in prison] while southern Somalia gets their institutions functioning and then we will hand them back. . . . Somaliland is increasingly showing itself as a credible partner so that the international community will see Somaliland as a state actor that can enter into formal contracts . . . and become a normal member of the international community.[28]

Along similar lines, a former minister framed the maintenance of peace in Somaliland and the conflict in other Somali territories through an explicit comparison of attitudes toward piracy:

> Imagine a nightmare. Imagine that Somalia had access to the Red Sea like Somaliland has. Imagine what would have happened. Imagine where the world would have been. Somaliland has maintained their coast—that gateway to the Red Sea, that trade route—as best as it could because we wish it to be safe. We wish it to be stable. So, I hope that the world will at least recognize and reward Somaliland and Somalilanders for having maintained the international waterways, free of disturbances.[29]

There were nearly 180 successful hijackings by Somali pirates between 2005 and 2012 (World Bank 2013, 41), with the vast majority of operations based in either Puntland or parts of Southern Somalia (particularly Hobyo and Xarardheere). The English language literature tends to attribute the near absence of piracy in Somaliland to being largely a function of Somaliland's institutional capacity. Stig Jarle Hansen notes:

> Somaliland's achievements in the struggle against piracy are amazing . . . Despite having a very weak coast guard service, pirate attacks in their part of the Somali maritime economic zone number less than one every two years over the last ten years. Somaliland reacts fast against rumoured pirate groups, catching pirates when they are in the process of organizing themselves. (Hansen 2009, 30)

Likewise, Jay Bahadur writes:

> The difference [between Puntland and Somaliland] is due to Somaliland's greater political stability . . . Its central government can exert control over its territory in a way that Puntland's leaders, who must navigate a much more fractured clan landscape, cannot. In the south, in short, the pirates had to fear other criminals; in Somaliland, the danger came from a more traditional source: the police. (Bahadur 2011, 39)

Maintaining this focus on Somaliland's formal governance institutions, the World Bank reported:

> Somaliland's relatively good antipiracy record has often been attributed to the stability achieved by the regime . . . the state has a monopoly on the use of force. Formal (though underfunded) military, police, and coast guard units have been established, with the last having antipiracy authority . . . A coastline of only several hundred kilometers makes Somaliland fairly manageable for a relatively small force. (World Bank 2013, 147)

However, within Somaliland the near absence of piracy is less likely to be attributed (by government officials and ordinary Somalilanders alike) to the authorities' ability to prevent it than to Somalilanders' supposedly innate proclivity against disorderly behavior. The government's official website to lobby for international recognition highlights Somaliland's dearth of piracy, though does not explicitly credit its own authorities for suppressing it: "Somaliland has effectively tackled piracy along its coastline, ensuring that the waters off Somaliland's coast are largely free from pirate attacks. Nearly 90 pirates are currently in prison in Hargeysa" (Government of Somaliland n.d.). The Executive Director of Somaliland's Counter-Piracy Coordination Office confirmed in 2015 that the coast guard did not have the ability to physically prevent piracy, hoping instead that "by the end of 2016 the Somaliland coast guard should have an operational capacity to police our waters . . . We don't yet have the capacity to do this."[30] That is, the government did not have this enforcement capacity when piracy was at its peak (2005–2012), suggesting that it was never really the coastguard that prevented piracy from becoming a problem in Somaliland (Hastings and Phillips 2018, 18). Additionally, Alice Hills notes that Somaliland's police force has a technical and institutional advantage of perhaps five years over Puntland's (Hills 2014, 96), which, if accurate, suggests that the difference in capacity between the two is not vast—certainly not vast enough to account for the dramatically different levels of piracy that occurred between Puntland and Somaliland. That is, Somaliland's authorities do not appear to have had substantially greater coercive power against piracy than Puntland's had.[31]

What is crucial to note about the government's operational capacity is that when attacks were thwarted, they were thwarted before they were launched. The Counter-Piracy Coordination Office director noted: "Piracy starts on land; they need a base. Somaliland authorities, with the cooperation of the local communities are refusing pirates to have bases alongside the Somaliland coast." He suggested that people reported suspicious activity because they did not want trade at Berbera Port to be disrupted, and because preventing piracy reflects Somalilanders' "desire to practice [being] a state, not to allow criminals into their space, and also to be part of the international community. There was a sense that this goes out to the person on the coast, who has an obligation to fulfill" (Hastings and Phillips 2018, 22). In this framing, the dearth of piracy is more attributable to Somalilanders' collective desire to be seen as good international citizens than it is to the investigative or coercive power of either the police or coast guard.

However, the supposed absence of piracy from Somaliland's territory raises a problem: it was not entirely absent, and a small number of attacks did emanate from Somaliland. The UN Monitoring Group on Somalia and Eritrea (UNSC 2010, 37–38) reported that there was a pirate network operating on the Sanaag coast between 2007 and 2009, and the UN Office on Drugs and Crime (UNODC) confirmed that it conducted five operations (cited in World Bank 2013, 147). The network was based in the town of Laas-qorey, which both Somaliland and Puntland claim as their territory, though neither actively administers. In 2009, Yemeni authorities captured its leader, Fou'ad Hanaano, and the network was deactivated (World Bank 2013, 147, cited in Hastings and Phillips 2018, 23).

The independence discourse is important here. Fou'ad Hanaano is a member of the Warsangeli clan, which is predominant in western Puntland and in parts of eastern Somaliland (which Puntland also claims). The World Bank notes that Hanaano had close clan-based ties to some members of the Puntland administration, and that they provided him with protection (World Bank 2013, 148). Therefore, while the physical location of the anchorage points used by Hanaano's network are inside the territory that is claimed by Somaliland, the criminal behavior of some of its (non-Isaaq clan) inhabitants tends to be either ignored or attributed to Puntland, discursively maintaining Somaliland's pirateless status.[32]

While the idea of a Warsangeli clan enclave in Laasqorey, with its implied clan connections to Puntland, sits comfortably with the independence discourse it unsettles a core component of Somaliland's legal claim of independence. As discussed in chapter 2, Somaliland argues that sovereign recognition would simply reinstate a previously sovereign entity, not create one anew. That entity existed within the colonial Anglo-Italian borders of British Somaliland and was recognized by 34 member states of the UN (including the Permanent Five) for five days in 1960 before it voluntarily united with Somalia. The Foreign Minister summarized this position in 2012, placing careful emphasis on Somaliland's historical claim to statehood when responding to a question about the impact of being unrecognized: "What worked for Somaliland was the commitment to independence and to building a nation-state based on a historical and political background as a country which had been independent previously and later joined voluntarily with Somalia."[33]

In this view, conferring sovereignty on Somaliland would not constitute secession—a justification that is important in trying to assuage fears that formal recognition would open a Pandora's box of other African secessionist movements. For the reinstatement argument to hold, therefore, the integrity of Somaliland's previously recognized borders is paramount. Somaliland's territorial and border-based claim of sovereignty is set against Puntland's genealogical-based claim to the parts of Sool, eastern Sanaag, and southern Togdheer (Hoehne 2015, 21) that are dominated by the Harti clan family.[34] This claim recognizes clan boundaries over those imposed by colonial powers. Therefore, in order to discursively maintain the notion that Somalilanders do not engage in piracy (and are thus more orderly than other Somalis), the border that Somaliland claims for its independent state is implicitly sacrificed, and Laasqorey is discursively forfeited to Puntland.

An anecdote from an interview with a local NGO worker illustrates this flexibility in practice: he described an incident in which he was personally involved, where a number of Somalilanders were kidnapped while working in Laasqorey in 2012. The kidnapping was apparently an attempt to coerce the release of some relatives from Hargeysa prison, who were being held on allegations of piracy. When asked why people from Laasqorey had been involved in piracy when Somalilanders so vocally disavow piracy, he responded that Laasqorey "was infected by Puntland . . . all of its interactions are with Puntland."[35] In other words, people's behavior and relationships—not their location—determines whether they are considered Somalilanders or Puntlanders (Hastings and Phillips 2018, 25). Should a person's behavior not cohere with the discursive construction of an orderly Somaliland, therefore, they may be categorized as a non-Somalilander. In Somaliland's independence discourse, territorial claims to its contested periphery may be sacrificed in order to uphold the, ultimately more important, narrative of Somaliland's inherent propensity for order, in which piracy has no place (25). That the discourse is implicitly maintained despite its inconsistencies with Somaliland's key legal claim to sovereignty is another indicator of how important the independence discourse is to the reproduction of political order in Somaliland.

The International Reproduction of the Independence Discourse: Good Somaliland, Bad Somalia

As noted in the introduction, there are some striking consistencies across the academic work that is produced about Somaliland, particularly that by scholars who have conducted most of their research in Hargeysa and its surrounds. Within this body of work, Somaliland is almost invariably held up as the silver lining to Somalia's dark and violent cloud (as indeed it is, to an extent, in this book's own introduction). A paradigmatic example:

In the midst of this dire landscape [that is, Somalia], it is all the more remarkable that an apparent oasis of stability has nonetheless emerged: the self-declared Republic of Somaliland. . . . Somalilanders have managed to not only establish external security and internal stability—enough of the latter, in fact, to have developed what is arguably the most democratic politics in the subregion—but have done so without the benefit of international recognition of their existence or much foreign development assistance. Thus the lessons from Somaliland's successful peace and state-building processes may be applicable not only to efforts to bring stability to other Somali areas, but also to postconflict situations elsewhere around the globe. (Pham 2012, 3)

A quick internet search reveals similar sentiments in media articles by Western journalists who have visited, with titles such as: "In Praise of Somaliland: A Beacon of Hope in the Thorn of Africa" (Tatchell 2007); "Somaliland: Open for Business" (Tran 2012); "Somaliland: A Pocket of Stability in a Chaotic Region" (Muchler 2012); "In Somaliland, Less Money Has Brought More Democracy" (Eubank 2011); and, "Somaliland: The Former British Colony that Shows Africa Doesn't Need Our Millions to Flourish" (Birrell 2011). One of the most eminent Western anthropologists of Somalia, Ioan Lewis, writes: "What a pity that in this extraordinary record of material and human destruction, none of the [international] policy leaders was able to recognize and follow the relatively successful experience of state building in the Republic of Somaliland" (Lewis 2009, 91). Aisha Ahmad (2012, n.p.) makes a similar comparison between Somalia and Somaliland:

While southern Somalia has burned in turmoil, the north has become an oasis of security, reconciliation, and cooperation. Why have the north and south experienced such different results? "We were very fortunate," explained Minister of Finance and former Somali National Movement leader Mohamed Hashi Elmi. "Somaliland was without international interference. Freedom from foreigners caused our success." . . . As the chairman of the ruling Kulmiye party and former Somali National Movement fighter Muse Bihi said, "Our unique success was because we had no interference."

This latter quote reiterates points made previously about the lack of external intervention during Somaliland's formational years. It is presented here to underscore the consistency with which this narrative is offered to—and reflected by—foreign researchers (myself included). There is, of course, empirical validity to it, but the consistency of its presentation warrants analysis. Is it only consistent because it is true? As discussed previously, discourses have truth-effects but do not reveal unmediated facts about the social world that would be accepted as either ideologically neutral or common sense in all places at all times. There is human agency and purpose entailed in how Somaliland's independence is articulated to external observers. One of these purposes is to build international support for the recognition of Somaliland's independence from Somalia.

Within Somaliland, there is studious attention paid to the international coverage that the country receives. Local media agencies tend to hastily republish even the most obscure publications that mention the country. There is also a high level of knowledge among the Hargeysa elite about what is being said about Somaliland in the international media and academic spaces. In 2013, the government hired an international lobbying and communications company (Glover Park Group) for $22,500 per month to help disseminate messages in favor of Somaliland's formal independence (Palmer and Tau 2013).[36] This is a considerable sum when one considers that the entire budget for that year was only $125 million.

The extraordinary generosity and patience of Somalilanders in speaking with foreign researchers (many of whom—myself included—invariably ask some very similar questions) also points, at least in part, to a broader desire to articulate the legitimacy of Somaliland's independence to an international audience. There may also be sanctions applied to those who do appear to deviate from the broad tenets of the independence discourse. In 2012, the government closed down the private television station, Horn Cable TV, and arrested eight of its journalists for broadcasting reports about clan meetings in the contested district of Sool, where participants declared the independence of Sool from Somaliland. President Silayno blamed the station for promoting the division of Somaliland, calling it a "national destructor" in a speech to Parliament (Thanki 2012). In 2015, members of one of Somaliland's most popular bands were arrested at Hargeysa airport for allegedly waving a Somali flag during a concert they played in Mogadishu (BBC 2015).

Anthropologist Markus Hoehne laments that during his fieldwork he was labelled *Somaliland-diid*—someone who rejects Somaliland, who is anti-Somalilander—by some in Hargeysa because he became seen as a spokesperson for Dhulbuhante clan views (Hoehne 2015, 11), which was presumably taken to suggest that he opposed Somaliland's claim of independence. His book, *Between Somaliland and Puntland*, opens with a lengthy discussion "stating that I am biased" where he outlines his scholarly and personal reasons for deviating from the "'Hargeysa point of view' [that] has, as far as I can see, dominated the academic output concerning Somaliland and northern Somalia in general" (9–12). His apparent concern in doing so is suggestive about what may be at stake in being seen to diverge from the point of view that is so widely reiterated within Hargeysa's elite circles. As is true of anywhere, and whether they are aware of it or not, foreign researchers navigate issues of access when they interpret and publish information that they gather during fieldwork. Being seen to question the legitimacy or viability of Somaliland's independence trespasses against the foundations of the independence discourse and potentially puts researchers at risk of being seen as being ideologically biased or untrustworthy by their interlocutors. This may also be seen as a betrayal of those who generously gave their time to be interviewed by the researcher.

President Egal argued in 1999 that if Somaliland wanted to achieve international recognition, it was vital that it begin to conform to Western norms of good governance by transitioning to a multiparty political system (Bradbury, Abokor and Yusuf 2003, 463) with universal suffrage. This change came into effect when the country's constitution was approved by referendum in 2001, and the ICG noted shortly afterwards that the change did indeed increase the level of international attention that Somaliland received (ICG 2003, 7). Egal understood the premium that Western donors place on governance models that resemble their own, but by realigning Somaliland's domestic politics in this way, he also changed the degree to which the country looked beyond its borders for solutions to internal issues. To an extent this is inevitable in a globalized world, but it signaled a more outward-looking tone to Somaliland's political dynamics where, in sharp contrast to its formative years, external legitimacy became a driver of domestic political discourses. An indication of that outward shift is in the Constitution itself, which states: "the Republic of Somaliland shall oppose terrorism (and similar acts), regardless of the motives for such acts" (Article 10:7). This article is singled out as an "achievement" in the Somaliland Government's Recognition Campaign website (Government of Somaliland n.d.). President Dahir Rayale Kahin also highlighted it in a 2008 interview where he discussed Somaliland's normative claims to sovereignty: "We're also trying our best to fight the terror—We're the only Muslim country that has that in the constitution. . . .

If the elections are held and are perceived as legitimate and fair, that will be a major step toward recognition" (cited in Reerink 2008). President Rayale's interview aligned Somaliland's quest for formal independence from Somalia with two issues that are emotive for a Western audience: terrorism and elections.

On one hand, therefore, the independence discourse subverts the fragile states discourse about the role and desirability of international intervention in establishing and maintaining civil order in the Global South. On the other hand, by so purposefully highlighting Somaliland's transition to multiparty electoral democracy and its commitment to counterterrorism and counterpiracy, the discourse actively and quite skillfully inhabits some of the normative content of the fragile states discourse about the modes of governance that states should aspire to (Mahmood, 2005, 22).[37] It does so, however, to achieve the "self-directed goal" of formal independence (172) and is, as such, an expression of agency rather than an act of passivity. In this sense, it is redeploying the internationally dominant discourse about fragile statehood in the expectation of achieving other gains in exchange for that stance. At the same time, it challenges that discourse by claiming that Somalilanders do not need external financial assistance and, in fact, got to where they are today because they did not receive it.

Despite this, the ability of Somalilanders to thrive in the absence of recognition and external finance is sometimes paradoxically used as a justification for Somaliland to now receive both. The logic appears to be that if international recognition is warranted (at least partially on the basis of Somalilanders' inherent ability to maintain peace and order), there is no basis for Somaliland to be treated differently to other states—particularly when others have achieved much less with much more external assistance.

Hostages to Peace

The independence discourse expresses a deep cognizance of Somaliland's proximity, both historical and structural, to the violence that continued to immerse much of the rest of Somalia long after war ended in Somaliland. Peace is widely framed as being maintained through the fear of war, and war and peace are implicitly cast as mutually constitutive rather than as binary opposites. As one local analyst explained in a documentary about the peace process: "What gives advantage to Somaliland is that they have touched the bottom of hell" (Responding to Conflict 2010).[38] This point conjures Ole Wæver's (1996) point about the establishment of the European Union. He argues that the EU was not created to differentiate itself from an external or geographically different other but from a fear of returning to its own violent past: "Europe's Other is Europe's own past which should not be allowed to become its future" (Wæver 1996, 122; see also Hansen 2006, 46). Somaliland too invokes a temporal other to credibly maintain the notion that just as peace flows out of war, so might that tide reverse. There is an implied continuity of war and peace within the Somaliland identity, rather than a peaceful iden-tity simply being a negation of a war identity. As a result, the discourse dif-ferentiates Somalilanders from two others: Somalis more broadly, and that of their own violent recent past, which still threatens to re-emerge if not ac-tively kept at bay by the affirmations of peace that Somalilanders make in their daily lives.[39]

The effects of the independence discourse on practice in this regard are evident in Somalilanders' apparent collective caution in protesting unpopu-lar political decisions, which is widely referred to by Somalilanders as being held hostage to peace (Human Rights Watch 2009; see also Bryden 2003, 363; Stremlau 2013).[40] This phrase is so common that when Human Rights Watch published a report on the status of Somaliland's democratic institutions in 2009, it used the phrase "Hostages to Peace" as its title. The interview-based report cited a member of parliament for the opposition who lamented that Somalilanders were disinclined to oppose constrictions of political space for fear that doing so would threaten the peace: "We have avoided fighting too much about all of these issues for the security of the country. This country is hostage to peace" (Human Rights Watch 2009, 48). The report noted that "many Somalilanders" refer to themselves as hostages because they are "so desperate to avoid the risk of instability that they look the other way even when their rights have been infringed" (15). The report argues that this de-sire to prevent instability is so widespread that it "often preclude[s] any kind of effective opposition," and that a hallmark of Somaliland's politics is that "as always . . . all of the key actors quickly [move] towards compromise rather than risk an open confrontation that could threaten Somaliland's stability" (15 and 48 respectively). In emphasizing the idea of being held hostage—a concept brimming with potential violence—the maintenance of peace is framed as bearing the seeds of its own demise by existing in a tense equilibrium with its other: war.

In a report by another international organization (the International Crisis Group—ICG), a civil society leader was quoted making a similar observation about the desire for peace several years later: "the . . . population doesn't care who becomes president. . . . As long as there is peace, they don't care" (cited in ICG 2015, 7). Like Human Rights Watch, the ICG concluded: "Somaliland's institutions incline toward preserving stability rather than upholding the rule of law or constitutionality, and the public, for the most part, seems to support this" (ICG 2015, 7).

The dialectic relationship between war and peace is a theme in many of Somaliland's most celebrated poetic works. Its poets are widely credited as having been "one of the main channels" that persuaded militia leaders to accept disarmament in the 1990s (Kaariye 2016). However, while poetry plays an important role in calling for peaceful mediation, it is also used to urge people to war, the possibility of which is understood to intensify the pressure for effective mediation (Cabdillaahi 2009, 123; 154). In his anthology of Somali literature, simply titled *War and Peace*, Rashiid Sheekh Cabdillaahi implies that war cannot be contained to one side of a war/peace binary. This is because the threat of war is so consciously used to compel people to make peace that the two must be seen as existing in equilibrium. Analyzing Faraax Nuur's famous poem "Giving Each Other Up," (Nuur n.d., cited in Cabdillaahi 2009, 154–55) Cabdillaahi suggests that the line "The peace which has been agreed on at this time will not work" highlights the level of choice inherent to the maintenance of peace. He writes: "Peace is therefore something which is desired in its own right, and this inherent desire is a dynamic force which mobilizes the strength to ultimately bring it about by whatever ways or means possible, even if that means through war" (Cabdillaahi 2009, 123).

Such ambiguities surrounding the boundaries between war and peace are not particular to Somalia, though they are seldom the subject of investigation. Tarak Barkawi (2016, 202) argues, for example, that ambiguous boundaries are common to most experiences of conflict outside (though, really even within) major European wars: "war shades into coercion when violence is not reciprocated. A short step further and violence sublimates into the coercive threat behind lawful governance" (205). If Somaliland is not idiosyncratic in this, then its experiences offer insights beyond its borders. What is more unusual in the Somaliland case is that it has so explicitly mobilized a reasonably common experience of war's ambiguities in a way that delegitimizes violence. Though even that can be seen elsewhere too.

In Yemeni tribal conflicts, the goal is generally less to vanquish an opponent than to employ symbolic violence in defense of one's position from which to negotiate a solution where both sides retain honor. For this reason, the number of casualties caused by tribal conflicts is usually dramatically less than the amount of firepower used might lead one to expect (Phillips 2011, 128; Caton 1990, 12). Drawing on the philosophy of Henri Bergson, Steven Caton extends on this in his in observations of poetry in Yemeni tribal mediation practices. He argues that the ambiguity and uncertainty over when violence may begin and end is a necessary condition of the mediation process, "for it is this ambiguity that allows room for maneuvering and pressure by all the parties in the dispute" (Caton 2014, 243). It is not the case, Caton remarks, "that violence begins and mediation stops or vice versa . . . but rather that they co-endure" (247). This ambiguity is important for Somaliland's independence discourse because it too rests on an acute sensitivity to the velocity of war and the ease with which peace may give way to war, which is then used to discursively reiterate the responsibility of Somalilanders to ensure that peace remains in the ascendant.

Noah Coburn's anthropological study of a relatively violence-free town in Afghanistan also offers insights into the ways that war's ambiguities can dampen the likelihood of violence. He argues that in modern democratic systems:

> What generates stability is the fact that competition is regulated by the shared understanding of members of society that, while they may be defeated on one political issue, the system guarantees them the ability to return the next day and compete for other resources. (Coburn 2011, 216)

Since no such guarantees exist in Afghanistan, Coburn suggests that stakeholders may perceive that the outcomes of violence are unpredictable, which increases not only its potential rewards but also its potential costs. As a result, violence can lose its appeal as a political strategy (Coburn 2011, 219). Coburn uses this insight to show how the town's powerbrokers engaged in what he refers to as "masterly inactivity," where they sought to preserve their power precisely by going out of their way to avoid the appearance of doing anything that could upset the town's delicate political balance, even if that meant missing out on economic benefits or development projects (146). In being willing to forgo the possible benefits of potentially destabilizing activity, Coburn's masterly inactivity resonates with Somaliland's narrative about being held hostage to peace.

Anthropologist Sami Hermez discusses the role of war memories in constraining violence in postwar Lebanon. He credits the country's uneasy peace to what he refers to as the policy of "no victor no vanquished," wherein "politicians announce that any act destabilizing the status quo, their power, or the current structure of power sharing . . . will inevitably produce war" (Hermez 2017, 7). This has similarities to the hostages to peace narrative in Somaliland because both mobilize beliefs and memories about the dangers of violence to dissuade its re-emergence in the future, legitimizing a status quo that might otherwise not endure. Both express powerful ideas that constrain the possibilities for seeking either justice (in Lebanon) or inclusive development (in Somaliland). They differ, however, in that "no victor no vanquished" asks people to act as if they have *forgotten* the grievances and victimhood that they suffered during the war. This is an act of power by the war's protagonists because so many were in fact vanquished and being required to act as if they were not for the sake of peace appears to have sharpened grievances (Hermez 2017, 182). As Hermez notes, the politics of "No Victor No Vanquished" has meant that small moments of anger can tap deep roots of resentment, leading quickly to violence. The notion of Somalilanders as hostages to peace on the other hand, has people *remembering* war—a different, though related, act of power by the war's participants. Somalilanders are reminded of war and its consequences by the ongoing violence elsewhere in Somalia from which they stridently differentiate themselves and by the widely articulated view that it is only their actions as Somalilanders that prevented—and can continue to prevent—violence from subsuming them again. In both narratives, however, the challenge to prevailing power hierarchies is framed as being against the interests of both the individual and society while also justifying considerable sacrifices (justice in Lebanon and inclusive development in Somaliland).

The Independence Discourse and the Danger of Violence

This discussion of the independence discourse has suggested that the relationship between strong rule-based institutions and violence levels is not necessarily inversely proportional. Rather, it is mediated by the complex interactions of learning agents within (and beyond) the institutional framework. Thus, the 2003 presidential election was resolved peacefully despite its obviously questionable results (and the capacity of the aggrieved party to have violently sought redress), piracy has not emerged as a significant issue within the parts of Somaliland that produce the independence discourse, and a reasonably strong sense of public security is widely perceived despite people's awareness that the police and armed forces cannot provide a robust guarantee of that security.

In Somaliland, political competitors and their followers were scarred by years of violence and deeply conscious of the consequences of potentially jeopardizing the peace that had been achieved through recourse to politically motivated violence—as indicated by the wide refrain of being hostages to peace. This chapter has argued that the country's peace and relative stability have not been the products of state institutions or even the clan-based institutions that can provide many of their functional equivalents. Rather, they are products of local power being precariously—and perhaps only temporarily (Coburn 2011, 217)—balanced between potential competitors who participate in a discourse that foregrounds the notion that peace can unravel quickly and beyond the control of any protagonist. The cognizance that war and peace exist alongside and in tension with one another is interwoven in the discourse, as is the knowledge that one may intensify quickly as the other recedes. The ambiguity over the manner in which that intensification might occur has embedded political mobilization with caution.

War played a role in the centralization of power in Somaliland, but not in the way that Charles Tilly's argument for the state-making function of war in Europe might suggest (1975; 1990).[41] For Tilly, and other historical sociologists (see Evans, Rueschemeyer, and Skocpol 1985; Elias 1993/1994; Porter 1994), the effort required to fight wars against external enemies fostered the capacity of state institutions to extract and centrally administer revenue, and to more effectively discipline a civilian population. The impact of Somaliland's wars in the 1990s—though still critical to the type of political arrangements that emerged—was more ideational than technical.

Somaliland's wars did not give rise to the effective bureaucracy that Tilly describes in the European experience, although they do appear to have driven the elite economic collusion and monopolies that both he, and Norbert Elias before him, discuss (1939/1982, 320–329). Rather than building the capacity for either military adventurism or protection from external forces, the primary aim for Somaliland's elites (and the public more broadly) at the end of the war was to avoid the type of violence that it had just experienced and that continued to consume much of the rest of Somalia. For Somalilanders, the threat of violence was less from an external invasion than an internal combustion, which has had a profound impact on the discursive retelling of the national identity and historical experience, in which violence is understood to be dangerously uncontrollable (and thus nonlinear and unpredictable) once employed. Protection from violence was viewed as an internal matter, and if local actors had employed violence in the recent past it was believed that they could do so again with little warning (see Coburn 2011, 219). The country's peace and relative stability are not merely the products of formal state institutions, or even the structures, rules, or informal guarantees provided by the clans, but rather the discursive naturalization of the historically grounded sense that peace can subside quickly and beyond the control of anyone.

CONCLUSION

Why Aid Matters Less than We Think

Lest there be ambiguity, I begin this chapter by clarifying its title: "Why Aid Matters Less than We Think." This book was not conceived as another contribution to the anti-aid list, but neither was it intended to help reform a fixable system by making external development assistance, in its many variations, function more efficiently.[1] My argument has been that making such assistance the central issue is to ask the wrong question. It is a distraction. It keeps the focus on how external actors can intervene smarter while failing to honestly interrogate the things about the world that make intervention seem necessary in the first place. It is a question that whitewashes power asymmetries and, by that sleight of hand, facilitates their endurance. Aid matters less than we think it does because it is does not alter the asymmetries that make it difficult for countries in the Global South to extract themselves from violence and poverty (Engel 2014, 1385). In fact, it expresses those asymmetries. As long as the fragile states discourse provides the dominant framework for understanding violence and poverty in the south, exploring the levers for change that exist in the north will remain an illogical, and generally unthinkable, first step.

Then-US secretary of state Hillary Clinton articulated how the responsibility for global harm (and repair) is constructed in the fragile states discourse when she responded to strong Pakistani opposition to an American aid package in 2009:

> For the United States Congress to pass a bill unanimously saying that we want to give $7.5 billion to Pakistan in a time of global recession when we have a 10 percent unemployment rate, and then for [the] Pakistani press and others to say we don't want that, that's insulting—I mean, it was shocking to us. So clearly, there is a failure to communicate effectively." (cited in Nadim, 2019)

A US Congressional Research Service (CRS) report referred to a "representatively rancorous statement" by a Pakistani commentator, who called the bill "less an assistance program than a treaty of surrender" (CRS 2013, 18). To Secretary Clinton, the reason that many Pakistanis opposed the package (which tripled nonmilitary aid) was that the US had failed to communicate its benefits effectively. This implies that the problem was technical and that finessing a communication strategy would make it acceptable. But Pakistani concerns were about the power asymmetries they saw nested within the bill: that it called for democracy despite America's overwhelming historical support for Pakistan's military dictators; that it meddled in (and expected oversight of) sensitive internal politics; that it seemed either oblivious to, or unconcerned by, the fact that it was picking sides in a partisan struggle between the civilian government and the military; that it expected Pakistan to shoulder the burden of what many saw as America's war in Afghanistan; and that it essentially blamed Pakistan's military for al-Qa'ida's endurance (CRS 2013; Nadim 2019). But it was also about the level of change that the US suggested could be achieved in a sovereign state for just $8 per person, per year (for five years), which was decried as "peanuts" (Rafique 2011, 278).

For Clinton, the issue was to better explain the political, social, and economic changes that the bill intended to support. Within Pakistan, however, the bill could not be disentangled from the way that powerful states both pick sides in domestic conflicts and assign blame for global harm regardless of historical context. Clinton's remarks, which were indicative of the US government's position, foreclosed the possibility that northern actors have a responsibility to do other than to craft better interventions to fix the problems in Pakistan. Her presumption that America's aid package was so benevolent that opposition to it was insulting illustrates the naturalization of intervention as the only appropriate response to violence and poverty.

The fragile states discourse offers a story about how to transform the dysfunctional political arrangements that appear to keep so many countries in the Global South poor and at greater risk of violent conflict. As chapter 1 illustrated, it is myopically domestic in its vision of what drives conflict and developmental malaise in the states that it targets. Comparing Somaliland's relative isolation from the international system to Somalia's deep entanglement in it, this book has attempted to situate those domestic factors within the wider power relationships between donor and target states, in which official development assistance—aid—is but one aspect of many. As a result, external peace-building, state-building, and development interventions may be quite peripheral to the ability of a society to find either peace or prosperity for reasons that lie, to a significant degree, beyond the state in question.

The fragile states discourse attempts to solve a problem. It takes the world as it is and seeks to reform it within the confines of its existing structures (Cox 1980). If one accepts its logic then conventional peace/state-building and development interventions appear to be necessary and inevitable for reversing the problem of fragility that it describes (DFAT 2005, 7). The inevitability that the discourse constructs helps to explain why such interventions remain so overwhelmingly prescribed despite their well-documented failures. If, on the other hand, one applies a more critical stance, fragility is less a problem to be solved than a construction held in place by power relations. This stance requires one to interrogate how those relationships were established and what permits them to endure (Cox 1980, 129) to reveal that global politics could be different to how they appear today.

As Somaliland's early years are the closest we have to a counterfactual case of nonintervention in fragile states, its experience offers important avenues for exploring how intervened upon states might look outside the fragile states discourse. First, the lack of intervention left clear imprints on the trajectory of Somaliland's political economy. Its key stakeholders were unable to access external advantage and were thus mutually dependent for their ability to survive and prosper. This appears to have limited the perceived likely benefits of large-scale predation and violence—or at least, this is how it is widely recalled. The self-reliance that Somaliland's early autonomy nurtured also features heavily in the way that the independence discourse frames the country's peacefulness as being a function of Somalilanders' true nature, which could be expressed because they had autonomy.

Second, Somaliland's independence discourse presents an alternative lens through which to see the impact of external intervention on the process of state formation and postconflict reconstruction more broadly. Whereas the fragile states discourse takes state/state-like governance institutions as a universal point of origin for developmental change, Somaliland's independence discourse illustrates the pivotal role of context and identity within institutions. They are so pivotal, in fact, that even Somalilanders' lack of confidence in the ability of their institutions to reliably constrain large-scale violence helps to limit political violence by framing violence as a self-defeating and thus illogical act. Mobilizing for political violence not only risks revisiting the trauma of war but also dissolves the difference that the discourse constructs between peaceful Somalilanders and nonpeaceful Somali others. Much of the legal and moral justification for an independent Republic of Somaliland rests upon this construction.

Somaliland's experience contradicts another core assumption of the fragile states discourse: that ineffective governance institutions cause violence. It shows that peace can be sustained not only when but even partly because governance institutions are incapable of reliably enforcing constraints to large-scale violence. In Somaliland, there were no enforceable sanctions to large-scale violent action, and yet, as was clearly articulated in the defused standoff over the 2003 presidential election, the understanding expressed by the key political stakeholders and their constituencies was that violence posed too great a risk to be a viable political strategy. The political arrangements that resulted from the traumatic experience of war were based on the notion that the maintenance of peace outweighed all other political and economic matters. This placed an apparent ceiling on the prospects for more inclusive development, as the widely-used characterization of Somalilanders as hostages to peace suggests, but the bargain is still generally seen as preferable to the likely perceived alternative of renewed civil war, the possibility of which remains ever present.

Somaliland's discourse about independence also challenges the war/peace binary that structures Eurocentric thinking about large-scale violence

(Barkawi 2016) and, as a result, the ways that postconflict reconstruction is typically pursued by northern actors. The discourse illuminates how the absence of war is sustained by its presence through its representation of the precarious balance between war and peace. The precarity of this balance also reminds us of its inherent sensitivity to external intervention.

Influence beyond Aid

The fragile states discourse constructs a world where the responsibility for harm is, for the most part, domestically bounded. Even if we exclude the corrosive ramifications of historical colonialism, the global factors that sit outside its diagnostic frame include: the international borrowing privileges granted to sovereign governments and the often-crippling debt repayments associated with this long after; that the rates of global credit to southern states are governed by conditions in northern states (DiGiuseppe, Barry, and Frank 2012); the illicit flight of capital from south to north through widespread transfer mispricing and trade misinvoicing practices used by large international corporations (to the extent that Africa may be a net creditor to the rest of the world—see Ndikumana and Boyce 2011; Kar 2016; Eurodad 2014); the prevalence of strategic and resource rents in the global political economy that delivers funding to sovereign governments and partially obviates the need for them to extract money directly from the population; the protectionist policies of wealthy states that deny a level playing field to newer entrants to the market; the vastly disproportionate voting rights maintained by several wealthy northern states in the World Bank, IMF, and World Trade Organization; the ready availability of sophisticated weaponry to repressive governments; and the dominant discourse about what states should look like, which presupposes that governance institutions can and should be strengthened with external assistance as the most expeditious path to security and development.

These external matters are integral to the formation and evolution of the political arrangements in the states that external peace/state-building actors target. Nevertheless, the fragile states discourse has bracketed them out of its conception of what drives in/security and under/development in the Global South. Its focus remains squarely on the capacity of domestic state (or state-like) governance institutions to deliver political and economic services to citizens and on the kinds of internal changes that may be required to improve such delivery.

Against a background of global power inequalities, domestic problems may appear as relatively low-hanging fruit—and the fragile states discourse encourages a focus on these. Through the lens of state fragility domestic problems appear more tangible, measurable, and malleable than those that exist outside of this sphere. This is partly because if interveners attempted to engage directly with the complex linkages between transnational and national structures of power and wealth, the assumption that state fragility or failure is a symptom of only domestic configurations quickly becomes untenable. And if that becomes untenable so too may the organizations whose mandates are to reform those domestic configurations.

A key practical implication of this book is, therefore, that external actors who wish to foment significant societal change cannot expect to do so when only domestic issues are on the table. This requires, at a start, a critical reckoning with the ways in which practices at home are implicated in the political arrangements abroad that these actors seek to transform. Of course, even the major development agencies may, quite reasonably, cite their lack of purchase on entrenched global power asymmetries, all of which exist well beyond their organizational mandate of intervention, or alternatively providing expertise on intervention (Lemay-Hébert and Mathieu 2014, 242). Development organizations are structured and funded to provide development programs; state-building organizations provide institutional capacity-building programs; and peace-building facilitate dialogue and provide technical assistance programs. They do not challenge extractive industry contracts, rewrite global trade policy, forgive debt, campaign for the payment of reparations by colonial powers, chase transnational tax evaders, or confront the global arms trade. Most of this, of course, sounds ridiculous because these tasks sit so far outside the activities that they are structured and funded to perform. Their task is, at least at first glance, more modest: to reform an imperfect system under which (usually) northern actors intervene in southern states to alter their institutional settings and, ostensibly, their developmental trajectories. But in helping to make this appear the more modest task, they construct the necessity of their actions.

The Necessary Fiction of Neo-Weberian Statehood

The practice of intervention in fragile states rests on a necessary fiction: that states are held together—or torn apart—by the quality of their domestic governance institutions. This is fiction, first, because it disregards the global context in which violence is exercised and the role that powerful states, corporations, and international institutions can play in the destruction of social and political fabrics (Goetze 2016, 143–44). Second, it is well known that states do not always seek to strengthen their institutions, monopolize violence, make and enforce binding rules, or collect tax, and that the institutions that interveners seek to empower are often those that citizens see as self-serving and predatory (Kabamba 2012; Akhtar and Ahmed 2015; Perera 2017b). The establishment of institutions that monopolize legitimate violence is not something that is universally seen as optimal for managing state-society relations (Phillips 2017; 2019a).

Despite this, the empowerment of rational-legal state institutions is portrayed in the fragile states discourse as a prerequisite for any society's transition from violence or poverty. Chapter 2 illustrated how in Somalia in the early 1990s the UN played local actors against one another in an apparent attempt to centralize peace-making efforts under its own auspices and preserve the unitary state of Somalia, with Mogadishu as its capital (Renders 2012, 119, 123). To most Somalilanders, whose local peace conferences were actively disrupted by the UN in this process, it seemed that the international community had inexplicably prioritized its attempt to salvage predatory state structures over the creation of durable peace.

The protection of predatory state structures and actors is not confined to Somalia and can be seen even where northern intelligence agencies suspect states of facilitating international security threats. In Yemen, for example, the international community delivered massive amounts of money, weapons, and international legitimacy to the regime of President Ali Abdullah Saleh from 2006 until Saleh was forced from office in late 2011 by the protest movement. These goods were ostensibly given to aid in the fight against al-Qa'ida but were offered despite widespread allegations by Yemenis that the regime was actively facilitating al-Qa'ida fighters in an effort to maintain its own power. As the antiregime protests built throughout 2011, local activists become more outspoken with these allegations—allegations that chimed with those made by American diplomats in classified cables (Miller 2011). Despite this, the

United States vocally committed itself to supporting the Saleh regime as "the best [counter-terrorism] partner we're going to have . . . [which will hopefully] survive because I certainly would hate to start over again in what we've tried to build" (deputy assistant secretary of defense for special operations and combating terrorism, Garry Reid, cited in Phillips 2011, 140).

The neo-Weberian state is thus not only a fiction constructed by the fragile states discourse,[2] but it is a *necessary* fiction because without it, external intervention ceases to be inevitably useful. Without the narrative of the nascent neo-Weberian state that will, once fully established, decrease global security threats and reduce its citizens' vulnerability to harm, there is considerably less for interveners to construct. This fiction therefore offers an otherwise absent coherence to mainstream peace/state-building, development, and stabilization interventions. Intervention is perpetuated because it relies on the assumptions of its own necessity.

The self-evident usefulness of international intervention in situations defined as fragile also requires an ontology of global politics where domestic and international spheres are, more or less, divisible. However, one of the primary insights of postcolonial scholars is the mutual constitution of the West and non-West, colonizer and colonized, where each are products of their interactions and imaginings of the other (Said 1978; Sabaratnam 2017, 30). Global politics cannot be disentangled from their domestic manifestations.

Particular or Generalizable?

Somaliland's experience is not replicable by transporting the state or clan institutions that helped to establish peace to other contexts, such as the open-ended nature of the clan conferences or the establishment of other new institutions like the *Guurti*. Neither would this be possible by simply following the lack of intervention to its logical conclusion by withdrawing all external funding and political support to other postconflict states. This would be to misunderstand the constitutive nature of institutions and the discourses that give them meaning.

In one sense, Somaliland's experience of ending organized political violence is idiosyncratic. The country's level of detachment from most of the usual international systems and processes stands it alone in a number of respects. For this reason, some country-specialists have been reticent to draw too many wider lessons from Somaliland's experience. In his review of Michael Walls's 2014 book, *A Somali Nation-State*, Markus Hoehne critiques Walls for suggesting that Somaliland "offers real lessons beyond its borders" (cited in Hoehne 2016, 127). Hoehne argues instead that one of the key "factors that decisively limit[s] the scope of the lessons that can be learned from" Somaliland's experience is:

> the political identity of Somalilanders (prevalent in the capital and the central regions) developed against the backdrop of Somalia's continued failure. *At moments of crisis, the desire not to become "like Mogadishu" kept ordinary people in Somaliland motivated to carry on and to pressure their political elites to stay on course.* This background cannot be replicated and therefore limits what can be learned from Somaliland for other cases; it makes Somaliland *sui generis* (Hoehne 2016, 127—emphasis added).

However, the sui generis argument only holds if one is seeking a blueprint from which to engineer specific outcomes. Such an attempt upholds the presumption of the fragile states discourse that governance institutions, as tangible things out there in the world, are the engine of political life. If we turn this around to see institutions as constitutive of ideas, identities, and discourses then, far from excluding Somaliland from offering lessons, its idiosyncrasies may indeed serve as a basis for them. In Somaliland, we have an unusually clear case of the indivisibility of civil order and popular discourses about civil order, to the extent that the independence discourse quite clearly limits the circumstances that violence would be seen as a logical response to a political grievance.

Moreover, Somalilanders' fear of becoming like Mogadishu helps to limit the possibilities under which violence makes sense in ways that resonate elsewhere too. As the examples from Yemen, Afghanistan, and Lebanon suggest, people recall proximate violence in how they understand the likely consequences of further political violence, which can make it seem illogical—if it is even considered at all.

What happened in Somaliland may not predict developments elsewhere—a remark that may be disappointing to those seeking to reproduce its relatively positive trajectory. However, this does not mean the underlying drivers of its trajectory do not have broader relevance. Within Somaliland's independence discourse we glimpse ways in which uncertainty and institutional weakness can take on meanings that help to support the maintenance of political order. Being built on a discursive foregrounding of its own susceptibility to instability, violence, and war, these mechanisms are deeply self-referential. Stability is a function of readily shiftable ideas about what stability means. The ideas underlying political order shift all the faster when external actors intervene to reduce the cost of violence for local actors by offering political, economic, or military support.

Just as importantly, the relative absence of violence does not make violence impossible. In fact, because violence is framed as inimical to that which makes Somaliland worthy of formal independence from Somalia, violence is always present. The independence discourse expresses the mutual constitution of war and peace and, in affirming the precariousness of peace, appears to have contributed to its endurance. Neither of these factors are a function of evolutionary or linear processes. Nor are they (only) products of competition over material resources, political or economic disempowerment, or the rational decision making of game theoretic models (Coburn 2011, 218). Rather, in displaying an awareness of, and deep sensitivity to the tenuousness of its own foundations, the independence discourse has harnessed an apparent propensity to disorder as a source of order. It has done so in a way that the fragile states discourse, and the international interventions that enact it, can neither process nor replicate.

NOTES

Introduction

1. For variations on these notions set out by other foreign researchers, see Karl Sandstrom (2013, 122–23), who writes: "The legitimacy of the state institutions appears to be mainly based on a shared wish for it to succeed on some level rather than actual capacity and their real influence. . . . There appears to be no real national plan beyond peace and recognition." Mark Bradbury notes in the conclusion to his widely-cited book that "it is debatable where the real source of [Somaliland's] security and rule of law lies, but given the poverty of the security forces and the judicial system, an argument can be made that law and order is really sustained by the citizens, rather than enforced by the government" (Bradbury 2008, 248–49).

2. Casualty figures are notoriously difficult to estimate due to the lack of reporting and investigation at the time. The World Peace Foundation (2015) at Tufts University discusses the various figures that are available and estimates that the number of civilians that died (1988–1993) as a direct result of violence was between 50,000 and 100,000. The victims of the famine can be viewed as a direct result of violence, which adds between 250,000 and 500,000 deaths to that toll.

3. The most influential scholar in this group is Charles Tilly (1975, 1985, 1990). Others prominent works include Porter 1994; Diamond 1999; Luttwak 1999; Bates 2001;

Cramer 2006; Niemann 2007; Taylor and Botea 2008; Keen 2008; North, Wallis and Weingast 2009; Giustozzi 2011; Morris 2014. Charles Tilly does not suggest that his argument about the state-building properties of war holds outside the European context or for contemporary state formation, and in fact quite he explicitly doubts that it does: "Contrary to the apparent teaching of European history, the growth of big government, arbitrary rule, and militarization now seem to be going hand in hand" (1990, 204). Writing on Somaliland specifically, Dominik Balthasar (2013, 219) argues that Somaliland's experience in the 1990s does point to the potential state-building properties of war in the contemporary era—a contention that is taken up further in chapter 2.

4. This body of work is also expansive. Important works include Herbst 1990; Kaldor 1999; Jung 2003; Reno 2001, 2004; Leander 2004; Ferguson 2006; Meagher 2012.

5. The online database maintained by the Uppsala Conflict Data Program (UCDP) shows that between 1997 and 2017 there were 226 casualties of conflict in Somaliland. There were, however, border skirmishes in mid-2018 that killed at least 100 people and that had not yet been included in the database.

6. The UCDP online database (https://www.pcr.uu.se/research/ucdp/) records 26,019 conflict casualties for all of Somalia during this period. The figure of 25,793 is the total when Somaliland's figures are removed.

7. These casualties have been the result of clashes between the Somaliland armed forces and either the Puntland State of Somalia or militias associated with the Khatumo administration in south-eastern Togdheer—that is, groups actively opposed to Somaliland's claim of independence. On the basis of their opposition to Somaliland's independence, these forces are considered by proindependence Somalilanders as external forces.

8. It is worth noting that I began this project intending to map the processes by which Somalilanders forged peace and to explore how these processes related to the absence of external intervention. The more people I spoke to, the clearer it became that the story that I had encountered in various forms in the literature about Somaliland's peace process had taken on a rarefied form, but that people were also acutely aware—indeed, fearful of—its precarity. As the research progressed, I focused in on this perceived precarity and what I came to understand as its role in sustaining civil order.

9. This has changed considerably over time, not only from Western donors, but also—and more significantly—from states like China, Turkey and, more recently, the United Arab Emirates. The long-awaited Somaliland Development Fund also came into effect in early 2014. Established through negotiations between the minister of planning and the British and Danish governments, it aims to provide money that is administered by an external fund manager, offering a channel through which the Somaliland government can apply for funds.

10. It is estimated that international actors have now spent more than $8 billion on state-building efforts in Somalia (Gettleman 2008).

11. Prominent works include: Anderson 1999; Duffield 2001; Chandler 2006; Easterly 2007; Riddell 2007; Moyo 2009; Suhrke 2011; Banerjee and Duflo 2011.

12. Somaliland declared its independence from the rest of Somalia in May 1991, and its constitution was approved by referendum in 2001. However, other lines could potentially be drawn for determining its key formational years. For example, peace was con-

solidated at the Hargeysa Conference that ended in early 1997. By 1999, President Egal was purposefully lobbying the international community to grant Somaliland sovereign recognition, and by 2002, the quest for self-determination had become a key theme of all election campaigns (Hoehne 2009, 265). I use 2001 to delimit its formational years because the approval of the constitution clearly marked Somaliland's pivot from a polity that was largely sustained by domestic sources of revenue and legitimacy to one that more explicitly sought revenue and legitimacy from external sources.

13. My Somali language skills barely pass the exchange of pleasantries, though my knowledge of Arabic was sometimes of use. I had a wonderful research assistant who translated where necessary. However, being focused largely on an urban elite sample—the limitations of which are noted—most of my interlocutors were conversant in English.

14. See also the open letter "A Collective Response to Dr. Markus Hoehne and the Somaliland Journal of African Studies" that was published on Facebook and has been signed by hundreds of Somali scholars.

15. Interview with senior researcher at an externally funded research institute. Hargeysa: March 24, 2013.

16. Interview with a former minister, Hargeysa: March 24, 2013. Somaliland now has six regions, not five. The newest region, Saaxil, covers Berbera city and is thus considered part of central (and predominantly Isaaq) Somaliland.

17. There are a number of reasons for this focus on Hargeysa beyond the usual tendency of researchers to congregate in capital cities for reasons of access and comfort. It has also become quite expensive for foreigners to lawfully leave Hargeysa. Government checkpoints surround the city, and foreigners are required to have at least one armed guard with them, which can be costly, as can the four-wheel drive car that is needed to reliably navigate roads that are either in serious disrepair or may flood with little notice.

18. These three chapters update and adapt some material from Phillips 2013.

1. The Imperative of Intervention

1. See, for example, Kaplan 2008; Pham 2012; Eubank 2012.

2. The Republic of Somalia was estimated to have an external debt of around US $4.6 billion to twenty-seven creditors at the end of 2017, though this did not include significant debts to a number of other bilateral and multilateral creditors (Somalia NGO Consortium 2018, 4–5).

3. See, for example, Rotberg 2004; Ghani and Lockhart 2008; Stewart and Brown 2009; Collier 2009; Acemoglu and Robinson 2012; Brock et al. 2012.

4. There has been a longstanding critique against describing states as either failed or fragile. Some relevant examples from a large body of work include Morton 2005; Hameiri 2007; Call 2008; Hagmann and Hoehne 2009; Nuruzzaman 2009; Eriksen 2011; Wai 2012; Grim, Lemay-Hébert, and Nay 2015.

5. For an analysis of the many different actors involved in attempting to categorize and measure state fragility, see Ferreira 2017.

6. For example, USAID 2005, 1; UNDP 2012, 16; Independent Commission for Aid Impact 2015, 1.

7. See Sachs 2005; DFID 2005; Doyle and Sambanis 2006; Collier 2008, 2009.

8. While many southern states reject the label of fragility, there are some, like Rwanda (Beswick 2013), Uganda (Fisher 2014), and the signatories to the g7+ *New Deal on Fragile States* (International Dialogue on Peacebuilding and Statebuilding 2011), that use it in self-reference and engage directly with donor programs on fragility. The official pilot states for the New Deal were Afghanistan, Central African Republic, Democratic Republic of the Congo (DRC), Liberia, Sierra Leone, South Sudan and Timor-Leste. Somalia, Comoros, Guinea-Bissau, and Togo subsequently agreed to implement the deal.

9. Skype interview with bureaucrat at Australia's Department of Foreign Affairs. Canberra, February 2013.

10. See, for example, the discussion of how international actors can alter domestic policy dynamics in World Bank (2017, 257–59), or the reference to the lack of success by "benevolent external architects" in IGC (2018, 8).

11. See, for example, Fanon 1963; Mudimbe 1988; Mbembe 2001; Gruffydd Jones 2013; Rutazibwa and Shilliam 2018.

12. Wai is referring specifically to Africa, but the point can be applied to other postcolonial contexts as well.

13. The report does not explicitly define "fragility." This definition is contextually inferred from how it is referred to throughout.

14. The literature on this point is expansive. Some prominent examples include Fearon and Laitin 2003; Paris 2004; Krasner 2004; Call and Cousens 2008; De Rouen et al. 2010; Gleditsch and Ruggeri 2010.

15. For a more recent version of this view, and one which illustrates how little it appears to change, see the International Growth Centre's *Commission on State Fragility, Growth and Development*: "Part of the explanation for the persistence of state fragility is thus that some polities have not yet built the institutional framework needed for effective and inclusive government" (IGC 2018, 8).

16. See also Boege et al. 2009; Renders and Terlinden 2010; Kibble and Walls 2010; Mac Ginty 2011; Meagher 2012; Bagayoko, Hutchful, and Luckham 2016; Colona and Jaffe 2016; Wallis et al. 2018.

17. These terms refer to two overlapping networks of (northern—predominantly US- and UK-based) development actors. See https://www.odi.org/sites/odi.org.uk/files /odi-assets/events-documents/5149.pdf and http://publications.dlprog.org/TWP.pdf.

18. Like state fragility, the issue of what precisely constitutes a political settlement is contested. I have also published a number of pieces that have used a political settlements framework as a means of organizing my analysis of domestic political arrangements and modes of legitimacy (Phillips 2011, 2013, 2016, 2017). These were funded by the Developmental Leadership Program, which receives funding from Australia's Department of Foreign Affairs and Trade (DFAT), and the UK's DFID.

19. There are some exceptions to the latter point, such as Tobias Hagmann (2016, 12) who noted in a piece funded by the Political Settlements Research Program that in the case of Somalia, "Local political settlements . . . cannot be studied independently of foreign actors and their agendas, because political rule in the country has been strongly internationalized."

20. See, for example, Sachs 1992; Hurrell and Woods 1999; Mudimbe 1998; Mamdani 2001; Pietrese 2002; Wade 2004; Ferguson 2006; Wai 2007; Held and Kaya 2007; Pogge 2010; Muppidi 2012; Dasandi 2014; Braithwaite et al. 2016; Hickel 2017.

21. See Dasandi (2014, 206–7) for quantitative analysis of structural international inequalities.

22. For arguments that illicit outflows dwarf aid inflows in southern states/regions, see Ndikumana and Boyce 2011; Kar and Freitas 2012; Eurodad 2014; GFI 2015, 2017. Maya Forstater (2015) argues, however, that these claims are overstated.

23. Grimmett and Kerr (2012) note that the lion's share of transfers is from the US: "In 2011, the United States ranked first in arms transfer agreements with developing nations with over $56.3 billion or 78.7% of these agreements, an extraordinary increase in market share from 2010, when the United States held a 43.6% market share. In second place was Russia with $4.1 billion or 5.7% of such agreements. In 2011, the United States ranked first in the value of arms deliveries to developing nations at $10.5 billion, or 37.6% of all such deliveries. Russia ranked second in these deliveries at $7.5 billion or 26.8%."

24. Between 2011 and 2015, the United States exported 33 percent of the world's arms. Russia exported 25 percent, while China exported 5.9 percent. France, Germany, and the United Kingdom exported 5.6, 4.7, and 4.5 percent, respectively (SIPRI 2016).

25. The US Government Accountability Office says of FMF that "under this procurement channel, the U.S. government buys the desired item on behalf of the foreign country . . . generally employing the same criteria as if the item were being procured for the U.S. military" (cited in Sharp 2016, 16).

26. The video is available at https://www.youtube.com/watch?feature=youtu.be&v=Snd6idHeGfg&app=desktop.

2. Somaliland's Relative Isolation

1. Interview with Somaliland government minister, Hargeysa, November 20, 2011.

2. When Somalia was a proxy state of the Soviet Union earlier in the 1970s, it generally received equipment (military and industrial) and assistance with large industrial and state farm projects rather than large amounts of foreign exchange. The swap to the US side therefore represented a very significant change (Simons 1995, 52).

3. The US ambassador to Somalia (1984–1987) reported that the USAID office had around three times the number of American staff than did the military assistance mission, and it was so powerful that it acted quite independently of the embassy (Bridges 2000, cited in Kapteijns 2013a, 94).

4. While January 1991 is usually cited as the point at which the Somali conflict began, this is only when the government collapsed and the nature of the conflict shifted. Somalia had experienced large-scale organized violence since the late 1980s, with the most obvious increase in opposition levels occurring when Siyad Barre was injured in a car accident in May 1986. After this time, the internal regime rivalries became more open and violent rebellion by various armed groups across the country increased.

5. UNITAF was preceded by UNOSOM I (June 1991–February 1992), which consisted primarily of a food airlift and a tiny UN peacekeeping mission (Kapteijns 2013b, 424).

6. Michael Walls (2014, 187–88) notes that the standing committee of the London Conference of Somaliland Intellectuals Abroad (April 1995) was charged with raising funds for peace-building delegations to travel to Somaliland and Ethiopia. The committee was initially only permitted to source funding from Somaliland diaspora communities but later gained $5,000 from the United Nations Development Programme (UNDP) in Ethiopia. A very small amount of assistance was also provided by a London-based NGO, and some in-kind support was offered by the governments of Ethiopia and Djibouti. In other words, external support was negligible.

7. Most of these have been boycotted by Somaliland.

8. The report states that "In October 2014, budget support from development partners totaled $87 million, compared with $82 million in domestic revenue."

9. Lewis is quoting and refuting the arguments of Catherine Besteman (1996).

10. See Kapteijns (2004, 1–4) and much of the commentary surrounding the #CadaanStudies movement.

11. Ioan Lewis points out that in Somalia, this does not necessarily preclude other "contracts of government" from functioning at the same time (Lewis 1961, 94).

12. Of course, one may add that this salience may be either driven or outweighed by the other hierarchies that Besteman (1996, 1998) documents.

13. The Isaaq is not always accepted as a clan family, and some maintain that the Isaaq is part of the Dir clan family.

14. Thanks to an anonymous reviewer for raising this point. See Kapteijns 2013a (particularly chapter 2) for a discussion of how clan identities were constructed and maintained during this period.

15. Interview, Hargeysa, November 26, 2012.

16. Interview, Hargeysa, November 20, 2011.

17. The north did experience a drought and famine in the mid-1970s, after which a considerable number of Somalilanders left to go abroad. It experienced another in 2017.

18. Ethiopia did provide a base and some logistical assistance for SNM fighters in between 1984 and 1988, until Ethiopia's President Mengistu signed a peace treaty with Siyad Barre in 1988 (Compagnon 1998, 80). From then it provided a sanctuary for refugees but almost no financial assistance, which caused the SNM to change tactics and attack Hargeysa and Borco, leading to the regime's devasting reprisal. The little external military assistance that the SNM did receive came from the People's Democratic Republic of Yemen (Bradbury 2008, 69).

19. Ingiriis (2016, 247) suggests that as many as 100,000 people may have been killed, though this is higher than the figure of around 50,000 that is usually proffered.

20. The UN's Food Security and Nutritional Analysis Unit (FSNAU) estimated in 2013 that remittances to all regions of prewar Somalia (that is, including Somaliland) amounted to at least $1.2 billion per year. Hagmann and Stepputat (2016, 11) note that remittances are received in much higher volumes in the north of Somalia. Indicative of the difficulty of compiling reliable data in Somalia, another UN agency, the UNDP

Somalia (2012, 25), estimated in 2012 that the total amount of remittances "could be as high as \$2.3 billion."

21. Contrary to popular perceptions, a 2012 survey by the UN's International Labour Organization (ILO) found that the largest employer in Somaliland is the sales and services sector (ILO 2012, ix) rather than the livestock sector.

22. The goal of (re)unification was never explicitly stated by UNOSOM II officials but, according to Gerard Prunier (1996, 64), was considered common knowledge throughout Somalia.

23. UNOSOM's head of political affairs, Leonard Kumango, eventually warned Somaliland's President Egal that he could deploy militarily in Somaliland without Egal's consent. Egal warned Kumango that Hargeysa "would become the United Nations' Dien Bien Phu" and gave UNOSOM 24 hours to leave Somaliland (Renders 2012, 122).

24. Although Puntland actively disputes the border in the east, disputed borders do not necessarily undermine a claim to statehood under international law, as the cases of Israel and Palestine, and India and Pakistan, among others, illustrate.

25. These passports are not widely accepted, though the list of countries that will accept it as a valid travel document is slowly increasing. The Somaliland Government's Recognition Campaign claims on its website that "people have travelled with the Somaliland passport to South Africa, Kenya, Djibouti and Ethiopia, Uganda, UK, Sweden, USA." (Government of Somaliland n.d.). This phrasing implies that its holders are not automatically granted entry with this passport, however. In 2018, the United Arab Emirates also announced that would accept the Somaliland passport.

26. The majority of funds are extracted through customs duties rather than on production.

27. Its ability to do so is dwarfed by that of the private sector, however.

28. President Dahir Rayale Kahin was from the Gadabursi clan.

29. Ismail's paper cites other examples from within Africa as evidence of withdrawal from voluntary unions (Senegal and Mali—1960; Rwanda and Burundi—1962; Cape Verde and Guinea-Bissau—1975), though each of these were cases of immediate postindependence withdrawal from colonial entities rather than withdrawal from longstanding post-colonial entities as was the case with Somalia/Somaliland.

30. Of course, no society is completely homogenous and there were important divisions along class, clan, and other socioeconomic lines (Cassanelli, 2003: 14).

31. There were rumors in Hargeysa that Egal's secret hope in asserting the political strength of Somaliland was to gain momentum that would carry him to the presidency of a unified Somalia (Hoehne 2009, 264; see also Bradbury 2008, 250).

32. These figures are not known for certain and are highly controversial. The UNFPA *Population Estimation Survey of Somalia* estimates that the Sool and Sanaag regions contain approximately 871,000 people (UNFPA 2014, 32). It is here that anti-independence sentiment runs highest, though there are considerable pockets of it in southern Togdheer and, to a lesser extent, in Awdal. The UNFPA estimated the total population in the five (now six) regions claimed by Somaliland to be just over 3.5 million people.

33. Interview with a former minister, Hargeysa, June 12, 2013. The three regions that he was referring to are Awdal, Sool, and Sanaag.

34. The companies have the same controlling shareholder in Mogadishu, Ali Ahmed Nur Jimcaale.

35. The remainder of this money went to the semi-autonomous region of Puntland. Marleen Renders also notes that a level of foreign assistance has been long standing, and that by 1998 donor agencies pledged over $5 million for projects that the government outlined in its development plan for the forthcoming year (Renders 2012, 169).

36. The US-funded International Republican Institute (IRI) reported that there were 427 NGOs registered with Somaliland's Ministry of Planning and International Cooperation in 2012 (IRI 2012, 44). Many of these organizations are inactive, however.

37. It is impossible to determine exactly how much Somaliland receives as a separate entity because UN agencies and many other donors do not differentiate between what they spend in Somaliland and Somalia and simply classify all spending as being allocated to Somalia. Greg Mills reported that by 2014, external aid was estimated to be around $120 million (Mills 2015, 476).

38. The Minister of Planning estimated that international donors funded approximately 75 percent of the cost of the 2010 presidential elections and about two-thirds of the cost of the 2012 local elections. Interview, Hargeysa, March 2013. Western donors have contributed significant funds to all of Somaliland's elections since the first local council elections were held in 2002.

39. This was widely reiterated in interviews with both Somalilanders and donors throughout 2011–2015, though the perception that this was occurring appeared to be more prevalent later. Karl Sandstrom (2013, 122) highlights this point as well.

40. Interview with minister of planning and international cooperation, Saad Shire. Hargeysa, March 21, 2013.

41. Interview with senior UN official, based in Nairobi. Hargeysa, March 27, 2013.

42. Interview with senior official and technical advisor at the Ministry of Education. Hargeysa, November 14, 2011.

43. Interview with the head of a local advocacy group. Hargeysa, November 20, 2011.

44. Interview with senior official in the Ministry of Foreign Affairs, November 15, 2011. This person felt that openly articulating this view could put their job at the ministry in jeopardy.

45. Interview, Hargeysa, March 24, 2013.

46. Interview with senior official and technical advisor at the Ministry of Education. Hargeysa, November 14, 2011.

47. Interview with the head of a local NGO that partners with the UN and INGOs. Hargeysa, November 14, 2011.

48. Interview with senior official and technical advisor at the Ministry of Education. Hargeysa, November 14, 2011.

49. Interview with Somaliland Minister. Hargeysa, November 14, 2011.

50. Interview with Somaliland Minister. Hargeysa, November 20, 2011.

3. Self-Reliance and Elite Networks

1. As is discussed in the following chapter regarding taxation, the government is widely perceived to have become even more beholden to the business community under the administration of President Silanyo (2010–present) than it was under previous administrations.

2. The degree to which this is sustainable in the future remains an open bet, however.

3. This section draws from Phillips 2016.

4. Interview with the deputy chairman of a prominent civil society organization. Hargeysa, March 27, 2013.

5. Interview with a former member of Uffo (who did not attend Sheekh School). Hargeysa, November 19, 2011.

6. Interview with early SNM leader. Hargeysa, December 1, 2012.

7. Technically, Sheekh Secondary School was an intermediate school prior to becoming a full secondary school under Richard Darlington.

8. President Dahir Rayale Kahin also served as vice president from 1993 until the death of President Egal in 2002, when he became president.

9. Interview with Sheekh School graduate, Class of 1974. Hargeysa, December 2, 2012.

10. Sheekh School was reopened in 2003.

11. Interview with Sheekh School graduate, Class of 1974. Hargeysa, December 4, 2012.

12. Amoud School was first opened in 1952 (Samatar 2001, 647).

13. Interview with Sheekh School graduate, Class of 1974. Hargeysa, December 2, 2012.

14. Interview with Sheekh School graduate, Class of 1973. Hargeysa, October 5, 2015. For a more extensive critique of colonial education in Africa and how it taught values that presumed the "superiority of the colonizer," see Nyamnjoh (2012, 130).

15. Interview with Sheekh School graduate, Class of 1974. Hargeysa, December 2, 2012.

16. Interview with Sheekh School graduate, Class of 1974. Hargeysa, December 4, 2012.

17. Interview with Sheekh School graduate, Class of 1974. Hargeysa, December 4, 2012.

18. Interview with Sheekh School graduate, Class of 2009. Hargeysa, December 2, 2012.

19. Interview with Somaliland planning minister, Saad Shire. Hargeysa, March 21, 2013.

20. This paragraph draws from Phillips 2016.

21. Interview with early SNM leader, Hargeysa, December 1, 2012.

22. When news of the stir caused by the London movement reached Siyad Barre he dispatched his (Isaaq/Habar Jalo) minister of commerce, Mohamed Ahmed Silanyo—Somaliland's president at the time of writing. He earned the respect of the group and by 1984 served as the SNM's chairman.

23. Interview with early SNM leader, Hargeysa, December 1, 2012.

24. Recruitment and organization was also carried out by clan elders in the refugee camps that bulged after the violence in 1988, particularly in the Hartisheikh camp in Ethiopia.

25. The 1997 Hargeysa National Conference stipulated that members of the House of Representatives must have attended secondary school, but this was not made necessary for the Guurti.

26. The Guurti's mandate was formalized at the Hargeysa conference in February 1997, but most of its members had served since the Boorama conference in 1993. Many of the original members have since passed away and been replaced by family members.

27. There are some discrepancies in the number of traders listed as having contributed to this loan. Renders (2012, 127) says that there were ten traders, eight of whom were Habar Awal. Marchal (1996) says there were less than ten. The figure of eight was from Adan Du'ad Egal (Weli), the director of planning and statistics at Somaliland's Ministry of Finance, who was in that position back when the loan took place and listed each lender (interview, Hargeysa, June 13, 2013). There are also discrepancies in the amount of that loan, with Renders (2012, 127) citing it as $3 million, though noting that other sources place it between $6 million and $7 million. Again, the figure used in this piece is from the director of planning and statistics at Somaliland's Ministry of Finance.

28. Interview with the director of planning and statistics at Somaliland's Ministry of Finance, Adan Du'ad Egal (Weli). Hargeysa, June 13, 2013.

29. The Habar-Awal traders were: Ibrahim Abdi Kahin (Ibrahim Dheere was by far the largest contributor to President Egal, lending him around 70 percent of the total amount that he received. In addition to providing this loan, he also started to pay the insurance costs for large ships landing in Berbera Port carrying essential foodstuffs because at the time, no one else would insure them); Jama Omar Saeed (who runs the Omar Import/Export Company and is now believed to be the richest man in Somaliland); Ahmed Dahir Oman (who runs the Bahsane Group, which is the largest real estate company in Hargeysa and also imports car tires and engines); Ali Maweli (who runs the Maweli Group, which imports food and construction materials); Mohamed Jama Caraale (Juujuule, a major importer of food); and Omar Obokor Tani (Mulac). The non-Habar Awal traders were: Abdi Awad Ali (who runs the Indhadeero Group, a major importer of essential foods and livestock exporter from the Habar Jalo clan); Osman Geli Farax (who ran the Gelle Group, was also a major importer of construction materials and, now, also owns the Coca-Cola factory, DHL, and Miligo Digital. Gelle Arab was from the Isaaq/Arab clan).

30. Interview with the director of planning and statistics at Somaliland's Ministry of Finance, Adan Du'ad Egal (Weli). Hargeysa, June 13, 2013. The rest of the information in this paragraph is from this interview.

31. This and the following paragraph draw from Phillips 2016.

32. Egal had more shillings printed in 1996 and 1999, in both cases funded by loans from business elites (interview with director of planning and statistics at Somaliland's Ministry of Finance, Adan Du'ad Egal [Weli], Hargeysa, June 13, 2013). See also Bradbury (2008, 111–12). The next printing was in 2002 under President Dahir Rayale

Kahin, but he was not able to access this kind of money. Ibrahim Dheere was critical for Egal in this venture too, and offered Egal his contacts in London and Djibouti to facilitate both the printing and the international money transfer, respectively.

33. A more detailed discussion of this conflict is offered in chapter 4.

34. This paragraph draws from Phillips 2016.

35. Interview with Shukri Harir Ismail, Hargeysa, December 2, 2012.

36. Interview with Shukri Harir Ismail, Hargeysa, December 2, 2012.

37. Interview with Shukri Harir Ismail, Hargeysa, December 2, 2012.

38. Interview with Annab Omer Eleye, Hargeysa, December 2, 2012.

39. Interview with Annab Omer Eleye, Hargeysa, December 2, 2012.

4. Local Ownership and the Rules of the Game

1. This is less true for the Dhulbuhante and Warsangeli clans that live in the far eastern areas of Sool and Sanaag that are simultaneously claimed by Puntland.

2. Interview with Somali political analyst. Nairobi, January 30, 2013.

3. Also spelled "Calan Cas."

4. See Renders (2012, 132) for further historical background to their rivalry.

5. Interpeace notes that there remains disagreement over whether the formula used at Boorama should be traced to the one established as the basis for representation in the 1960 Parliament or the one that was used by the SNM in Baligubadle (Interpeace 2008, 51).

6. Michael Walls (2014, 176) notes that the foundations for this level of formalization had been laid by President Tuur at the Sheekh conference.

7. Of these participants, only 150 were official delegates. Most sources estimate the number of participants at around 2,000 though Michael Walls (2014, 177) suggests that it was between 700 and 1,000.

8. As discussed further in chapter 2, there was around $100,000 in contributions from various Western donors for the Boorama conference.

9. Activists say that a number of women wrote a letter to the chairman of the Guurti and the central committee in 1997 requesting that they be included as members of the constitutional committee. They were initially granted only six observer roles, which was later increased to eleven: "The discussion on the constitution was open to us but not the vote. We wanted the vote. . . . We were very annoyed." Interview with Shukri Harir Ismail. Hargeysa, December 2, 2012.

10. Somaliland's government employs considerable numbers of traditional leaders. Balthasar reports that in 2011 there were 937 traditional leaders officially on the books, and that they each received a monthly salary of between $50 and $100 (Balthasar 2012, 212).

11. Somaliland has had the following elections: 2002 district elections—which created first the three political parties that are permitted by the constitution; 2003 presidential elections; 2005 parliamentary elections; 2010 presidential elections; 2012 district elections; 2017 presidential elections.

12. I was an international observer to these elections.

13. There was one candidate from Habar Jalo, who reportedly tried to trade on the fact that his mother was from the Saad Musa clan. He was unsuccessful.

14. After the elections, the victorious Kulmiye Party did make a significant move against clan-based power, however, and in 2013 it implemented a policy to shift all governors outside of their local areas—thereby disrupting power systems constructed around clan monopolies across government institutions.

15. It should be noted, however, that the levels of trust expressed in either the government police or the statutory courts were lower in regions outside of Somaliland, particularly in Mogadishu, the capital of the Federal Republic of Somalia (Observatory of Conflict and Violence Prevention 2011).

16. Interview with local businessman and an NGO worker who were both recently involved in clan-based negotiations over fatal incidents. Hargeysa, October 2, 2015.

17. I was present in Somaliland as this case unfolded.

18. Interview with a member of the telecommunications association. Hargeysa, November 10, 2011.

19. The companies and individuals that contributed were: Telesom ($1.2 million); Dahabshiil ($750,000); Ali Warabe (a livestock exporter—$500,000); Jama Omar Saeed ($200,000); Mohamed Aw Saeed (Somcable—$200,000); Mohamed "Ina" Dable (the owner of a bedding factory—$100,000). Interview with the director of planning and statistics at Somaliland's Ministry of Finance. Hargeysa, June 13, 2013.

20. Interview with the director of planning and statistics at Somaliland's Ministry of Finance. Hargeysa, June 13, 2013.

21. Another reason for this increase was that the government changed the exchange rate of the Somaliland shilling to the dollar from 6,000/$1 to 6,500/$1. Interview with a senior official in the Ministry of Finance. Hargeysa, November 20, 2011.

22. This is up from $51 million in 2010. Budget figures received from the Somaliland Ministry of Finance (Hargeysa) in June 2013.

23. Interview with a political analyst working on Somaliland for a large Western donor. Nairobi, April 12, 2013. This was not confirmable (as the opacity of the figure is the problem) but chimes with other estimates given to the author.

24. Interview with the director of planning and statistics at Somaliland's Ministry of Finance. Hargeysa, June 13, 2013.

25. Interview with the director of planning and statistics at Somaliland's Ministry of Finance. Hargeysa, June 13, 2013.

26. Interview with Kulmiye member of Parliament. Hargeysa, March 24, 2013.

27. Interview, Hargeysa, December 5, 2012.

28. Telesom publicly maintains that the issue of interconnections is a technical one. However, there was a brief period when connections were possible between the subscribers of all other telecommunications companies. At that time Telesom insisted upon charging between double and triple the rate that the other carriers were charging for the service, and the government did not intervene. One person who was involved in this process claims that members of the Telecommunications Ministry were actively involved in "unplugging the servers" to disrupt the ability for customers to call across networks, ultimately scuttling it. Interview with an employee at a competing telecommunications company. Hargeysa, December 5, 2012.

29. Telesom later successfully demanded a hand in drafting the legislation that regulated the industry (Iazzolino 2015, 22).

30. Interview, Hargeysa, March 24, 2013.

31. The view that Silanyo's administration is dependent on Dahabshiil financially is widespread.

32. Interview with observer to the conference. Hargeysa, June 11, 2013.

33. Interview with a small business owner who imports basic commodities. Hargeysa, March 21, 2013.

34. Interview with senior official in the Education Ministry. Hargeysa, November 9, 2011.

35. Interview with Somaliland Minister. Hargeysa, November 14, 2011.

36. Interview with a senior executive of Telesom. Hargeysa, November 26, 2011.

5. War and Peace in the Independence Discourse

1. The levels of trust expressed in either the government police or the statutory courts were lower in regions outside of Somaliland, particularly in Mogadishu, the capital of the Federal Republic of Somalia (Observatory of Conflict and Violence Prevention 2011).

2. Interview with the research director at a local institute. Hargeysa, March 24, 2013.

3. Interview with member of parliament. Hargeysa, November 12, 2011.

4. Interview with member of parliament. Hargeysa, November 12, 2011.

5. Interview with local researcher and freelance consultant to a number of INGOs. Hargeysa, March 22, 2013.

6. Comment made by a former minister at a public forum, Hargeysa Cultural Centre, October 1, 2015.

7. Interview with the chairman of an opposition political party. Hargeysa, November 16, 2011.

8. Kulmiye Party press conference, Hargeysa, Somaliland, April 22, 2003. Partial transcripts are with the author.

9. Press conference held in Hargeysa, Somaliland, April 22, 2003. Partial transcripts of the event are held by the author.

10. This particular phrasing was used by a senior official in the Ministry of Justice to refer to the absence of piracy from Somaliland, but it is representative of that used by many interviewees and informal conversations between 2011 and 2015. Interview, Hargeysa, November 30, 2012.

11. Hargeysa, November 18, 2011.

12. Hargeysa, November 28, 2012.

13. The largest sum that the presenter could recall hearing was $900.

14. Interview with a former minister. Hargeysa, December 3, 2012.

15. Interview with Somaliland Minister. Hargeysa, November 20, 2011.

16. Hargeysa, October 1, 2015.

17. Hargeysa, October 1, 2015. Another member of the audience then clarified that he had helped to deliver $100,000 in foreign donations to the conference in Boorama on

behalf of two organizations: The Life and Peace Institute from Sweden and the Mennonites from the United States.

18. Interview with Somalilander researcher and freelance consultant to a number of INGOs. Hargeysa, March 22, 2013.

19. Interview with local researcher at a think tank. Hargeysa, December 1, 2012.

20. Hargeysa, November 15, 2011.

21. I was an international observer to these elections. Marleen Renders made a similar observation when she observed the presidential elections in 2003: "'Go tell your countrymen that Somaliland now deserves to be recognized,' voters told the international observers" (Renders 2012, 244).

22. This section draws from interviews and analysis presented in Hastings and Phillips 2018.

23. Interview with a senior official in the Ministry of Justice. Hargeysa, November 30, 2012.

24. Interview with a former minister. Hargeysa, December 3, 2012.

25. Interview with senior official in the Ministry of Foreign Affairs. Hargeysa, November 15, 2011.

26. Interview, Hargeysa, September 29, 2015.

27. This issue was raised during a number of conversations with the author in 2012.

28. Interview with foreign minister, Mohamed Abdulahi Omar. Hargeysa, December 4, 2012.

29. Comment made by a former minister at a public forum. Hargeysa Cultural Centre, October 1, 2015.

30. Interview with executive director of Somaliland's Counter-Piracy Coordination Office, Mohamed Osman Ahmed. Hargeysa, October 3, 2015.

31. There are other explanations for the discrepancy between the two locations that are facially plausible, such as other structural economic, geographic, or political differences—but in a detailed analysis of these hypotheses elsewhere, Hastings and Phillips (2018) find each to be unconvincing on their own.

32. During the two years that Hanaano's network was operational, Laasqorey was essentially a Warsangeli "clan enclave" (World Bank 2013, 147) that declared itself the Maakhir State of Somalia between July 2007 and January 2009. The short-lived state was opposed to the territorial claims of both Somaliland and Puntland, though it has been politically closer to Puntland than Somaliland since its dissolution.

33. Interview with foreign minister, Mohamed Abdulahi Omar. Hargeysa, December 4, 2012.

34. The Harti clan family includes the Warsangeli and Dhulbuhante clans.

35. Interview with a local NGO worker who was working with the group of people who were kidnapped in Laasqorey at the time of the incident in 2012. Hargeysa, September 27, 2015.

36. The contract was renewed again in 2017, with a more explicit aim of improving relations with the United States.

37. Thanks to Eda Gunaydin for pointing this out.

38. The analyst is not named in the documentary.

39. I am grateful to Eda Gunaydin for this point.

40. This is not intended to imply that political protests have never occurred, only that they are approached with a high degree of caution.

41. Charles Tilly explicitly doubts that his argument holds for non-Western contexts (Tilly 1990, 204).

Conclusion

1. There has been a long public exchange between William Easterly and Jeffrey Sachs on the impact and proper role of official development assistance in reducing poverty. Their key books during this period were Sachs (2005); Easterly (2007). See also Collier (2008); Moyo (2009). Susan Engel (2014, 1383) offers an insightful critique of the parameters of this debate and the ways that it has maintained the focus on aid as the key driver of either positive or negative change, while obfuscating the "broader processes and systems that produce inequality."

2. Some scholars see the universalism that is so widely attached to Max Weber's definition of statehood as a misreading of the broader cannon of Weber's work, which is interpretivist and opposed to essentialized thinking. See Lottholz and Lemay-Hébert (2016) and Goetze (2016). They suggest that such readings, including their inordinate focus on institutions, be referred to as neo-Weberian rather than Weberian.

REFERENCES

Abokor, Adan Y., Steve Kibble, Mark Bradbury, Haroon Ahmed Yusuf, and Georgina Barrett. 2006. *The Somaliland Parliamentary Elections, September 2005*. London: Progressio. http://www.progressio.org.uk/sites/default/files/Further-steps-to-democracy.pdf.

Acemoglu, Darren, and James Robinson. 2012. *Why Nations Fail: The Origins of Power, Prosperity, and Poverty*. London: Crown Business.

ADB (Asian Development Bank). 2011. *Country Partnership Strategy: Papua New Guinea, 2011–2015 Supplementary Document*. Asian Development Bank. https://www.adb.org/sites/default/files/linked-documents/cps-png-2011-2015-oth-04.pdf.

Africa Research Institute. 2013. *After Borama: Consensus, Representation and Parliament in Somaliland*. ARI. May 2013. http://www.africaresearchinstitute.org/newsite/wp-content/uploads/2013/05/PV-After-Borama-HR-for-website.pdf.

African Union Commission. 2005. *Resume, AU Fact-Finding Mission to Somaliland*. Unpublished Report, Addis Ababa. Ethiopia: African Union.

Ahmad, Aisha. 2012. "Agenda for Peace or Budget for War? Evaluating the Economic Impact of International Intervention in Somalia." *International Journal* 67, no. 2: 313–24.

Ahmed, Ismail I., and Reginald Herbold Green. 1999. "The Heritage of War and State Collapse in Somalia and Somaliland: Local-Level Effects, External Interventions and Reconstruction." *Third World Quarterly* 20, no. 1: 113–27.

Aid and International Development Forum. 2018. "Cholera Outbreaks Dramatically Decline in Yemen Following New DFID Prediction Method." August 29, 2018. http://www.aidforum.org/topics/health-and-wash/cholera-outbreaks-dramatically-reduce-in-yemen-following-new-dfid-predictio/.

Aidid, Safia. 2015. "The New Somali Studies." *The New Inquiry*, April 15, 2015. https://thenewinquiry.com/the-new-somali-studies/.

Akhtar, Aasim Sajjad, and Ali Nobil Ahmed. 2015. "Conspiracy and Statecraft in Postcolonial States: Theories and Realities of the Hidden Hand in Pakistan's War on Terror." *Third World Quarterly* 36, no. 1: 94–110.

Amnesty International. 2015. "Yemen: Call for Suspension of Arms Transfers to Coalition and Accountability for War Crimes." October 7, 2015. https://www.amnesty.org/en/latest/news/2015/10/yemen-call-for-suspension-of-arms-transfers-to-coalition-and-accountability-for-war-crimes/.

Anderson, Mark. 2012. "Somaliland Says New Laws Show Intent to Fight Piracy." Reuters, February 22. http://www.reuters.com/article/2012/02/22/ozatp-somalia-somaliland-piracy-idAFJOE81L09620120222.

Anderson, Mary B. 1999. *Do No Harm: How Aid Can Support Peace—or War.* Boulder, CO: Lynne Rienner Publishers, 1999.

Anghie, Antony. 2004. *Imperialism, Sovereignty and the Making of International Law.* Cambridge: Cambridge University Press.

APD (Academy for Peace and Development). 2002. *Consolidation and Decentralization of Government Institutions.* Hargeysa: APD. https://www.somali-jna.org/downloads/Jimcaale%20-%20APD%20Governance%20and%20Dcentralisation%20of%20Institution.pdf.

Arnoldy, Ben. 2010. "Afghanistan War: How USAID Loses Hearts and Minds." *Christian Science Monitor*, July 28, 2010. https://www.csmonitor.com/World/Asia-South-Central/2010/0728/Afghanistan-war-How-USAID-loses-hearts-and-minds.

Arteh, Hibo, and Ahmed A. Dualeh. 2011. *Securing the Peace in Somaliland: The Role of the Somaliland Business Sector.* Rift Valley Institute, Academy for Peace and Development. Research Report 2.

Autesserre, Severine. 2010. *The Trouble with the Congo: Local Violence and the Failure of International Peacebuilding.* Cambridge: Cambridge University Press.

———. 2012. "Dangerous Tales: Dominant Narratives on the Congo and their Unintended Consequences." *African Affairs* 111, no. 443, 202–22.

———. 2014. *Peaceland: Conflict Resolution and the Everyday Politics of International Intervention.* Cambridge: Cambridge University Press.

Ayoob, Mohammed, 1995. *The Third World Security Predicament: State Making, Regional Conflict, and the International System.* Boulder, CO: Lynne Reinner.

Bacevich, Andrew. 2015. "ISIS Is Using US Military Hardware to Fight the Iraqi Army." *The Nation*, June 19, 2015. https://www.thenation.com/article/isis-is-using-us-military-hardware-to-fight-the-iraqi-army/.

Bagayoko, Niagale, Eboe Hutchful, and Robin Luckham. 2016. "Hybrid Security Governance in Africa: Rethinking the Foundations of Security, Justice and Legitimate Public Authority." *Conflict, Security & Development* 16, no. 1: 1–32.

Bahadur, Jay. 2011. *The Pirates of Somalia: Inside their Hidden World.* New York: Vintage.

Bakonyi, Jutta. 2009. "Moral Economies of Mass Violence: Somalia 1988–1991." *Civil Wars* 11, no. 4: 434–54.

Balthasar, Dominik. 2012. "State-Making in Somalia and Somaliland: Understanding War, Nationalism and State Trajectories as Processes of Institutional and Socio-Cognitive Standardization." PhD diss., London School of Economics.

——. 2013. "Somaliland's Best Kept Secret: Shrewd Politics and War Projects as Means of State-Making." *Journal of Eastern African Studies* 7, no. 2: 218–38.

——. 2014. "Thinking beyond Roadmaps in Somalia: Expanding Policy Options for State Building." Washington, DC: Center for Strategic and International Studies. https://csis-prod.s3.amazonaws.com/s3fs-public/legacy_files/files/publication/141118_Balthasar_ThinkingBeyondRoadmaps_Web.pdf.

Balthasar, Dominik, and Janis Grzybowski. 2012. "Between State and Non-state: Somaliland's Emerging Security Order." In *Small Arms Survey 2012: Moving Targets*, 146–73. Cambridge: Cambridge University Press.

Banerjee, Abhijit, and Esther Duflo. 2011. *Poor Economics: A Radical Rethinking of the Way to Fight Global Poverty.* New York: PublicAffairs.

Banta, Benjamin. 2012. "Analysing Discourse as a Causal Mechanism." *European Journal of International Relations* 19, no 2: 379–402.

Barkawi, Tarak. 2016. "Decolonising War." *European Journal of International Security* 1, no. 2: 199–214.

Bates, Robert H. 2001. *Prosperity and Violence: The Political Economy of Development.* New York: W.W. Norton.

——. 2009. *When Things Fell Apart: State Failure in Late-Century Africa.* Cambridge: Cambridge University Press.

BBC. 2015. "Somaliland's Horn Stars Band Arrested over Somali Flag." September 28, 20154. https://www.bbc.com/news/world-africa-34378350.

BBC Somalia Service. 2003. Interview with Ahmed Mohamed Silanyo. Hargeysa, June 9.

Bell, Christine. 2015. "What We Talk about When We Talk about Political Settlements: Towards Inclusive and Open Political Settlements in an Era of Disillusionment." Political Settlement Research Programme, Working Paper 1, September 1, 2015.

Belloni, Roberto. 2012. "Hybrid Peace Governance: Its Emergence and Significance." *Global Governance* 18, no. 1: 21–38.

Besteman, Catherine. 1996. "Representing Violence and 'Othering' Somalia." *Cultural Anthropology* 11, no. 1: 120–33.

——. 1998. "Primordialist Blinders: A Reply to I. M. Lewis." *Cultural Anthropology* 13, no. 1: 109–20.

Beswick, Danielle. 2013. "From Weak State to Savvy International Player? Rwanda's Multi-level Strategy for Maximising Agency." In *African Agency in International Politics*, ed. William Brown, and Sophie Harman, 158–74. London: Routledge.

Birrell, Ian. 2011. "Somaliland: The Former British Colony that Shows Africa Doesn't Need Our Millions to Flourish" *Daily Mail.* July 24, 2011. https://www.dailymail.co.uk/news/article-2018055/Somaliland-The-British-colony-shows-Africa-doesnt-need-millions-flourish.html.

Blyth, Mark, 2002. *Great Transformations: Economic Ideas and Institutional Change in the Twentieth Century.* New York: Cambridge University Press.

———. 2011. "Ideas, Uncertainty and Evolution." In *Ideas and Politics in Social Science Research*, ed. Daniel Beland and Robert Henry Cox, 83–101. Oxford: Oxford University Press.

Boege, Volker, Anne Brown, Kevin Clements, and Anna Nolan. 2009. "Building Peace and Political Community in Hybrid Political Orders." *International Peacekeeping* 16, no. 5: 599–615.

Börzel, Tanja A. and Thomas Risse. 2016. "Dysfunctional State Institutions, Trust, and Governance in Areas of Limited Statehood." *Regulation & Governance* 10: 149–60.

Bradbury, Mark. 2008. *Becoming Somaliland*. Bloomington: Indiana University Press.

———. 2010. *State-Building, Counterterrorism, and Licensing Humanitarianism in Somalia*. Feinstein International Center, Tufts University. September 2010. http://fic.tufts.edu/assets/state-building-somalia.pdf.

Bradbury, Mark, Adan Yusuf Abokor, and Haroon Ahmed Yusuf. 2003. "Somaliland: Choosing Politics over Violence." *Review of African Political Economy* 30, no. 97: 455–78.

Braithwaite, Alex, Niheer Dassandi, and David Hudson. 2016. "Does Poverty Cause Conflict? Isolating the Causal Origins of the Conflict Trap." *Conflict Management and Peace Science* 33, no.1: 45–66.

Brautigam, Deborah, and Tania Diolle. 2009. *Coalitions, Capitalists and Credibility: Overcoming the Crisis of Confidence at Independence in Mauritius*. Developmental Leadership Program Research Paper 4, April 2009.

Bridges, Peter. 2000. *Safirka: An American Envoy*. Kent, OH: Kent State University Press.

Brock, Lothar, Hans-Henrik Holm, Georg Sorenson, and Michael Stohl. 2012. *Fragile States: Violence and the Failure of Intervention*. Cambridge: Polity Press.

Bryden, Matt. 2003. "The 'Banana Test': Is Somaliland Ready for Recognition?" *Annales d'Ethiopie* 19: 341–64.

Buh, Abdikarim. 2010. "Somaliland's Summer of Trial: Looking beyond the Lean Cabinet." *Wardheer News*, August 2, 2010. https://www.mareeg.com/fidsan.php?sid=16855.

Bush, Kenneth D. 1997. "When Two Anarchies Meet: International Intervention in Somalia." *Journal of Conflict Studies* 17, no. 1. https://journals.lib.unb.ca/index.php/JCS/article/view/11732/12485.

Cabdillaahi, Rashiid Sheekh. 2009. *War and Peace: An Anthology of Somali Literature*. Translated by Martin Orwin with help from Maxamed Xasan "Alto." London and Pisa: Progressio and Ponte Invisibile.

Call, Charles T. 2008. "The Fallacy of the 'Failed State.'" *Third World Quarterly* 29, no. 8: 1491–1507.

Call, Charles, and Elizabeth Cousens. 2008. "Ending Wars and Building Peace." *International Studies Perspectives* 9, no. 1: 1–21.

Campos, J. Antonio. 2016. "On Taxes and Suspicion: Ambivalences of Rule and the Politically Possible in Contemporary Hargeisa, Somaliland." DIIS Working Paper no. 5. Copenhagen: Danish Institute for International Studies. http://pure.diis.dk/ws/files/609871/DIIS_WP_2016_5.pdf.

Carrier, Neil, and Emma Lochery. 2013. "Missing States? Somali Trade Networks and the Eastleigh Transformation." *Journal of Eastern African Studies* 7, no. 2: 334–52.

Cassanelli, Lee V. 2003. "Explaining the Somali Crisis." In *The Struggle for Land in Southern Somalia: The War behind the War*, ed. Catherine L. Besteman and Lee V. Cassanelli, 13–26. London: Haan Publishing.

Caton, Steven C. 1990. *"Peaks of Yemen I Summon": Poetry as Cultural Practice in a North Yemeni Tribe*. Berkeley: University of California Press.

———. 2014. "Henri Bergson in Highland Yemen." In *The Ground Between: Anthropologists Engage Philosophy*, ed. Veena Das, 234–53. Durham, NC: Duke University Press.

Chandler, David C. 2006. *Empire in Denial: The Politics of State-Building*. London: Pluto Press.

———. 2017. *Peacebuilding: The Twenty Years' Crisis, 1997–2017*. Cham, Switzerland: Palgrave Macmillan.

Chandy, Laurence, Brina Seidel, and Christine Zhang. 2016. "Aid Effectiveness in Fragile States: How Bad Is It and How Can It Improve?" Washington, DC: Brookings Institute. https://www.brookings.edu/wp-content/uploads/2016/12/global_121616_brookeshearer.pdf.

Chossudovsky, Michel. 2003. *The Globalization of Poverty and the New World Order*. 2nd ed. Quebec, Canada: Global Research.

Ciabarri, Luca. 2010. "Trade, Lineages, Inequalities: Twists in the Northern Somali Path to Modernity." In *Peace and Milk, Drought and War: Somali Culture, Society and Politics*, ed. Markus Hoehne and Virginia Luling, 67–86. London: Hurst and Company.

Clapham, Cristopher, Holger Hansen, Jeffrey Herbst, J. Peter Pham, Patrick Mazimhaka, Susan Schulman, and Greg Mills. 2011. *African Game Changer? The Consequences of Somaliland's International (Non) Recognition*. A Brenthouse Foundation Discussion Paper. May 2011. http://www.somalilandlaw.com/Brenthurst_paper_2011-05_african_game_changer_SL_recognition.pdf.

Coburn, Noah. 2011. *Bazaar Politics: Power and Pottery in an Afghan Market Town*. Stanford, CA: Stanford University Press.

Cockburn, Andrew. 2016. "Acceptable Losses: Aiding and Abetting the Saudi Slaughter in Yemen." *Harpers Magazine*, September 2016. https://harpers.org/archive/2016/09/acceptable-losses/.

Collier, Paul. 2000. "Doing Well War: Economic Perspectives." In *Greed & Grievance: Economic Agendas in Civil Wars*, ed. Mats R. Berdal and David Malone, 91–112. Boulder, CO: Lynne Reiner.

———. 2007. *The Bottom Billion: Why the Poorest Countries Are Failing and What Can Be Done about It*. Oxford: Oxford University Press.

———. 2009. "The Political Economy of State Failure." *Oxford Review of Economic Policy* 25, no. 2: 219–40.

———. 2011. *Wars, Guns and Votes: Democracy in Dangerous Places*. New York: Random House.

Collins, Gregory. A. 2009. "Connected: Developing Somalia's Telecoms Industry in the Wake of State Collapse." PhD diss., University of California.

Colona, Francesco, and Rivke Jaffe. 2016. "Hybrid Governance Arrangements." *European Journal of Development Research,* 28, no. 2: 175–83.

Comaroff, Jean, and John L. Comaroff. 2012. "Theory from the South: Or, How Euro-America Is Evolving toward Africa." *Anthropological Forum* 22, no. 2, 113–31.

Compagnon, Daniel. 1990/1. "The Somali Opposition Fronts: Some Comments and Questions." *Horn of Africa* 13, no. 1–2: 29–54.

——. 1998. "Somali Armed Movements: The Interplay of Political Entrepreneurship and Clan-Based Factions." In *African Guerrillas*, ed. Christopher Clapham, 73–90. Oxford: James Currey.

Connolly, William. 1991. *Identity/Difference: Democratic Negotiations of Political Paradox*. Minneapolis: University of Minnesota Press.

Cox, Robert W. 1980. "Social Forces, States and World Orders: Beyond International Relations Theory." *Millenium Journal of International Studies* 10, no. 2: 126–55.

Cramer, Christopher. 2006. *Civil War is Not a Stupid Thing: Accounting for Violence in Developing Countries*. London: Hurst and Company.

CRS (Congressional Research Service). 2013. *Pakistan: U.S. Foreign Assistance.* R41856, July 1, 2013. https://www.everycrsreport.com/files/20130701_R41856_0ffac3bb726dc4 6cf10da53a560c2f2c8b7aea96.pdf.

Dasandi, Niheer. 2014. "International Inequality and World Poverty: A Quantitative Structural Analysis." New Political Economy 19, no. 2: 201–26.

Daud, Abdillahi. 2003. "Ahmed Silanyo: The Man Who Saved Somaliland from Civil War." *Somaliland Times*, no. 73. http://somalilandtimes.net/2003/73/7322.shtml (accessed using Wayback Machine).

Deaton, Angus. 2013. *The Great Escape: Health Wealth and the Origins of Inequality*. Princeton, NJ: Princeton University Press.

De Rouen, Karl Jr, Mark J. Ferguson, Samuel Norton, Young Hwan Park, Jenna Lea, and Ashley Streat-Bartlett. 2010. "Civil War Peace Agreement Implementation and State Capacit." *Journal of Peace Research* 47, no. 3: 333–46.

De Waal, Alex. 1996. "Class and Power in a Stateless Somalia: A Discussion Paper." August 1996. http://justiceafrica.org/wp-content/uploads/2016/07/DeWaal_ClassandPower inSomalia.pdf.

——. 1997. *Famine Crimes: Politics and the Disaster Relief Industry*. Oxford, Bloomingdale and Indianapolis: James Currey and Indiana University Press.

——. 2015. *The Real Politics of the Horn of Africa: Money, War and the Business of Power*. Cambridge: Polity Press.

DFAT (Department of Foreign Affairs and Trade). 2005. *Fragile States*. http://dfat.gov .au/about-us/publications/Documents/focus_jun05_6.pdf.

DFID (Department for International Development). 2005. "Why We Need to Work More Effectively in Fragile States: A DFID Practice Paper." Department for International Development, January 2005. https://www.jica.go.jp/cdstudy/library/pdf/2007 1101_11.pdf.

——. 2010. "Building Peaceful States and Societies: A DFID Practice Paper." Department for International Development. https://www.gov.uk/government/publications /building-peaceful-states-and-societies-a-dfid-practice-paper.

Diamond, Jared. 1999. *Guns, Germs, and Steel: The Fates of Human Societies* New York: W. W. Norton.

DiGiuseppe, Matthew R., Colin M. Barry, and Richard W. Frank. 2012. "Good for the Money: International Finance, State Capacity, and Internal Armed Conflict." *Journal of Peace Research* 49, no. 3: 391–405.

Dini, Shukria. 2008. "Somali Women Respond to State Collapse and Civil War: Two Decades of Collective Self-Organizing in Somaliland and Puntland." PhD Diss., York University, Toronto.

Doornbos, Martin. 2010. "Researching African Statehood Dynamics: Negotiability and its Limits." *Development and Change* 41, no. 4, 747–69.

Doty, Roxanne Lynn. 1996. *Imperial Encounters*. Minneapolis: University of Minnesota Press.

Doyle, Michael, and Nicholas Sambanis. 2006. *Making War and Building Peace: United Nations Peace Operations*. Princeton, NJ: Princeton University Press.

Drysdale, John. 1992. *Somaliland: The Anatomy of Secession*. Hove, UK: Global-Stats Ltd.

Dua, Jatin. 2011. "Piracy and the Narrative of Recognition: The View from Somaliland." Social Science Research Council [online], New York: SSRC. http://www.ssrc.org/pages /Piracy-and-the-Narrative-of-Recognition-The-View-from-Somaliland/.

Duffield, Mark. 2001. *Global Governance and New Wars: The Merging of Development and Security*. London: Zed Books.

Easterly, William. 2007. *The White Man's Burden: Why the West's Efforts to Aid the Rest have Done So Much Ill and So Little Good*. New York: Penguin.

Ebrahim, Alnoor, and Steven Herz. 2011. "The World Bank and Democratic Accountability: The Role of Civil Society." In *Building Global Democracy? Civil Society and Accountable Global Governance*, ed. Jan Aart Scholte, 58–77. Cambridge: Cambridge University Press.

The Economist. 2008. "Piracy and Much Worse." October 2, 2008. http://www.economist .com/node/12341825.

———. 2015, "*The Economist* Explains Why Somaliland Is Not a Recognised State." November 1, 2015. http://www.economist.com/blogs/economist-explains/2015/11/economist -explains.

Elder, Claire. 2019. "The Politics of Diaspora Return: From State Collapse to a New Federal Somalia and Somaliland, 1985–2018." Unpublished PhD Diss., Oxford University.

Elias, Norbert, 1939/1982. *The Civilising Process*. Vol. 2, *State Formation and Civilization*. Oxford: Blackwell.

———. 1939/1994. *The Civilizing Process*. Vol. 1, *The History of Manners and State Formation and Civilization*. Oxford: Blackwell.

Engel, Susan. 2014. "The Not-So-Great Aid Debate." *Third World Quarterly* 35, no. 8: 1374–89.

Englebert, Pierre. 2006. "Sovereignty Globalization and the Violent Reproduction of a Weak State." In *Globalization, Self-Determination and Violent Conflict*, ed. Valpy FitzGerald, Frances Stewart and Rajesh Venugopal, 119–46. New York: Palgrave Macmillan.

———. 2009. *Africa: Unity, Sovereignty and Sorrow*. Boulder, CO: Lynne Rienner.

Epstein, Charlotte. 2008. *The Power of Words in International Relations: Birth of an Anti-Whaling Discourse*. Cambridge, MA: MIT Press.

Eriksen, Stein. 2011. "'State Failure' in Theory and Practice: The Idea of the State and the Contradictions of State Formation." *Review of International Studies* 37: 229–47.

Escobar, Arturo. 1995. *Encountering Development: The Making and Unmaking of the Third World*. Princeton, NJ: Princeton University Press.

Eubank, Nicholas. 2011. "In Somaliland, Less Money Has Brought More Democracy." *The Guardian*. August 26, 2011. https://www.theguardian.com/global-development /poverty-matters/2011/aug/26/somaliland-less-money-more-democracy.

——. 2012. "Taxation, Political Accountability and Foreign Aid: Lessons from Somaliland." *Journal of Development Studies* 48, no. 4: 465–80.

Eurodad (European Network on Debt and Development). 2014. "The State of Finance for Developing Countries, 2014." December 17, 2014. http://www.eurodad.org/finance _for_developing_countries.

Evans, Peter, Dietrich Rueschemeyer, and Theda Skocpol. 1985. *Bringing the State Back In*. Cambridge: Cambridge University Press.

Fanon, Frantz. 1963. *The Wretched of the Earth*. New York: Grove Press.

Farah Ahmed Y., and Ioan M. Lewis. 1993. *Somalia: The Roots of Reconciliation: Peace Making Endeavours of Contemporary Lineage Leaders: A Survey of Grassroots Peace Conferences in "Somaliland."* London: ActionAid.

——. 1997. "Making Peace in Somaliland." *Cahiers d'études africaines* 37, no. 146: 349–77.

Fartaag, Abdirazak. 2012. *Audit Investigative Report—2011: Transitional Federal Government—2011*. February 20, 2012. http://web.archive.org/web/20160406001813/http://www .somaliareport.com/downloads/Audit_Investigative_Report___2011_Consolidatedx .pdf.

Farzin, Y. Hossein. 1991. "Food Aid: Positive or Negative Economic Effects in Somalia." *Journal of Developing Areas* 25, no. 2: 261–82.

Fearon, James D. 2010. "Governance and Civil War Onset." Background paper for the World Bank *World Development Review 2011*. August 31, 2010. http://siteresources .worldbank.org/EXTWDR2011/Resources/6406082-1283882418764/WDR _Background_Paper_Fearon.pdf.

Fearon, James D., and David D. Laitin. 2003. "Ethnicity, Insurgency, and Civil War." *American Political Science Review,* 97, no. 1: 75–90.

Federal Government of Somalia. 2018. "Citizens' Guide to the 2018 Budget." https://www .unicef.org/esa/sites/unicef.org.esa/files/2019-04/Citizens-Budget-in-Somalia -%282018%29.pdf.

Ferguson, James. 2006. *Global Shadows: Africa in the Neo-Liberal World Order*. Durham, NC: Duke University Press.

Ferreira, Ines A. 2017. "Measuring State Fragility: A Review of the Theoretical Groundings of Existing Approaches." *Third World Quarterly* 38, no. 6: 1291–1309.

Fisher, Jonathan. 2014. "When It Pays to Be a 'Fragile State': Uganda's Use and Abuse of a Dubious Concept." *Third World Quarterly* 35, no. 2, 316–32.

Forstater, Maya. 2015. "Can Stopping 'Tax Dodging' by Multinational Enterprises Close the Gap in Development Finance?" CGD Policy Paper 069. Washington, DC: Center for Global Development. https://www.cgdev.org/publication/can-stopping-tax-dodging -multinational-enterprises-close-gap-development-finance.

Foucault, Michel. 1980. *Power/Knowledge: Selected Interviews and Other Writings, 1972– 1977*. New York: Vintage.

Freedom House. 2012. *Freedom in the World 2012—Somaliland*. https://freedomhouse.org /report/freedom-world/2012/somaliland.

Fund for Peace. 2019. *Fragile States Index: Annual Report 2019*. Washington, DC: Fund for Peace. http://fundforpeace.org/wp-content/uploads/2019/04/9511904-fragil estatesindex.pdf.

Gandrup, Tobias. 2016. *Enter and Exit: Everyday State Practices at Somaliland's Hargeisa Egal International Airport*. DIIS Working Paper no. 3. http://pure.diis.dk/ws/files /579529/DIIS_WP_2016_3.pdf.

Geddes, Barbara. 1990. "How the Cases You Choose Affect the Answers You Get: Selection Bias in Comparative Politics." *Political Analysis* 2: 131–50.

Gellner, Ernest. 2000. "Trust, Cohesion, and the Social Order." In *Trust: Making and Breaking Cooperative Relations*, ed. Diego Gambetta, 142–57, electronic edition. Oxford: Department of Sociology, University of Oxford.

Geshekter, Charles. 2001. "The Search for Peaceful Development in a Century of War: Global Restraints on 20th Century Somali Socio-Economic Development." In *What Are Somalia's Development Perspectives: Science between Resignation and Hope*, ed. Jorg Janzen, 9–34. Berlin: Das Arabische Buch.

Gettleman, Jeffrey. 2008. "Anarchy-Cursed Nation Looks to Bottom-Up Rule." *New York Times*. August 17, 2008. https://www.nytimes.com/2008/08/18/world/africa/18somalia .html.

GFI (Global Financial Integrity). 2017. *Illicit Financial Flows to and from Developing Countries: 2005–2014*. April 2017. https://www.gfintegrity.org/wp-content/uploads /2017/05/GFI-IFF-Report-2017_final.pdf.

Ghani, Ashraf, and Clare Lockhart. 2008. *Fixing Failed States: A Framework for Rebuilding a Fractured World*. Oxford: Oxford University Press.

Giddens, Anthony. 1985. *A Contemporary Critique of Historical Materialism*. Vol. 2, *The Nation State and Violence*. Berkeley: University of California Press.

Giustozzi, Antonio. 2011. *The Art of Coercion: The Primitive Accumulation and Management of Coercive Power*. New York: Columbia University Press.

Gleditsch, Kristian Skrede, and Andrea Ruggeri. 2010. "Political Opportunity Structures, Democracy, and Civil War." *Journal of Peace Research,* 47, no. 3: 299–310.

Goetze, Catherine. 2016. "Warlords and States: A Contemporary Myth of the International System." In *Myth and Narrative in International Politics: Interpretive Approaches to the Study of IR*, ed. Berit Bliesemann de Guevara, 129–46. Basingstoke, UK: Palgrave Macmillan.

Government of Somaliland. n.d. *The Recognition of Somaliland: Achievement against All the Odds*. http://recognition.somalilandgov.com/wp-content/uploads/2013/01/The -recognition-of-Somaliland-Achievements-Againt-all-odds.pdf.

Graham-Harrison, Emma. 2016. "British and US Military 'In Command Room' for Saudi Strikes on Yemen." *The Guardian*, January 15, 2016. http://www.theguardian .com/world/2016/jan/15/british-us-military-in-command-room-saudi-strikes -yemen.

Grawert, Elke, and Zeinab Abul-Magd. 2016. *Businessmen in Arms: How the Military and Other Armed Groups Profit in the MENA Region*. New York: Rowman & Littlefield.

Grimm, Sonja, Nicolas Lemay-Hébert, and Olivier Nay. 2014. "'Fragile States': Introducing a Political Concept." *Third World Quarterly* 35, no. 2: 197–209.

Grimmett, Richard F., and Paul K. Kerr. 2012. *Conventional Arms Transfers to Developing Nations, 2004–2011.* Congressional Research Service. https://fas.org/sgp/crs/weapons/R42678.pdf.

Gruffydd Jones, Branwen. 2013. "Slavery, Finance and International Political Economy: Postcolonial Reflections." In *Postcolonial Theory and International Relations: A Critical Introduction*, ed. Sanjay Seth, 49–65. London: Routledge.

Gulrajani, Nilima. 2011. "Transcending the Great Foreign Aid Debate: Managerialism, Radicalism and the Search for Aid Effectiveness." *Third World Quarterly* 32, no. 2: 199–216.

Gundel, Joakim. 2009. *Clans in Somalia.* Rev. ed. COI Workshop Vienna. May 15, 2009. http://www.ecoi.net/file_upload/90_1261130976_accord-report-clans-in-somalia-revised-edition-20091215.pdf.

Hagmann, Tobias. 2016. "Stabilization, Extraversion and Political Settlements in Somalia." Rift Valley Institute, Political Settlements Research Program. riftvalley.net/download/file/fid/4139.

Hagmann, Tobias, and Markus V. Hoehne. 2007. "Failed State or Failed Debate? Multiple Somali Political Orders within and beyond the Nation-State." *Politorbis: Zeitschrift zur Aussenpolitik* 42: 20–26.

Hagmann, Tobias, and Didier Péclard. 2011. "Introduction." In *Negotiating Statehood: Dynamics of Power and Domination in Africa*. Chichester, UK: Wiley-Blackwell, 1–23.

Hagmann, Tobias, and Finn Stepputat. 2016. *Corridors of Trade and Power: Economy and State Formation in Somali East Africa.* Danish Institute for International Studies. Working Paper 8. https://rucforsk.ruc.dk/ws/files/59114463/DIIS_WP_2016_8.pdf.

Hameiri, Shahar. 2007. "Failed States or Failed Paradigm? State Capacity and the Limits of Institutionalism." *Journal of International Relations and Development* 10: 122–49.

——. 2011. "A Reality Check for the Critique of the Liberal Peace." In *A Liberal Peace? The Problems and Practices of Peacebuilding*, ed. Susanna Campbell, David Chandler, and Meera Sabaratnam, 191–208. London: Zed Books.

Hammond, Laura. 2012. "The Absent but Active Constituency: The Role of the Somaliland UK Community in Election Politics." In *Politics from Afar: Transnational Diasporas and Networks*, ed. Terrence Lyons and Peter G. Mandaville, 157–80. London: C. Hurst.

Hampel, Karl Adalbert. 2015. "The Dark(er) Side of 'State Failure': State Formation and Socio-Political Variation" *Third World Quarterly* 36, no. 9: 1629–48.

Hansen, Lene. 2006. *Security as Practice: Discourse Analysis and the Bosnian War.* London: Routledge.

Hansen, Stig Jarle. 2009. "Piracy in the Greater Gulf of Aden: Myths, Misconceptions and Remedies." Oslo: Norwegian Institute for Urban and Regional Research. https://gsdrc.org/document-library/piracy-in-the-greater-gulf-of-aden-myths-misconceptions-and-remedies/.

Harper, Mary. 2012. *Getting Somalia Wrong? Faith and War in a Shattered State.* London: Zed Books.

Hartung, William. 2013. "Risks and Returns: The Economic Illogic of the Obama Administration's Arms Export Reforms." *International Policy Report*, August 2013, Cen-

ter for International Policy. http://web.archive.org/web/20180220223149/http://www
.ciponline.org/images/uploads/Hartung_IPR_0713_Economic_Illogic_Arms
_Export.pdf.

Hastings, Justin, and Sarah G. Phillips. 2015. "Maritime Piracy Business Networks and
Institutions in the Horn of Africa and the Gulf of Guinea." *African Affairs* 114, no. 457:
555–76.

———. 2018. "Order beyond the State: Explaining Somaliland's Avoidance of Maritime
Piracy." *Journal of Modern African Studies* 56, no. 1: 5–30.

Healy, Sally, and Hassan Sheikh. 2009. *Somalia's Missing Millions: The Somali Diaspora
and its Role in Development*. United Nations Development Programme Somalia.
March 2009. http://www.undp.org/content/dam/somalia/docs/undp_report_onsomali
_diaspora.pdf.

Helander, Bernhard. 2005. "Who Needs a State? Civilians, Security and Social Services
in North-East Somalia." In *No Peace, No War: The Anthropology of Contemporary
Armed Conflicts*, ed. Paul Richards, 93–202. Athens: Ohio University Press.

Held, David, and Asye Kaya, eds. 2007. *Global Inequality: Patterns and Explanations*.
Cambridge: Polity Press.

Hellman, Joel. 2013. "Surprising Results from Fragile States." *Future Development: Economics to End Poverty* (a World Bank blog). October 15, 2013. http://blogs.worldbank
.org/futuredevelopment/surprising-results-fragile-states.

Helmke, Gretchen, and Steven Levitsky. 2004. "Informal Institutions and Comparative
Politics: A Research Agenda." *Perspectives on Politics* 2, no. 4: 725–40.

Herbst, Jeffrey. "War and the State in Africa." *International Security* 14, no. 4: 117–39.

Hermez, Sami, 2017. *War Is Coming: Between Past and Future Violence in Lebanon*. Philadelphia: University of Pennsylvania Press.

Hesse, Brian J. 2010. "Where Somalia Works." *Journal of Contemporary African Studies*
28, no. 3: 343–62.

Hickel, Jason, 2017. *The Divide: A Brief Guide to Global Inequality and Its Solutions*. London: William Heinemann.

Hickey, Sam. 2013. *Thinking about the Politics of Inclusive Development: Towards a Rela-
tional Approach*. ESID Working Paper No. 1.

Hills, Alice. 2014. "Somalia Works: Police Development as State Building." *African
Affairs* 113, no. 450: 88–107.

Hironaka, Ann. 2005. *Never Ending Wars: The International Community, Weak States,
and the Perpetuation of Civil War*. Cambridge, MA: Harvard University Press.

Hoehne, Markus V. 2009. "Mimesis and Mimicry in Dynamics of State and Identity Formation in Northern Somalia." *Africa: Journal of the International African Institute* 79,
no. 2: 252–81.

———. 2010. "People and Politics along and across the Somaliland-Puntland Border." In
Border and Borderlands as Resources in the Horn of Africa, ed. Dereje Feyissa and Markus
Hoehne, 97–121. Oxford: James Currey.

———. 2011. "Not Born as a De Facto State: Somaliland's Complicated State Formation." In *Regional Security in the Post-Cold War Horn of Africa*, ed. Roba Sharamo and
Berouk Mesfin, 309–46. Institute for Security Studies: Monograph 178. https://www
.files.ethz.ch/isn/137519/Mono178.pdf.

———. 2013. "Limits of Hybrid Political Orders: The Case of Somaliland." *Journal of Eastern African Studies* 7, no. 2: 199–217.

———. 2015. *Between Somaliland and Puntland: Marginalization, Militarization and Conflicting Political Visions*. London: Rift Valley Institute.

———. 2016. Review of *A Somali Nation-State: History, Culture and Somaliland's Political Transition*, by Michael Walls. *Africa Spectrum* 1: 125–28.

Holden, Paul. 2016. *Indefensible: Seven Myths that Sustain the Global Arms Trade*. London: Zed Books.

House of Congress, Foreign Affairs Committee Hearing. 2013. "Export Control Reform: The Agenda Ahead," April 24, 2013, Washington, DC.

Human Rights Watch. 2009. *Hostages to Peace: Threats to Human Rights and Democracy in Somaliland*. New York: HRW. http://www.hrw.org/sites/default/files/reports /somaliland0709web.pdf.

———. 2015. "UN: Rights Council Fails Yemeni Civilians." https://www.hrw.org/news /2015/10/02/un-rights-council-fails-yemeni-civilians.

Hurrell, Andrew, and Ngaire Woods. 1999. *Inequality, Globalization, and World Politics*. Oxford: Oxford University Press.

Hussein, Abdi. 2011. "Somaliland's Military is a Shadow of the Past." *Somalia Report*, August 13. http://piracyreport.com/index.php/post/1299/Somalilands_Military_is_a _Shadow_of_the_Past_.

Hussein, Shamis. 1997. "Somalia: A Destroyed Country and a Defeated Nation." In *Mending Rips in the Sky: Options for Somali Communities in the 21st Century*, ed. Hussein M. Adam and Richard Ford, 165–92. Lawrenceville, NJ: Red Sea Press.

Iazzolino, Gianluca. 2015. "Following Mobile Money in Somaliland." Research Report No. 4, London: Rift Valley Institute. http://riftvalley.net/publication/following-mobile -money-somaliland#.XOOaCcZL1gc.

Ibrahim, Mohamed Hassan, and Ulf Terlinden. 2008. "Making Peace, Rebuilding Institutions: Somaliland—A Success Story?" In *Somalia: Current Conflicts and New Chances for State Building*, ed. Axel-Harneit-Sievers and Dirk Spilker, 52–69. Berlin: Heinrich Böll Foundation.

———. 2010. "Somaliland: 'Home Grown' Peacemaking and Political Reconstruction." In "Whose Peace Is it Anyway? Connecting Somali and International Peacemaking," ed. Mark Bradbury and Sally Healy. *Accord*, no. 21: 76–79. https:// www.c-r.org/accord-article/somaliland-home-grown-peacemaking-and-political -reconstruction.

ICG (International Crisis Group). 2003. *Democratisation and Its Discontents*. International Crisis Group Africa Report 66. July 28, 2003. https://www.crisisgroup.org/africa/horn -africa/somaliland/somaliland-democratisation-and-its-discontents.

———. 2006. *Somaliland: Time for African Union Leadership*. International Crisis Group Africa Report 110. May 23, 2006. https://www.crisisgroup.org/africa/horn-africa /somalia/somaliland-time-african-union-leadership.

———. 2011. *Somalia: The Transitional Government on Life Support*. International Crisis Group Africa Report 170. February 21, 2011. https://www.crisisgroup.org/africa/horn -africa/somalia/somalia-transitional-government-life-support.

———. 2015. *Somaliland: The Strains of Success.* Crisis Group Africa Briefing 113. October 5, 2015. https://d2071andvip0wj.cloudfront.net/b113-somaliland-the-strains-of-success.pdf.

IEG (Independent Evaluation Group). 2016. *World Bank Group Engagement in Situations of Fragility, Conflict, and Violence: An Independent Evaluation.* Washington, DC: International Bank for Reconstruction and Development/The World Bank. http://ieg.worldbankgroup.org/evaluations/fragility-conflict-violence.

IGC (International Growth Center). 2018. *Escaping the Fragility Trap.* International Growth Centre, Commission on State Fragility, Growth and Development. https://www.theigc.org/wp-content/uploads/2017/06/Escaping-the-fragility-trap_Aug-2018.pdf.

ILO (International Labour Organization). 2012. *Labour Force Survey Somaliland 2012: Report on Borama, Hargeisa & Burao.* http://www.ilo.org/wcmsp5/groups/public/@africa/@ro-addis_ababa/@sro-addis_ababa/documents/publication/wcms_234412.pdf.

Independent Commission for Aid Impact. 2015. *DFID's Scale-Up in Fragile States: Terms of Reference.* https://icai.independent.gov.uk/wp-content/uploads/Fragile-States-ToRs-Final.pdf.

Indian Ocean Newsletter. 2016. "Will Telesom's Optical Fibre Sink in the Gulf of Aden?" *ION* no. 1426 (May 6, 2016).

———. 2017. "Berbera May Not Be a Haven of Peace for DP World." *ION* no. 1447 (March 24, 2017).

Ingiriis, Mohamed Haji. 2016. "'We Swallowed the State as the State Swallowed Us': The Genesis, Genealogies, and Geographies of Genocides in Somalia." *African Security* 9 no. 3: 237–58.

———. 2017. "Clan Politics and the 2017 Presidential Election in Somaliland." *Journal of Somali Studies* 4, nos. 1–2: 117–33.

Initiative & Referendum Institute. 2001. *Final Report of the Initiative & Referendum Institute's Election Monitoring Team: Somaliland National Referendum.* Washington, DC: Citizen Lawmaker Press. http://www.iandrinstitute.org/docs/Final-Somaliland-Report-7-24-01-combined.pdf.

International Aid Transparency, 2012. "Annex 2a: Democratic Republic of Congo Question and Report Matrix." In *Study on Better Reflecting Aid Flows in Country Budgets to Improve Aid Transparency and Public Financial Management.* www.aidtransparency.net/wp-content/uploads/2013/05/Annex-2a-DRC-Matrix.doc.

International Dialogue on Peacebuilding and Statebuilding. 2011. *The "New Deal" on Fragile States.* http://www.pbsbdialogue.org/media/filer_public/07/69/07692de0-3557-494e-918e-18df00e9ef73/the_new_deal.pdf.

Interpeace. 2008. "Peace in Somaliland: An Indigenous Approach to State-Building." The Search for Peace: Somali Programme. Somaliland: Academy for Peace and Development. https://apd-somaliland.org/wp-content/uploads/2014/12/Peace-in-Somaliland-an-indigenous-Approach-to-State-building-.pdf.

———. 2009. "The Search for Peace: A History of Mediation in Somalia since 1988." The Search for Peace: Somali Program. The Center for Research and Dialogue. https://

www.interpeace.org/wp-content/uploads/2009/05/2009_Som_Interpeace_A
_History_Of_Mediation_In_Somalila_Since_1988_EN.pdf.

IRI (International Republican Institute). 2011. *Somaliland Opinion Survey—Hargeisa District.* September 28–October 8, 2011. http://www.iri.org/sites/default/files/2011%20
November%2016%20Survey%20of%20Somaliland%20Public%20Opinion,%20Sep-
tember%2028-October%208,%202011_0.pdf.

——. 2012. "Somaliland International Democratization Support Strategy." http://www
.iri.org/sites/default/files/flip_docs/Somaliland%20Democratization%20Strat-
egy%20Blog%20Post%20-%20E%20Lewis%20OME/files/assets/basic-html/toc
.html.

Ismail, Edna Aden. 2006. "The Case for Unitary Government." Conference on Ethnicity and Federalism in Africa, Lagos: February 20–23, 2006. http://www.somalilandsun
.com/somaliland-the-case-for-unitary-government/.

Jama, Ibrahim Hashi. 2010. "Making the Somaliland Constitution and its Role in Democratization and Peace." In *Whose Peace Is it Anyway?*, ed. Mark Bradbury and Sally
Healy, 89–91. https://www.c-r.org/downloads/21_Somalia_2010_ENG_F.pdf.

Jama, Jama Muse. 2003. *A Note on "My Teachers' Group": News Report of an Injustice.*
Hargeisa: Ponte Invisibile Edizioni.

Jimcaale, Cabdiraxmaan. 2005. "Consolidation and Decentralisation of Government Institutions." In *Rebuilding Somaliland: Issues and Possibilities*, 49–121. Trenton, NJ:
WSP International, Red Sea Press.

Jones, Amir, Charlotte Jones, and Susy Ndaruhutse. 2014. *Higher Education and Developmental Elites: Ghana Case Study.* Research paper no. 26. Birmingham, UK: University of Birmingham. Developmental Leadership Program. March 2014. http://
publications.dlprog.org/Higher%20Education%20and%20Developmental%20
Leadership%20-%20The%20Case%20of%20Ghana.pdf.

Jørgensen, Marianne W., and Louise J. Phillips. 2002. *Discourse Analysis as Theory and
Method.* London: Sage.

Jung, Dietrich. 2003. "A Political Economy of Intra-State War: Confronting a Paradox."
In *Shadow Globalization, Ethnic Conflicts and New Wars—A Political Economy of Intra-
State War*, 9–25. London: Routledge.

Kaariye, Barkhad M. 2016. "The Role of Somali Poetry for Somaliland Disarmament."
Unpublished paper. Hargeysa, Somaliland, September 2016. http://ocvp.org/docs
/Cahort1/4.pdf.

Kabamba, Patience. 2012. "The Real Problems of the Congo: From Africanist Perspectives to African Prospectives." *African Affairs Comments*, March, 2012, n.p.

Kaldor, Mary. 1999. *New and Old Wars: Organized Violence in a Global Era.* Stanford,
CA: Stanford University Press.

Kaplan, Eben. 2006. "Somalia's Terrorist Infestation." Council on Foreign Relations,
June 6, 2006. https://www.cfr.org/backgrounder/somalias-terrorist-infestation.

Kaplan, Seth. 2008. "The Remarkable Story of Somaliland." *Journal of Democracy* 19,
no. 3: 143–57.

Kapteijns, Lidwien. 2004. "I. M. Lewis and Somali Clanship: A Critique." *Northeast African Studies* 11, no. 1: 1–23.

———. 2013a. *Clan Cleansing in Somalia: The Ruinous Legacy of 1991*. Philadelphia: Pennsylvania University Press.

———. 2013b. "Test-Firing the 'New World Order' in Somalia: The US/UN Military Humanitarian Intervention of 1992–1995." *Journal of Genocide Research* 15, no. 4: 421–42.

Kar, Dev. 2016. "Financial Flows and Tax Havens: Combining to Limit the Lives of Billions of People." Global Financial Integrity. December 5, 2016. http://www.gfintegrity .org/report/financial-flows-and-tax-havens-combining-to-limit-the-lives-of-billions -of-people/.

Kar, Dev, and Sarah Freitas. 2012. *Illicit Financial Flows from Developing Countries 2001– 2012*. Washington, DC: Global Financial Integrity.

Keen, David. 2008. *Complex Emergencies*. Cambridge: Polity Press.

Khan, Mushtaq. 2010. *Political Settlements and the Governance of Growth-Enhancing Institutions*. School of Oriental and African Studies (SOAS), draft paper in the research paper series on "growth-enhancing governance," SOAS, London. http://eprints.soas .ac.uk/9968/.

Kibble, Steve, and Michael Walls. 2010. "Beyond Polarity: Negotiating a Hybrid State in Somaliland." *Africa Spectrum* 45: 1.

Koddenbrock, Kai. 2012. "Recipes for Intervention: Western Policy Papers Imagine the Congo. *International Peacekeeping* 19, no. 5: 549–64.

———. 2014. "Malevolent Politics: ICG Reporting on Government Action and the Dilemmas of Rule in the Democratic Republic of Congo." *Third World Quarterly* 35, no. 4: 669–85.

Kothari, Uma. 2005a. "From Colonial Administration to Development Studies: A Post-Colonial Critique of the History of Development Studies." In *A Radical History of Development Studies: Individuals, Institutions and Ideologies*, 47–66. London: Zed Books.

———. 2005b. "Authority and Expertise: The Professionalisation of International Development and the Ordering of Dissent." *Antipode* 37, no. 3: 425–46.

Krasner, Stephen D. 2004. "Sharing Sovereignty: New Institutions for Collapsed and Failing States." *International Security* 29, no. 2: 85–120.

Kuperman, Alan J. 2015. *Constitutions and Conflict Management in Africa Book: Preventing Civil War through Institutional Design*. Philadelphia: University of Pennsylvania Press.

Kurki, Milja. 2007. "Critical Realism and Causal Analysis in International Relations." *Millennium* 35, no. 2: 361–78.

Lambach, Daniel. 2006. "Security, Development and the Australian Security Discourse about Failed States." *Australian Journal of Political Science* 41, no. 3 (September): 407–18.

Laws, Edward. 2012. *Political Settlements, Elite Pacts, and Governments of National Unity: A Conceptual Study*. Developmental Leadership Program, Background Paper 10. https://www.dlprog.org/publications/background-papers/political-settlements-elite -pacts-and-governments-of-national-unity-a-conceptual-study.

Leander, A. 2004. "War and the Un-Making of States: Taking Tilly Seriously in the Contemporary World." In *Copenhagen Peace Research: Conceptual Innovation and Contemporary Security Analysis*, ed. Stephan Guzzini and Dietrich Jung, 69–80. London: Routledge.

Lemay-Hébert, Nicolas, and Xavier Mathieu. 2014. "The OECD's Discourse on Fragile States: Expertise and the Normalisation of Knowledge Production." *Third World Quarterly* 35, no. 2: 232–51.

Leonard, David K., and Mohamed S. Samantar. 2011. "What Does the Somali Experience Teach Us about the Social Contract and the State?" *Development and Change* 42, no. 2: 559–84.

Le Sage, Andre. 2005. "Stateless Justice in Somalia: Formal and Informal Rule of Law Initiative." Geneva: Centre for Humanitarian Dialogue. https://gsdrc.org/document -library/stateless-justice-in-somalia-formal-and-informal-rule-of-law-initiatives/.

Levi, Margaret. 1988. *Of Rule and Revenue*. Berkeley: University of California Press.

Lewis, Ioan M. 1961. "Force and Fission in Northern Somali Lineage Structure." *American Anthropologist* 63, no. 1: 94–112.

——. 1994. *Blood and Bone: The Call of Kinship in Somali Society*. Trenton: Red Sea Press.

——. 1998. "Doing Violence to Ethnography: A Response to Catherine Besteman's 'Representing Violence and "Othering" Somalia.'" *Cultural Anthropology* 13, no. 1: 100–108.

——. 2004. "Visible and Invisible Differences: The Somali Paradox." *Africa* 74, no. 4: 489–515.

——. 2009. *Understanding Somalia and Somaliland*. London: Hurst Publishers Ltd.

——. 2010. *Making and Breaking States in Africa: The Somali Experience*. New Jersey: Red Sea Press.

Lindeman, Berit Nising, and Stig Jarle Hansen. 2003. *Somaliland: Presidential Election 2003*. Norddem Report 08/2003. Oslo: The Norwegian Resource Bank for Democracy and Human Rights (NORDEM). http://web.archive.org/web/20120804062950 /http://www.jus.uio.no/smr/english/about/programmes/nordem/publications /nordem-report/2003/08/nordem_report-contents.html.

Lindemann, Stefan. 2011. "Inclusive Elite Bargains and the Dilemma of Unproductive Peace: A Zambian Case Study." *Third World Quarterly* 32, no. 10: 1843–69.

Little, Peter. 2003. *Somalia: Economy without State*. Oxford: James Currey.

Lottholz, Philipp, and Nicolas Lemay-Hébert. 2016. "Re-Reading Weber, Re-Conceptualizing State-Building: From Neo-Weberian to Post-Weberian Approaches to State, Legitimacy and State-Building." *Cambridge Review of International Affairs* 29, no. 4: 1467–85.

Luciani, Giacomo, and Hazem Beblawi, eds. 1987. *The Rentier State*. London: Croom Helm.

Lund, Christian. 2006. "Twilight Institutions: Public Authority and Local Politics in Africa." *Development and Change* 37, no. 4: 684–705.

Luttwak, Edward N. 1999. "Give War a Chance." *Foreign Affairs*, no. 78 (July/August): 4.

Mac Ginty, Roger. 2011. *International Peacebuilding and Local Resistance: Hybrid Forms of Peace*. Basingstoke, UK: Palgrave.

Mac Ginty, Roger, and Oliver Richmond. 2016. "The Fallacy of Constructing Hybrid Political Orders: A Reappraisal of the Hybrid Turn in Peacebuilding." *International Peacekeeping* 23, no. 2: 219–39.

Mahmood, Omar, and Mohamed Farah. 2017. "High Stakes for Somaliland's Presidential Elections." *East Africa Report* 15. Institute for Security Studies and Academy for Peace and Development. October 2017. https://issafrica.s3.amazonaws.com/site/uploads/ear15.pdf.

Mahmood, Saba. 2005. *Politics of Piety: The Islamic Revival and the Feminist Subject.* Princeton, NJ: Princeton University Press.

Mallaby, Sebastian. 2002. "The Reluctant Imperialist: Terrorism, Failed States, and the Case for American Empire." *Foreign Affairs*, no. 2 (March/April).

Mamdani, Mahmood. 2001. "Beyond Settler and Native as Political Identities: Overcoming the Political Legacy of Colonialism." *Comparative Studies in Society and History* 43: 651–64.

Marchal, Roland. 1996. *The Post-Civil War Somali Business Class.* Nairobi: EC/Somalia Unit.

Mbembe, Achille. 1992. "The Banality of Power and the Aesthetics of Vulgarity in the Postcolony." *Public Culture* 4, no. 2: 1–30.

——. 2001. *On The Postcolony.* Berkeley: University of California Press.

Meagher, Kate. 2012. "The Strength of Weak States? Non-State Security Forces and Hybrid Governance in Africa." *Development and Change* 43, no. 5: 1073–1101.

Menkhaus, Ken. 2006/2007. "Governance without Government in Somalia: Spoilers, State Building, and the Politics of Coping." *International Security* 31, no. 3: 74–106.

——. 2012. "Somalia at the Tipping Point?" *Current History* 111, no. 745: 169–74.

Miller, Greg. 2011. "State Cables Show Rising Concern about al-Qaeda in Yemen." *Washington Post*, April 9, 2011. https://www.washingtonpost.com/world/state-cables-show-rising-concern-about-al-qaeda-in-yemen/2011/04/07/AFrH6EAD_story.html.

Milliken, Jennifer. 1999. "The Study of Discourse in International Relations: A Critique of Research and Methods." *European Journal of International Relations* 5, no. 2: 225–54.

Mills, Greg. 2015. *Why States Recover: Changing Walking Societies into Winning Nations, from Afghanistan to Zimbabwe.* London: C. Hurst & Co. Ltd.

Mills, Greg, J., Peter Pham, and David Kilcullen. 2013. *Somalia: Fixing Africa's Most Failed State.* Cape Town: Tafelberg Short. Kindle Edition.

Moore, Mick. 2016. "How Well Does the World Bank Serve Fragile and Conflict-Affected States?" Fragile States. http://www.fragilestates.org/2014/02/05/well-world-bank-serve-fragile-conflict-affected-states/.

Morris, Ian. 2014. *War! What Is It Good For? Conflict and the Progress of Civilization from Primates to Robots.* New York: Farrar, Straus and Giroux.

Morton, Adam David. 2005. "The 'Failed State' of International Relations." *New Political Economy* 10, no. 3: 371–79.

Moss, Todd, Gunilla Pettersson, and Nicolas van de Walle. 2006. "An Aid-Institutions Paradox? A Review Essay on Aid Dependency and State Building in Sub-Saharan Africa." *Centre for Global Development.* Working Paper No. 74, January 2006.

Moyo, Dambisa. 2009. *Dead Aid: Why Aid is Not Working and How There is a Better Way for Africa.* New York: Farrar, Straus and Giroux.

Mubarak, Jamil Abdulla. 1996. *From Bad Policy to Chaos in Somalia: How an Economy Fell Apart.* Westport, Greenwood Publishing Group.

Muchler, Benno. 2012. "Somaliland: A Pocket of Stability in a Chaotic Region." National Public Radio Inc. August 28, 2012. https://www.npr.org/2012/08/28/160117706/somaliland-a-pocket-of-stability-in-a-chaotic-region.

Mudimbe, Vumbi Yoka. 1988. *The Invention of Africa*. Bloomington: Indiana University Press.

Munter, Cameron. 2016. "Imagining Assistance: Tales from the American Aid Experience in Iraq in 2006 and Pakistan in 2011." Brookings Institute, Local Orders Working Group, Paper 1. https://www.brookings.edu/wp-content/uploads/2016/07/CMuntersLocalOrderWorkingPaperv5.pdf.

Muppidi, Himadeep. 2012. *The Colonial Signs of International Relations*. London: Hurst & Company.

Nadim, Hussain. 2019. "The Politics of the Security-Development Nexus: A Case Study of the Kerry-Lugar-Berman Act in Pakistan" Unpublished PhD diss., University of Sydney.

The National. 2017. "Abdirahman Irro Concedes Defeat, Calls for National Unity." November 22, 2017. http://web.archive.org/web/20180730150906/http://www.thenational-somaliland.com/2017/11/22/abdirahman-irro-concedes-defeat-calls-national-unity/.

Nay, Oliver. 2014. "International Organisations and the Production of Hegemonic Knowledge: How the World Bank and the OECD helped invent the Fragile State Concept." *Third World Quarterly* 35, no. 2, 210–31.

Ndikumana, Léonce, and James K. Boyce. 2011. *Africa's Odious Debts: How Foreign Loans and Capital Flight Bled a Continent*. London: Zed Books Ltd.

Nestle, Marion, and Sharron Dalton. 1994. "Food Aid and International Hunger Crises: The United States in Somalia." *Agriculture and Human Values* 11, no. 4: 19–27.

Niemann, Michael. 2007. "War Making and State Making in Central Africa." *Africa Today* 53, no. 3: 21–39.

Nordstrom, Carolyn. 2004. *The Shadows of War: Violence, Power and International Profiteering in the Twenty-First Century*. Berkeley: University of California Press.

North, Douglass C. 1990. *Institutions, Institutional Change and Economic Performance*. Cambridge: Cambridge University Press.

North, Douglass C., John Joseph Wallis, and Barry R. Weingast. 2009. *Violence and Social Orders: A Conceptual Framework for Interpreting Recorded Human History*. Cambridge: Cambridge University Press.

Nuruzzaman, Mohammed. 2009. "Revisiting the Category of Fragile and Failed States in International Relations." *International Studies* 46, no. 3: 271–94.

Nuur, Faraax. n.d. "Giving Each Other Up." In *War and Peace: An Anthology of Somali Literature* (2009), ed. Rashiid Sheekh Cabdillaahi, trans. Martin Orwin with help from Maxamed Xasan, 154–55. London: Progressio.

Nyamnjoh, Francis B. 2012. "'Potted Plants in Greenhouses': A Critical Reflection on the Resilience of Colonial Education in Africa." *Journal of Asian and African Studies* 47, no. 2: 129–54.

OAU (Organization of African Unity). 1963. *OAU Charter*. Addis Ababa, Ethiopia: OAU.

———. 1964. *Resolutions Adopted by the First Ordinary Session of the Assembly of Heads of State and Government*. Cairo, UAR, July 17–21. Addis Ababa, Ethiopia: OAU.

Observatory of Conflict and Violence Prevention. 2011. *Safety and Security Baseline Report: Mogadishu.* Hargeisa, Somaliland.

——. 2015. *Safety and Security Baseline Report: Borao.* Hargeisa, Somaliland.

OECD (Organisation for Economic Cooperation and Development). 2008. "Concepts and Dilemmas of State Building in Fragile Situations: From Fragility to Resilience." In *OECD-DAC Discussion Paper.* Paris: OECD.

——. 2010. *Do No Harm: International Support for Statebuilding.* Paris: OECD.

——. 2011. *Supporting Statebuilding in Situations of Conflict and Fragility: Policy Guidance.* Paris: OECD.

OECD DAC (Development Assistance Committee). 2015. "List of Fragile States and Economies Used for Preparing the 2015 OECD Report on States." https://www.oecd .org/dac/governance-peace/conflictandfragility/docs/List%20of%20fragile%20states .pdf.

Pachirat, Timothy. 2017. *Among Wolves: Ethnography and the Immersive Study of Power* (Routledge Series on Interpretive Methods). Milton Park, UK: Taylor and Francis. Kindle Edition.

Paice, Edward, and Hannah Gibson, eds. 2013. *After Borama: Consensus, Representation and Parliament in Somaliland*, Policy Voice series. London: Africa Research Institute.

Palmer, Anna, and Byron Tau. 2013. "Somaliland Signs with Glover Park Group." *Politico.* March 26, 2013. http://www.politico.com/tipsheets/politico-influence/2013/03 /somaliland-signs-with-glover-park-group-energy-drink-hiring-spree-continues -livestrong-increases-lobbying-presence-010302.

Paris, Roland. 2002. "International Peacebuilding and the 'Mission Civilisatrice.'" *Review of International Studies* 28, no. 4: 637–56.

——. 2004. *At War's End: Building Peace after Civil Conflict.* Cambridge: Cambridge University Press.

——. 2006. "Bringing the Leviathan Back In: Classical Versus Contemporary Studies of the Liberal Peace." *International Studies Review* 8, no. 3: 425–40.

Paris, Roland, and Timothy D. Sisk, eds. 2009. *The Dilemmas of Statebuilding: Confronting the Contradictions of Postwar Peace Operations.* London: Routledge.

Pegg, Scott and Michael Walls. 2018. "Back on Track? Somaliland after Its 2017 Election." *African Affairs* 117, no. 467: 326–37.

Perera, Suda. 2017a. "Bermuda Triangulation: Embracing the Messiness of Researching in Conflict." *Journal of Intervention and Statebuilding* 11, no. 1: 42–57.

——. 2017b. "Burning the Tent Down: Violent Political Settlements in the Democratic Republic of the Congo." *Journal of International Development* 29, no. 5, 628–44.

Pham, Peter. 2012. "The Somaliland Exception," *Marine Corps University Journal* 3 (1): Spring.

Phillips, Sarah G. 2011. *Yemen and the Politics of Permanent Crisis.* London: Routledge.

——. 2013. "Political Settlements and State Formation: The Case of Somaliland." The Developmental Leadership Program, Research Paper 23, December 2013.

——. 2016. "When Less Was More: External Assistance and the Political Settlement in Somaliland." *International Affairs* 92, no. 3: 630–45.

——. 2017. "The Norm of State-Monopolised Violence from a Yemeni Perspective." In *Against International Relations Norms: Postcolonial Perspectives*, ed. Charlotte Epstein. London: Routledge: 138–57.

——. 2019a (forthcoming). "Making al-Qa'ida Legible: Counter-Terrorism and the Reproduction of Terrorism." *European Journal of International Relations*.

——. 2019b. "Proximities of Violence: Civil Order beyond Governance Institutions." *International Studies Quarterly* 63, no. 3 (September): 680–91.

——. 2020 (forthcoming). "The Localisation of Harm: Why Local-Context Based Approaches to Poverty and Insecurity Still Tinker in the Margins." *Australian Journal of International Affairs*.

Phillips, Sarah G., and Jennifer S. Hunt. 2017. "'Without Sultan Qaboos We Would Be Yemen': The Renaissance Narrative and the Political Settlement in Oman." *Journal of International Development* 29, no. 5. https://onlinelibrary.wiley.com/doi/epdf/10.1002/jid.3290.

Pieterse, Jan Nederveen. 2002. "Global Inequality: Bringing Politics Back In." *Third World Quarterly* 23, no. 6: 1023–46.

Pogge, Thomas. 2010. *Politics as Usual: What Lies behind the Pro-Poor Rhetoric*. Cambridge: Polity, 2010.

Porter, Bruce. 1994. *War and the Rise of the State: The Military Foundations of Modern Politics*. New York: Free Press.

Prunier, Gerard. 1990/1991. "A Candid View of the Somali National Movement." *Horn of Africa* 13, nos. 3–4: 107–20.

——. 1996. "Somalia: Civil War, Intervention, and Withdrawal." *Refugee Survey Quarterly* 15, no. 1: 35–85.

——. 1998. "Somaliland Goes It Alone." *Current History* 97: 619.

PSRP (Political Settlements Research Programme). n.d.a. "Why?" Accessed May 24, 2019. http://www.politicalsettlements.org/about/why/.

——. n.d.b. "What? Navigating Inclusion." Accessed May 24, 2019. http://www.politicalsettlements.org/about/what/.

Qaq, Richard al-. 2015. "The United Nations in Africa: The Rise of Peacekeeping and the Case of Somalia." In *Readings in the International Relations of Africa*, ed. Tom Young, 192–204. Indianapolis: Indiana University Press.

Qoti, Mohamed Farah, ed. 2013. *Dhaxalkii Gobannimada* [The Origins of the Republic]. Hargeisa: Somaliland.

Raeymaekers, Timothy, Koen Vlassenroot, and Kenneth Menkhaus. 2008. "State and Non-State Regulation in African Protracted Crises: Governance without Government?" *Afrika Focus* 21, no. 2: 7–21.

Rafique, Najam. 2011. "Analyzing the Kerry-Lugar Bill." Institute of Strategic Studies Islamabad. http://issi.org.pk/wp-content/uploads/2014/06/1315811328_60436199.pdf.

Rawson, David. 1994. "Dealing with Disintegration: U.S. Assistance and the Somali State." In *The Somali Challenge: From Catastrophe to Renewal?*, ed. Ahmed I. Samatar, 147–88. Boulder, CO: Lynne Rienner.

Rayale, Siham. 2011. "Participation through Peacebuilding: Somaliland Women's Experiences Of Peace Initiatives in Somaliland Since 1991." *Somaliland Journal of Peace and Development* 1 (October): 24–40.

Reerink, Jack. 2008. "Interview-Somaliland Keen to Host US Base, Hopeful on Oil." Reuters. April 9, 2008. http://uk.mobile.reuters.com/article/article/idUKL09 87878420080409.

Reliefweb. 2000. "UNICEF Somalia Review March 2000." March 31, 2000. http:// reliefweb.int/report/somalia/unicef-somalia-review-march-2000.

Renders, Marleen. 2007. "Appropriate 'Governance-Technology'? Somali Clan Elders and Institutions in the Making of the 'Republic of Somaliland.'" *Afrika Spectrum* 42, no. 3, 439–59.

———. 2012. *Consider Somaliland: State Building with Traditional Elders.* Leiden, Netherlands: Brill.

Renders, Marleen, and Ulf Terlinden. 2010. "Negotiating Statehood in a Hybrid Political Order: The Case of Somaliland." *Development & Change* 41, no. 4: 723–46.

Reno, William. 2001. "How Sovereignty Matters: International Markets and the Political Economy of Local Politics in Weak States." In *Intervention and Transnationalism in Africa: Global-Local Networks of Power,* ed. Thomas M. Callaghy, Ronald Kassimir, and Robert Latham, 197–215. Cambridge: Cambridge University Press.

———. 2003. "Somalia and Survival: In the Shadow of the Global Economy." QEH Working Paper No. 100. Northwestern University, February 2003. https://www.qeh .ox.ac.uk/sites/www.odid.ox.ac.uk/files/www3_docs/qehwps100.pdf.

———. 2004. "Order and Commerce in Turbulent Areas: 19th Century Lessons, 21st Century Practice." *Third World Quarterly* 25, no. 4: 607–25.

———. 2006. "Somalia: State Failure and Self-Determination in the Shadow of the Global Economy." In *Globalization, Violent Conflict and Self-Determination*, ed. Valpy FitzGerald, Frances Stewart, and Rajesh Venugopal, 147–78. Hampshire: Palgrave Macmillan.

Responding to Conflict. 2010. "Only Through Dialogue: The Somali Way to Peace." Uploaded March 9, 2010. Vimeo video, 28:12. http://vimeo.com/10032698.

Richards, Paul, ed. 2005. *No Peace, No War: The Anthropology of Contemporary Armed Conflicts.* Athens: Ohio University Press.

Richards, Rebecca. 2015. "Bringing the Outside In: Somaliland, Statebuilding and Dual Hybridity." *Journal of Intervention and Statebuilding* 9, no. 1: 4–25.

Riddell, Roger C. 2007. *Does Aid Really Work?* Oxford: Oxford University Press.

Rocha De Siqueira, Isabel. 2014. "Measuring and Managing 'State Fragility': The Production of Statistics by the World Bank, Timor-Leste and the g7+." *Third World Quarterly* 35, no. 2: 268–83.

Rocha Menocal, Alina. 2015. "Inclusive Political Settlements: Evidence, Gaps, and Challenges of Institutional Transformation." Developmental Leadership Program. Birmingham: University of Birmingham.

Rotberg, Robert, ed. 2004. *When States Fail: Causes and Consequences.* Princeton, NJ: Princeton University Press.

Rutazibwa, Olivia U. 2013. "What If We Took Autonomous Recovery Seriously? A Democratic Critique of Contemporary Western Ethical Foreign Policy." *Ethical Perspectives* 20, no. 1: 81–108.

Rutazibwa, Olivia U., and Robbie Shilliam, eds. 2018. *Routledge Handbook of Postcolonial Politics.* London: Routledge.

Sabaratnam, Meera. 2017. *Decolonising Intervention: International Statebuilding in Mozambique.* London: Rowman & Littlefield International.

Sachs, Jeffrey. 2005. *The End of Poverty: Economic Possibilities for Our Time.* New York: Penguin.

Sachs, Wolfgang, ed. 1992. *The Development Dictionary: A Guide to Knowledge as Power.* London: Zed Books.

Said, Edward. 1978. *Orientalism: Western Representations of the Orient.* New York: Pantheon.

Samatar, Abdi Ismail. 1993. "Structural Adjustment as Development Strategy? Bananas, Boom, and Poverty in Somalia." *Economic Geography* 69, no. 1: 25–43.

——. 2001. "Somali Reconstruction and Local Initiative: Amoud University." *World Development* 29, no. 4: 641–56.

Samatar, Abdi Ismail, and Ahmed I. Samatar. 2005. "International Crisis Group Report on Somaliland: An Alternative Somali Response." *Bildhaan: An International Journal of Somali Studies* 5: 107–24.

Sandstrom, Karl. 2013. *Local Interests and American Foreign Policy: Why International Interventions Fail.* London: Routledge.

Schäferhoff, Marco. 2014. "External Actors and the Provision of Public Health Services in Somalia." *Governance: An International Journal of Policy, Administration, and Institutions* 27, no. 4: 675–95.

Schedler, Andreas. 2013. *The Politics of Uncertainty: Sustaining and Subverting Electoral Authoritarianism.* Oxford: Oxford University Press.

Schuenemann, Julia, and Amanda Lucey. 2015. "Success and Failure of Political Settlements: Defining and Measuring Transformation." Political Settlement Research Programme, Working Paper 2, September 2, 2015.

Sebudubudu, David. 2009. *Leaders, Elites and Coalitions in the Development of Botswana.* Developmental Leadership Program, Research Paper 2, April. https://res.cloudinary.com/dlprog/image/upload/vSnax9hVeFf58HC54DLUeR2sl3OBHPDQa8z5qThM.pdf.

Sharp, Jeremy M. 2016. "Egypt: Background and U.S. Relations." *Congressional Research Service*, February 25, 2016.

Shore, Luke. 2015. "In Addis Ababa." London Review of Book (blog), August 20, 2015. https://www.lrb.co.uk/blog/2015/08/20/luke-shore/in-addis-ababa/.

Simons, Anna. 1995. "Networks of Dissolution." *In Networks of Dissolution: Somalia Undone.* Boulder, CO: Westview Press.

SIPRI. 2015. "Trends in International Arms Transfers 2014." Stockholm International Peace Research Institute, March 2015. https://www.sipri.org/sites/default/files/files/FS/SIPRIFS1503.pdf.

Sisk, Timothy. 2013. *Statebuilding.* Cambridge: Polity Press.

Somalia NGO Consortium. 2018. *Debt Cancellation for Somalia: The Road to Peace, Poverty Alleviation and Development.* October 2018. http://www.somaliangoconsortium.org/download/5bb4595b62dd2/.

Somaliland Ministry of Finance. 2013 *Statement of Revenue by Heads and Sub-Heads of Last four Years Average Actual Revenue.* Hargeisa: Government of Somaliland.

Somaliland Ministry of Foreign Affairs. 2002. *The Case for Somaliland's International Recognition as an Independent State.* Hargeisa: Government of Somaliland.

SomTribune. 2018. "Somaliland: 2019 Budget 8 Per Cent More than Current Year." December 19, 2018. http://www.somtribune.com/2018/12/19/somaliland-2019-budget-8 -per-cent-more-than-current-year/.

SONSAF (Somaliland Non-State Actors Forum). 2012. *Citizens Dialogue: Pre-Election Consultation Forums on Upcoming Local Council Elections.* SONSAF. http://www .somalilandlaw.com/SONSAF_pre_2012_Election_Report.pdf.

Stavriankis, Anna. 2015. "Thinking Internationally about the Arms Trade." The Disorder of Things, October 2, 2015. https://thedisorderofthings.com/2015/10/02/thinking -internationally-about-the-arms-trade/#more-10912.

Stewart, Frances, and Graham Brown. 2009. "Fragile States." CRISE Working Paper No. 51, Centre for Research on Inequality, Human Security and Ethnicity, Oxford.

Stone, Jon. 2015. "Philip Hammond Says He Wants UK to Sell Even More Weapons to Saudi Arabia." *The Independent,* November, 11, 2015. http://www.independent.co.uk /news/uk/politics/philip-hammond-says-he-wants-to-sell-even-more-weapons-to-saudi -arabia-a6730066.html.

Stremlau, Nicole. 2013. "Hostages of Peace: The Politics of Radio Liberalization in Somaliland." *Journal of Eastern African Studies* 7, no. 2, 239–57.

Stremlau, Nicole, and Ridwan Osman. 2015. "Courts, Clans and Companies: Mobile Money and Dispute Resolution in Somaliland." *Stability: International Journal of Security & Development* 4, no. 1: 1–15.

Stuckler, David, and Sanjay Basu. 2010. "Six Concerns about Data in the (Dead) Aid Debate." Global Economic Governance Programme, University College, Oxford. Unpublished paper. Copy held by author.

Suhrke, Astri. 2011. *When More Is Less: The International Project in Afghanistan.* New York: Columbia University Press.

Tatchell, Peter. 2007. "In Praise of Somaliland: A Beacon of Hope in the Horn of Africa." *The Liberal.* http://www.theliberal.co.uk/issue_11/columns/tatchell_11 .html.

Taylor, Brian, and Roxana Botea. 2008. "Tilly Tally: War-Making and State-Making in the Contemporary Third World." *International Studies Review* 10, no. 1: 27–56.

Thanki, Nisha. 2012. "Wave of Media Intimidation in Somaliland." International Press Institute, January 18, 2012. https://ipi.media/wave-of-media-intimidation-in-soma liland/.

Thorpe, Rebecca U. 2014. *The American Warfare State: The Domestic Politics of Military Spending.* Chicago: University of Chicago Press.

Tilly, Charles. 1975. "Reflections on the History of European State-Making." In *The Formation of National States in Western Europe,* 3–83. Princeton, NJ: Princeton University Press.

———. 1985. "War Making and State Making as Organised Crime." In *Bringing the State Back In,* ed. Peter D. Evans, Dietrich Rueschemeyer, and Theda Skocpol, ", 169–91. Cambridge: Cambridge University Press.

———. 1990. *Coercion, Capital, and European States, AD 990–1990*. Cambridge: Basil Blackwell.

Titeca, Kristof, and Tom De Herdt. 2011. "Real Governance beyond the 'Failed State': Negotiating Education in the Democratic Republic of the Congo." *African Affairs* 110, no. 439: 213–31.

Tran, Mark. 2012. "Somaliland: Open for Business." *The Guardian*. March 2, 2012. https://www.theguardian.com/global-development/poverty-matters/2012/mar/01/somaliland-open-for-business.

Twigg, Stephen, MP. 2016. "Crisis in Yemen." Letter from the International Development Committee to Rt Hon Justine Greening MP, February 2, 2016. http://www.parliament.uk/documents/commons-committees/international-development/ChairtoSoSregardingYemen.pdf.

UCDP (Uppsala Conflict Data Program). 2019. "Somalia Data." https://www.pcr.uu.se/research/ucdp/.

UK Commons Select Committee. 2015. "Crisis in Yemen Inquiry Launched." Parliament.UK, November 19, 2015. http://www.parliament.uk/business/committees/committees-a-z/commons-select/international-development-committee/news-parliament-20151/yemen-launch-tor-yemen-15-16/.

UNDP (United Nations Development Programme). 2010. "Somaliland Progresses towards Police Reform." July 11, 2010. https://www.somaliaonline.com/community/topic/37175-undp-somaliland-progresses-towards-police-reform/.

———. 2012. *Governance for Peace: Securing the Social Contract*. New York: United Nations Development Programme. http://www.undp.org/content/dam/undp/library/crisis%20prevention/governance-for-peace_2011-12-15_web.pdf.pdf.

UNEP (United Nations Environment Programme). 2005. *The State of the Environment in Somalia*. Nairobi: United Nations Environment Programme. http://www.humanitarianlibrary.org/sites/default/files/2013/07/dmb_somalia.pdf.

UNFPA (United Nations Population Fund). 2014. *Population Estimation Survey for the 18 Pre-War Regions of Somalia*. Nairobi: Somalia Country Office.

UNSC (United Nations Security Council). 2002. *Final Report of the Panel of Experts on the Illegal Exploitation of Natural Resources and Other Forms of Wealth of the Democratic Republic of the Congo*. New York: United Nations Security Council. S/2002/1146. https://www.securitycouncilreport.org/atf/cf/%7B65BFCF9B-6D27-4E9C-8CD3-CF6E4FF96FF9%7D/DRC%20S%202002%201146.pdf.

———. 2010. *Report of the Monitoring Group on Somalia and Eritrea Pursuant to Security Council Resolution 1916 (2010)*. New York: United Nations Security Council. S/2011/433. https://undocs.org/S/2011/433.

USAID (United States Agency for International Development). 2005. "Fragile States Strategy." PD-ACA-999. http://www.au.af.mil/au/awc/awcgate/usaid/2005_fragile_states_strategy.pdf.

USDODIG (United States Department of Defense Inspector General). 2016. *The Army Did Not Implement Effective Controls to Maintain Visibility and Accountability of Iraq Train and Equip Fund Equipment*. Report DODIG-2016-134. https://www.gao.gov/assets/690/684935.pdf.

Vucetic, Srdjan. 2011. "Genealogy as a Research Tool in International Relations." *Review of International Studies* 37, no. 3: 1295–1312.

Wade, Robert Hunter. 2004. "On the Causes of Increasing World Poverty and Inequality, or Why the Matthew Effect Prevails." *New Political Economy* 9, no. 2: 163–88.

Wæver, Ole. 1996. "European Security Identities." *Journal of Common Market Studies* 34, no. 1: 103–32.

Wai, Zubairu. 2007. "Whither African Development? A Preparatory for an African Alternative Reformulation of the Concept of Development." *Africa Development* 32, no. 4: 71–97.

——. 2012. "Neo-Patrimonialism and the Discourse of State Failure in Africa." *Review of African Political Economy* 39, no. 131: 27–43.

——. 2018. "International Relations and the Discourse of State Failure in Africa." In *Recentering Africa in International Relations: Beyond Lack, Peripherality, and Failure*, ed. Iñiguez de Heredia, Marta, and Zubairu Wai, 31–58. New York: Palgrave Macmillan.

Wallis, Joanne, Lia Kent, Miranda Forsyth, Sinclair Dinnen, and Srinjoy Bose, eds. 2018. *Hybridity on the Ground in Peacebuilding and Development: Critical Conversations*. Acton, ACT: Australian National University Press.

Walls, Michael. 2009. "The Emergence of a Somali State: Building Peace from Civil War in Somaliland." *African Affairs* 108, no. 432: 371–89.

——. 2014. *A Somali Nation-State: History, Culture and Somaliland's Political Transition*. Pisa, Italy: Ponte Invisible.

Walter, Barbara F. 2015. "Why Bad Governance Leads to Repeat Civil War." *Journal of Conflict Resolution* 59, no. 7: 1242–72.

Weber, Max. 1919/1946. "Politics as a Vocation." In *Essays in Sociology*, ed. H. H. Garth and C. Wright Mills, 26–45. New York: Macmillian.

Webersik, Christian. 2005. "Fighting for the Plenty: The Banana Trade in Southern Somalia." *Oxford Development Studies* 33, no. 1: 81–97.

Weinstein, Jeremy M. 2005. "Autonomous Recovery and International Intervention in Comparative Perspective." Center for Global Development. Working Paper Number 57. https://www.cgdev.org/sites/default/files/2731_file_WP57.pdf.

Westendorf, Jasmine-Kim. 2015. *Why Peace Processes Fail: Negotiating Insecurity After Civil War*. Boulder, CO: Lynne Rienner Publishers.

Whitlock, Craig. 2015. "Pentagon Loses Track of $500 Million in Weapons, Equipment Given to Yemen." *Washington Post*, March 17, 2015. https://www.washingtonpost.com /world/national-security/pentagon-loses-sight-of-500-million-in-counterterrorism-aid -given-to-yemen/2015/03/17/f4ca25ce-cbf9-11e4-8a46-b1dc9be5a8ff_story.html.

Woods, Ngaire. 2006. *The Globalizers: The IMF, the World Bank, and Their Borrowers*. Ithaca, NY: Cornell University Press.

Woodward, Susan L. 2017. *The Ideology of Failed States*. Cambridge: Cambridge University Press.

World Bank. 1992. *Effective Implementation: Key to Development Impact. Report of the World Bank's Portfolio Management Task Force* (Wapenhans Report). Washington, DC: World Bank.

———. 2011. *World Development Report 2011: Conflict, Security, and Development.* Washington, DC: World Bank. https://openknowledge.worldbank.org/handle/10986/4389.

———. 2013. *Pirate Trails: Tracking the Illicit Financial Flows from Pirate Activities off the Horn of Africa.* A World Bank Study. Washington, DC: World Bank.

———. 2017. *World Development Report 2017: Governance and the Law.* Washington, DC: World Bank.

World Peace Foundation. 2015. "Somalia: Fall of Siad Barre and the Civil War." Mass Atrocity Endings, the Fletcher School, Tufts University. August 7, 2015. https://sites.tufts.edu/atrocityendings/2015/08/07/somalia-fall-of-siad-barre-civil-war/#_edn31.

Yemen Data Project. 2017. "Airwar" (database). https://yemendataproject.org/onewebmedia/Yemen%20Data%20Project%20Publication%20-%20Air%20raids%20database%20from%2026%20March%202015%20to%2020%20March%202019.csv.

Zierau, Tabea. 2003. "State Building without Sovereignty: The Somaliland Republic." *Mondes en développement* 3, no. 123: 57–62.

INDEX

loans, 184n27; from business elite, 94–97, 129. *See also* debt
local ownership, 21, 38–42, 49, 103–35
London Conference of Somaliland Intellectuals Abroad, 180n6
Lucey, Amanda, 40

Maakhir State of Somalia, 188n32
Madagascar, 52
Madar, Sheekh Ibrahim Sheekh Yusuf Sheek, 93
Mali, 52
Marehan clan, 83
Marshall Plan, 52
maternal lineage, 53
Mathieu, Xavier, 38
Mauritius, 82
Maweli, Ali, 184n29
memorials, 2
Mengistu, 180n18
Mennonites (US), 188n17
methodology, 12–15, 17–20, 177n13, 177n17
military aid: to Somalia, 9, 49; to Yemen, 45
military expenditure in fragile states, 43–44
Millennium Challenge Account, 28
Millennium Development Goals (MDG), 30
Milliken, Jennifer, 18
Mills, Greg, 25, 182n37
MOD (Marehan, Ogaden, and Dhulbuhante) alliance, 83
Mogadishu: military aid in, 9; trust in police, 186n15; violence in, 23, 50, 61, 95, 147, 173
Montevideo Convention on the Rights and Duties of States (1933), 63
Moore, Mick, 29
Moorgan, Maxamed (Butcher of Hargeysa), 57
Moss, Todd, 52
Moyo, Dambisa, 11
multi/international corporations, 43, 169, 171. *See also* arms transfers, global; power asymmetries
multiparty electoral system, 98, 121–25, 157–58. *See also* elections

National Charter, 115–16. *See also* Boorama Charter (1993)
National Electoral Commission, 140–41, 143

Nationlink Telecom, 69–70
neo-Weberian statehood, 171–72, 189n2
New Deal for Engagement in Fragile States, 39
Niger, 52
Nkurunziza, Pierre, 31
nongovernmental organizations (NGOs), 12, 70–74, 98, 131, 154, 180n6, 182n36. *See also* international nongovernmental organizations (INGOs)
Nordstrom, Carolyn, 16
North, Douglass, 7
Nuur, Faraax, "Giving Each Other Up," 160

Observatory of Conflict and Violence Prevention, 137
official development assistance (ODA), 9; fragile states and, 24, 28, 52
Ogaden clan, 83
Ogaden region, 66
Ogaden War, 83, 86
Oman, Ahmed Dahir, 184n29
Omar, Mohamed Abulahi, 150
Oodweyne, 20
order. *See* civil order and security
Organisation for Economic Co-operation and Development (OECD), 26, 125; Development Assistance Committee (OECD-DAC), 28; "List of Fragile Situations," 32; local context and, 38–39
Organisation of African Unity (OAU), 65. *See also* African Union (AU)

Pakistan, 37, 166–67
Papua New Guinea, 31–32
Parliament, 115, 120, 132
pastoral economy, 55–56, 58–59
patronage networks, 22, 25; clan leaders and, 92, 96, 98, 122; Cold War and, 57; military expenditure and, 43–44; in Somalia, 49, 55
peace: precarity of, and fear of violence, 8, 16–17, 22–23, 61, 104, 135, 138–40, 144–48, 158–64, 173, 176n8; Somalilanders as "hostages to peace," 158–63, 168; war and (as mutually constitutive), 4, 7–8, 16–17, 139, 158–62, 174. *See also* civil order and security
peace-building in Somaliland, 1–6; business elites and, 93–99, 102, 120; clan leaders and, 90–99; elite secondary schools and, 77–82;